PRAISE FOR *THE LOGISTICS AND SUPPLY CHAIN TOOLKIT,* SECOND EDITION

'A book that summarizes and explains many of the key techniques that make logistics the profession that it is. Certainly one that will not gather dust on a bookshelf, but will gather insight and understanding in the workplace.' **Professor Neil H Ashworth, Chief Executive Officer, Collect+, United Kingdom**

'A great resource that not only provides the tools but also gives you a plan. Sufficiently succinct to give comprehensive coverage of the subject, but in enough depth to work as a standalone reference. I thoroughly recommend it.' **Nigel Price, Managing Director, CRP, United Kingdom**

'An invaluable source of practical information on all aspects of the supply chain, which will be useful to both practitioners and those studying the subject at any academic level. The toolkit provides an excellent resource to help in this task. Enhanced by many illustrations and tables, with inputs from a range of companies and practitioners and references to useful websites and literature, this book is a must-buy for anyone interested in learning more about this fascinating industry.' **Dr Sharon Cullinane, Gothenburg Business School, Sweden**

'*The Logistics and Supply Chain Toolkit*, second edition, is a well-researched, substantial reference book. Packed full of clear examples and with a very structured approach, this is an excellent practical guide into the understanding of logistics tools and how to apply them in the real world. It's a must-read for anyone who is involved in logistics and supply chain management.' **Carole Verry, Consultant, France**

SECOND EDITION

The Logistics and Supply Chain Toolkit

GWYNNE RICHARDS
AND SUSAN GRINSTED

Kogan Page

LONDON PHILADELPHIA NEW DELHI

First published in Great Britain and the United States in 2013 by Kogan Page Limited
Second edition published in 2016

2nd Floor, 45 Gee Street	1518 Walnut Street, Suite 900	4737/23 Ansari Road
London EC1V 3RS	Philadelphia PA 19102	Daryaganj
United Kingdom	USA	New Delhi 110002
www.koganpage.com		India

© Gwynne Richards and Susan Grinsted, 2013, 2016

The right of Gwynne Richards and Susan Grinsted to be identified as the authors of this work has been asserted by them in accordance with the Copyright, Designs and Patents Act 1988.

ISBN   978 0 7494 7557 4
E-ISBN   978 0 7494 7558 1

British Library Cataloguing-in-Publication Data

A CIP record for this book is available from the British Library.

Library of Congress Cataloging-in-Publication Data

Names: Richards, Gwynne, author. | Grinsted, Susan, author.
Title: The logistics and supply chain toolkit : over 100 tools and guides for
  supply chain, transport, warehousing and inventory management / Gwynne
  Richards and Susan Grinsted.
Description: Second edition. | London ; Philadelphia : Kogan Page, 2016. |
  Includes bibliographical references and index.
Identifiers: LCCN 2016018652 (print) | LCCN 2016024356 (ebook) | ISBN
  9780749475574 (paperback) | ISBN 9780749475581 (ebook)
Subjects: LCSH: Business logistics–Management. | BISAC: BUSINESS & ECONOMICS
  / Production & Operations Management. | BUSINESS & ECONOMICS / Facility
  Management. | BUSINESS & ECONOMICS / Distribution.
Classification: LCC HD38.5 .R53 2016 (print) | LCC HD38.5 (ebook) | DDC 658.7–dc23

Typeset by SPi Global
Print production managed by Jellyfish
Printed and bound by CPI Group (UK) Ltd, Croydon, CR0 4YY

CONTENTS

Additional resources to accompany this text are available at the following urls.

A selection of tools are available at:

www.koganpage.com/TLASCT2 (please scroll to the bottom of the web page and complete the form to access these)

For a comprehensive set of tools go to:

http://howtologistics.com

LIST OF TOOLS

ACKNOWLEDGEMENTS

We thank our partners, Teresa Richards and Sidney Garber, respectively, for their support while we were updating this book.

We are also grateful to Suzanne Turner whose book, *Tools for Success: A manager's guide*, gave Gwynne the idea for this supply chain and logistics book.

We want to thank the following individuals and organizations for their support and contributions: Sherry Alexander, BCI Incorporated; Julian Amey, University of Warwick; Kate Barr, Fortna; Beth Barber-Atkinson, 512 Sheffield; Katie Barry, isixsigma; Natalie Beecroft, JDA; Mark Bergkotte; Erik Bootsma, Cap Gemini; Gordon Brace, formerly of Burman Associates and University of Warwick; Enrico Camerinelli; Carbon Trust; Chris Coles, Adaptive BMS; Steven Cross, ATMS Global; Phil Culling, RediRack; Richard Evans, Slimstock; Brian Fish, DFF; Joe Fogg, Arvato; Gary Frankham, Atlet; Richard Gibson; Jo Godsmark, Labyrinth; Monique Henry, ESC Rennes; John Hill, University of Warwick; Charles Intrieri; Aaron Lininger, West Monroe Partners; Martijn Lofvers, Supply Chain Media; Lynn Mentiply, CILTUK; Geoff Relph, Inventory Matters and University of Warwick; RHA; Janna Santala, Aalto University; John Skelton, Supply Chain Almanac; Alan Sommer, Six Sigma Material; Stephen Steele, Transport for London; Deborah Stevens, Belbin; Chris Sturman, FSDF; Bruce Taylor, Nissan; Jeroen van den Berg; Ruth Waring, Labyrinth; Tony Wallis, Toyota Forklifts; Roger Williams, UKWA.

Finally, we would like to thank Ed Mottram Breeze and Julia Swales from Kogan Page for their patience.

The authors have endeavoured to trace and acknowledge all sources. Should there be any errors or omissions, we will be pleased to know about them and make corrections in future.

Introduction

Today's logisticians are working in a fast-moving, ever-changing environment. The supply chain has become centre stage, providing competitive advantage to those who can master procurement, supplier management, inventory, warehouses and distribution. Getting the right product in the correct quantity to the right customer at the prescribed time in good condition at an acceptable cost is paramount to not only retaining but increasing sales and profitability. Supply chain and logistics managers are not only expected to be experts in their own field but also in human resource management, finance, customer service, supplier management and, at times, production. This book, written by supply chain and logistics practitioners, sets out to provide users with a handbook to enable them to keep pace with what's happening in this sector.

According to the *Collins English Dictionary*, a tool is 'anything that can be used as a means of performing an operation or achieving an end'. In this book we will introduce guides, frameworks, models, quick calculations and practical ideas, describing to the reader how to use the tools and under what circumstances. These guides and tools have been chosen to enable the reader to identify issues, produce solutions and thus improve operational efficiency and effectiveness. Some of these tools and spreadsheets can be downloaded from our website: http://howtologistics.com.

Have you ever wondered how you go about efficiently locating stock in your warehouse utilizing an ABC analysis, what is meant by the term 'slotting' or what your trucks' CO_2 emissions are? To answer these questions and more we thought it was time to bring these tools and calculations together in an easy-to-understand format with specific examples that relate to the supply chain and logistics sector.

The aim of this book is to provide today's managers with a toolbox of practical guides, ideas and information to help them in their day-to-day work. It explains a number of the major management tools and suggests areas within supply chain and logistics where they can be applied. We don't expect you to use all the tools and data but hope that you will find a number of them useful in your work.

The tools have been put into chapters, including supply chain, warehousing, transport and inventory. The supply chain is a demanding and challenging area and managers require all the assistance they can get to satisfy both internal and external customers. Where we believe that the reader's experience will be enhanced by further information on the tools discussed, we have identified and provided details of websites, software packages and companies that can further assist. These are included at the end of each tool. Each chapter provides guides and tools that enable the reader to tackle most problems faced in the above areas and thus improve efficiency and effectiveness. The chapters provide guidelines and suggestions as to how each tool can be used and show examples where needed to explain the tools further.

The book is split into nine chapters:

1 Warehouse management tools and guides

2 Transport management tools

3 Inventory management tools

4 Supply chain management tools

5 Outsourcing tools

6 General management tools

7 Performance management tools

8 Financial management tools and ratios

9 Problem-solving tools

The chapter on warehousing includes descriptions of the various types of item-pick methods, the use of ABC analysis to lay out the warehouse and the factors that need to be taken into account when deciding on a new location for a distribution centre.

The transport management chapter looks at areas such as carbon footprint measurement, fuel surcharge calculation and transport costs.

Within the inventory management chapter we discuss the various tools used in determining the optimum stock quantity, demand forecasting, how to calculate stock turn and carry out perpetual inventory counting.

The chapter on supply chain management looks at current tools such as SCOR®, factory gate pricing and supplier relationships.

Chapter 5 provides a step-by-step guide to logistics outsourcing, while the performance management section provides a number of relevant logistics targets and details on how to measure performance.

The tools set out in the general management, finance and problem-solving chapters can be used across the different logistics sectors.

Appendix 1 provides a list of useful websites, Appendix 2 provides useful measurements and conversions and Appendix 3 details the different auto ID options.

A glossary of terms and a list of useful acronyms can also be found, along with many of the tools in this book, on our website: http://howtologistics. com. A number of the examples and templates are free while others have been heavily discounted for purchasers of this book. The code to enable you to receive the discount is lsct0104.

This book is a quick reference guide for supply chain and logistics professionals who want immediate access to relevant tools and data to assist with their day-to-day work. We hope you enjoy it. If you have any ideas for other logistics-related tools please let us know and we will endeavour to include them in the next edition and on our website.

Warehouse management tools and guides

1.1 Warehouse audit

Introduction

This section provides an audit checklist for a warehouse and its operations. The list of questions is not exhaustive and can be added to by users to mirror their own operations.

Audits should be undertaken by an independent person from within the company or by an outside consultant. The purpose of the audit should be explained to the staff. Results need to be shared with all the staff, and they need to take ownership of any improvements necessary.

The audits are based on what we see as best practice in a warehouse. A full set of audit forms with over 100 questions can be purchased from http://howtologistics.com, discount code: lsct0104; an extract is shown in Table 1.1.

TABLE 1.1 Warehouse audit checklists – example questions

Carried out by:			Location:		Date:	
Item	No	Poor	Good	Excellent	N/A	Comments
Comprehensive signage for delivery drivers in multiple languages						
Stock adequately protected from theft and pilferage						

(Continued)

TABLE 1.1 Warehouse audit checklists – example questions
(Continued)

Carried out by:			Location:			Date:
Item	No	Poor	Good	Excellent	N/A	Comments
Escape routes clearly marked and obstruction free						
Is there disabled access into the building?						
Racking condition is checked regularly and reported						
Are there any overhanging pallets in the racks?						
Weight capacity visible on the end of the racks						
Are sufficient security measures in place for high-value items?						
Are sufficient safety measures in place for hazardous items?						
All electrical items tested (UK PAT test)						
Staff have correct licence for type of truck operated						
Responsible staff trained to operate MHE						
Record of safety training kept up to date						

Further information

Suggested reading to ensure safe and legal practices:

UK HSE – http://www.hse.gov.uk

UK COMAH – http://www.hse.gov.uk/comah/index.htm

UK SEMA – http://www.sema.org.uk/

USA OSHA – www.osha.gov/

USA EPA – http://www.epa.gov/lawsregs/regulations/

European Safety and Health at Work – https://osha.europa.eu/en/safety-and-health-legislation

Risk – www.ioshroutefinder.co.uk

References

Ackerman, K (2003) *Auditing Warehouse Performance*, Ackerman Publications, Columbus, OH

Richards, G (2014) *Warehouse Management,* 2nd edn, Kogan Page, London

United Kingdom Warehousing Association – www.ukwa.org.uk

1.2 5S or 5C, also known as Gemba Kanri

Introduction

5S, also known as 5C, has its origins in Japan. 5S focuses on organizing the workplace effectively and standardizing work procedures (see Figure 1.1). 5S simplifies processes and reduces waste and non-value-adding activities while improving quality, efficiency and productivity. Safety is sometimes included as a sixth S.

The tool is also effective in getting employees involved in the improvement process and 'owning' their area of work, taking pride in how it looks and performs.

When to use

When a company is looking to improve efficiency within the warehouse and instil a culture of continuous improvement.

FIGURE 1.1 The steps of 5S

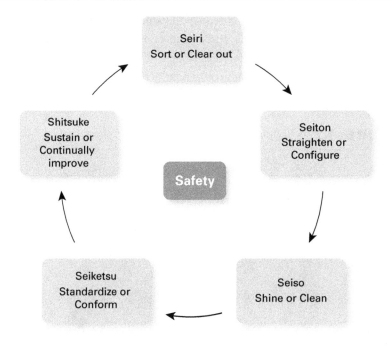

How to use

5S needs to be carried out in the correct order. You need to give individuals responsibility for each task and for their respective work areas within the warehouse:

a The first S (Sort or Seiri or Clear out) concentrates on removing any unnecessary items from the work area. This can include obsolete and damaged stock, over-stocks, defective equipment, broken pallets, waste packaging, etc. It can also refer to unnecessary movement within the warehouse. For example, the introduction of a cross-aisle within the picking area will reduce the amount of travel undertaken by the operators. Items marked for disposal can be put into a holding area until a consensus is reached as to what should be done with them.

b The second S (Straighten or Seiton or Configure) focuses on efficient and effective placement of items, for example location labelling and putting frequently used items in easy-to-access locations. Shadow boards can be used to ensure items are returned to their correct locations (see Figure 1.2). Directional signs in the warehouse are also part of this, as they should reduce the amount of time taken to find items. Items such as tools, empty pallets and packaging should be placed in easily accessible areas close to the point of need. Finally, parking areas for handling equipment need to be set up, with reminders to staff to put the equipment on charge if required.

FIGURE 1.2 Shadow boards courtesy of Fabufacture

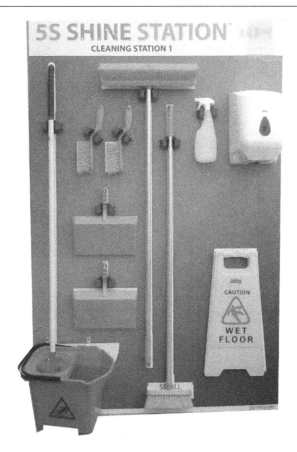

c The third S (Shine or Seiso or Clean) comes after you have cleared the area of any unnecessary items. Thoroughly clean the area and produce a timetable for cleaning. This can be done at the end of each shift, with defects to equipment reported immediately. Staff take pride in a clean work area, they work better and, from experience, clean warehouses tend to be more efficient! Suggestions include putting bins at the front of each aisle to capture waste paper, packaging and broken pallets and making brooms and dust pans easily accessible.

d The fourth S (Standardize or Seiketsu or Conform) is all about creating standards for each work area. Walk through each process with the relevant staff and then produce, document and display best practice procedures within the warehouse. Make them simple to read and understand. A photograph displaying the process with minimal text works well in this situation.

e The fifth S (Sustain or Shitsuke or Continually improve) ensures continuous improvement. Staff are encouraged not to return to previous work practices but to accept change and take things to a new level. Regular checks and audits need to be carried out, with the potential for bonus payments on achieving high performance scores.

More recently, companies have introduced a sixth S, which covers safety. It can be argued that safety is at the heart of the operation and therefore is a valuable addition to the 5S mentality.

An example of how to use the 5S tool is shown in Table 1.2. Companies that have instigated 5S have improved quality, increased efficiency, improved safety, reduced waste and given employees a sense of ownership.

TABLE 1.2 5S tool

5S	Actions	Person/Group responsible	Measurement	Checked by
Sort	Audit MHE and remove defective equipment	WM	Reduced maintenance costs, increased space	GM
	Identify obsolete stock and dispose of it	Inventory manager	Increased available locations, lower stock holding costs	GM
	Label locations. Introduce shadow boards	WM/external	No. of locations labelled/total no. of locations. All equipment in correct location	Put-away team. Housekeeping team

(Continued)

TABLE 1.2 5S tool *(Continued)*

5S	Actions	Person/Group responsible	Measurement	Checked by
Straighten	ABC analysis	WM	Increased pick productivity rates, shorter travel distances	GM
	Slotting analysis	WM	Increased pick productivity rates, shorter travel distances	GM
	Reduce pick travel time	Picking team	Increased items picked per hour	WM
Shine	Identify and remove broken pallets	Housekeeping	Visual	WM
	Provide bins at the end of each aisle	WM	Visual	GM
Standardize	Produce new procedures for each section	Team leaders	Visual	WM
	Set up a communication cell for each team	WM/Team leaders	Visual	GM
Sustain	Set up regular review meetings between staff and team leaders	WM/Team leaders	No. of improvement suggestions made per month. No. of improvements introduced	WM

Key

WM = Warehouse Manager

GM = General Manager

MHE = Mechanical or Materials Handling Equipment

TABLE 1.3 6S audit tool

1S – SORT – ACTIVITY DESCRIPTIONS		YES	NO
1	Only the required stock and packaging present in the work area		
2	Only the required tools and equipment are present in the work area		
3	Only the required paperwork is present in the work area (signage)		
4	Unnecessary items have been removed from the general area		
2S – STRAIGHTEN ACTIVITY DESCRIPTIONS			
5	Locations for all stock are clearly defined and labelled		
6	Equipment and tools are properly labelled and have a clearly defined storage location		
7	Paperwork/scanners/voice equipment is properly labelled and has a clearly defined location		
8	Walkways, access to equipment and work area boundaries are clearly defined and marked		
3S – SHINE – ACTIVITY DESCRIPTIONS			
9	Storage containers, shelving/racking and storage areas are clean and damage free		
10	Tools and equipment are clean, fully maintained and damage free		
11	Work surfaces are clean and damage free		
12	Walls and partitions are clean, uncluttered and damage free – no excessive signage		
13	Cleaning equipment available and neatly stored		
4S – STANDARDIZE – ACTIVITY DESCRIPTIONS			
14	Displayed KPIs are correct, relevant for the department and up to date		
15	Tools, equipment, paperwork stored neatly and returned immediately after use		
16	Maintenance records for tools and material handling equipment are easily accessible and up to date		
17	Waste products (waste oil, rubbish) consistently cleaned up and removed from the work areas		

(Continued)

TABLE 1.3 6S audit tool (Continued)

	5S – SUSTAIN – ACTIVITY DESCRIPTIONS	YES	NO
18	Is the 6S audit visible to all, up to date and shared with all staff?		
19	Recognition is given to teams who get involved in 6S activities		
20	Time and resources are continually allocated to 6S activities		
21	Has the team improved items that were not already identified on the previous audit?		
	6S – SAFETY – ACTIVITY DESCRIPTIONS		
22	Are employees wearing suitable PPE required for their current work?		
23	Walkways and access to safety equipment are clearly identified and unobstructed (no hazards or obstacles in the way of fire extinguishers, emergency access doors)		
24	Is the working environment suitable for the work in hand (lighting, air quality, temperature)?		
25	Are the equipment and tools provided correctly for the current work activity?		

Table 1.3 shows an audit tool which can be carried out in a work area, including offices. It can be adapted to work in most areas. An interactive version of this audit tool can be found at http://tools.adaptivebms.com/

Allied to 5S are the 7 Muda. These are as follows:

1 Inventory – wastes space, equipment, facilities, energy, administration and IT resources. It needs to be evaluated and adjusted as necessary.

2 Motion – any motion of a person or machine that does not add value needs to be removed.

3 Over-production – 'just in case' mentality. 'More than', 'faster than' or 'sooner than needed' have to stop.

4 Waiting – waiting is idle time. Created by imbalances of machinery or people. This needs to be reduced or eradicated.

5 Re-work – reject, repair, re-work causes a great waste of resources: materials, manpower and machinery. Although capturing value in the warehouse it shouldn't occur in the first place.

6 Processing – non-logical flow in the wrong sequence that adds no value – needs to be regularly evaluated – walk through the process regularly.

7 Conveyance – essential but adds no value. Every time you move something it adds cost. Reduce these movements.

Companies need to carry out an audit to identify areas that can be improved based on the 7 Muda. Discuss the process/procedures and how any changes can benefit the organization.

Further information

There is an abundance of literature on this topic and websites specifically for Six Sigma and Lean: www.isixsigma.com

References

http://tools.adaptivebms.com/ [accessed 3 March 2013]
Toyota TPS system. www.toyota-forklifts.co.uk

1.3   Pareto analysis, 80/20 rule, ABC analysis or the vital few analysis

Introduction

Vilfredo Pareto was an Italian economist who calculated that 80 per cent of the land in Italy was owned by 20 per cent of the population and that 20 per cent of his pea plants produced 80 per cent of the crop. This idea was taken further by Joseph Juran, a US consultant. It is now used by companies to identify and separate best-selling products and profitable customers from slow-moving products and less profitable customers.

The tool is used heavily within the warehouse environment. Examples are as follows:

20 per cent of the stock lines account for 80 per cent of sales;

20 per cent of the stock lines produce 80 per cent of the profit;

20 per cent of stock lines appear most frequently on orders;

20 per cent of the stock keeping units (SKU) account for 80 per cent of the stock value;

20 per cent of suppliers provide 80 per cent of the stock lines;

20 per cent of customers produce 80 per cent of turnover;

>20 per cent of customers cause 80 per cent of the problems;
>
>20 per cent of customers produce 80 per cent of the profit;
>
>20 per cent of the staff produce 80 per cent of the output;
>
>20 per cent of staff cause 80 per cent of problems.

These are all common rules of thumb used in business today. They may not be exact for every company, but most companies can relate to at least some of them. It is the 20 per cent figure (or the vital few) that we need to concentrate our efforts on; that is, our top 20 per cent of customers, suppliers, product lines and staff.

When to use

This tool can be used in many areas of logistics – the warehouse in particular. One of the most time-consuming operations within a warehouse is the picking of orders. It can take up to 60 per cent of the overall labour activity within the warehouse and, of that, half can be accounted for by travel to, between and from the pick locations. Thus, to reduce travel in the warehouse we need to place our most popular items in terms of order frequency (not sales volume) as close to the dispatch area as possible. To do this, we need to analyse our data.

How to use

If we take a company's order profile we can use Excel as a tool to list all of the products by sales frequency and use the 'Data Sort' function to list them from highest to lowest, as can be seen in Table 1.4. Once this analysis has been undertaken, you can revise the warehouse layout by having the top 20 per cent of popular stock lines (SKU), ie those that appear most often on orders, at the front of the warehouse closest to dispatch. Many companies use the total unit sales; however, this can provide a false picture in terms of warehouse layout as some items may sell in large quantities but only once a year, whereas others sell on a continuous basis.

As we can see in Table 1.4, the first four items have by far the most appearances on orders during the period. These are classified as fast movers, the next six as medium movers, and the following eight as class 'C' or slow movers. They are also referred to as runners, repeaters and strangers. As a rule of thumb 80 per cent of order frequency appearance tends to come from 20 per cent of the product lines (A items), 15 per cent of order frequency appearance from 35 per cent of the product lines (B items) and 5 per cent of order frequency appearance from 45 per cent of the product lines. The last two items have not

TABLE 1.4 ABC analysis of pick list frequency

Product code	Ranking (by order frequency)	Frequency in period	Cumulative frequency	Cumulative % of total frequency	Cumulative % of number of stock lines	Category
123	1	300	300	30	5	A
235	2	225	525	52.5	10	A
127	3	150	675	67.5	15	A
134	4	125	800	80	20	A
167	5	40	840	84	25	B
222	6	30	870	87	30	B
361	7	25	895	89.5	35	B
363	8	25	920	92	40	B
221	9	17	937	93.7	45	B
344	10	15	952	95.2	50	B
345	11	10	962	96.2	55	C
166	12	8	970	97	60	C
177	13	6	976	97.6	65	C
189	14	6	982	98.2	70	C
190	15	6	988	98.8	75	C
111	16	4	992	99.2	80	C
1035	17	4	996	99.6	85	C
1037	18	4	1,000	100	90	C
126	19	0	1,000	100	95	X
135	20	0	1,000	100	100	X
Total		1,000				

sold at all during the period, and need to be assessed by Sales, Marketing, Procurement and Finance to determine whether they are likely to be sold in the future, need to be put on special offer, returned to the suppliers or written off. In this example we have denoted them with an 'X' for further analysis.

This tool can also be used for perpetual inventory or cycle counting (see tool 3.5) and with activity-based costing (see tool 8.1) to determine which customers should be retained in terms of profitability and also how much sales time should be allocated to each customer. It is usually the case that the smaller customers demand more management time!

Provided that you have accurate information for each of these parameters, the 80/20 analysis can be a valuable tool in any company's armoury.

Further information

There is a significant amount of information on the web for ABC analyses in logistics. The author's own book, Richards, G (2014) has a section on the subject.

An Excel template can be downloaded from http://howtologistics.com; discount code: lsct0104.

Reference

Richards, G (2014) *Warehouse Management*, 2nd edn, Kogan Page, London

1.4   Choosing an order-picking strategy

Introduction

Many warehouses continue to pick orders individually; however, there are ways of combining orders to speed up the picking process. We also find that there is confusion between the different pick strategies in terms of how they are described. Below is our interpretation.

Pick by individual order

Line items are collected from all locations by an individual for a specific customer order. Once picked, the operator returns for the next order:

- Instructions can be via paper-based systems, scanners or voice technology.
- It is normally a single-stage process unless every order is checked on dispatch.

- Handling equipment can range from a trolley to a forklift truck.
- Prone to error if using paper-based system.
- Time-consuming.
- Training can be time-consuming for scanning and paper pick.

Cluster picking

Operators take several individual orders out into the warehouse at the same time:

- Operation is as per individual order pick otherwise.
- Order sizes are lower than for individual order picks.
- Orders are clustered in a particular area.
- Normally a single-stage process unless every order is packed and checked on dispatch.
- Handling equipment can range from a trolley to a forklift truck but requires segregated sections.
- Reliant on operator being accurate in sorting.
- System assistance required to ensure orders are clustered efficiently.
- Training can be very time-consuming.

Pick by batch

Large quantities of items are collected for a large number of orders that have the same product lines. All orders are consolidated onto one pick request:

- Typical use in e-commerce applications.
- One to five lines per order maximum.
- Can pick exact amount from reserve storage and allocate to zero or pick full cartons/pallets and return remainder to stock (pick by line) once allocation is completed.
- Handling equipment is mainly reach or forklift trucks for pallet quantities.
- Two-stage process – pick then sort and label. Possible return of unused stock.
- Requires additional space to sort and label.
- Reliant on system to consolidate orders.

Pick by zone

Products are categorized into specific groups and located in defined areas within the warehouse:

- Reduced walking distance as operator looks after small area.
- Picking can be simultaneous or sequential.
- Requires conveyors to transport orders around the warehouse.
- Essential to ensure each zone has near equal activity.
- Used with pick and put to light systems.
- High accuracy if combined with scanning.

Pick by waves

Large numbers of orders are picked during defined time periods:

- Any of the above pick methods can be used.
- Pick is associated with vehicle departures, shift changes, order deadlines, etc.

Goods to picker

Large number of orders can be picked at the same time:

- Initial orders are batched together.
- Picker remains in one position.
- Products are brought to the picker by conveyor or automated system.
- Operator uses put to light system to allocate items to individual orders.
- Little training required.

When to use

When looking to improve both productivity and accuracy within the warehouse.

How to use

Table 1.5 compares the methods discussed above.

Further information

There are a number of books and websites on the subject of picking; page 22 lists a few suggestions:

TABLE 1.5 Order-picking strategies comparison chart

Pick method	Typical applications	Benefits	Disadvantages
Pick by individual order	Most operations	• Single-stage operation • Flexible • Quick implementation • Ability to isolate urgent orders • Picker able to decide pick path if using paper pick system • Utilize manual or technology systems	• Low pick rate • Very labour intensive • Can result in bottlenecks at the pick face • Training can take some time depending on the tools used
Cluster picking	Most operations with low cube items	• Multiple orders picked at the same time • Reduce travel in the warehouse if orders clustered in a particular area • Reduce overall pick time	• Training can take some time • Accuracy can be an issue if no technology is used • Urgent orders cannot be separated easily • Requires equipment to hold multiple orders • Requires low cube items in the main • Requires system assistance to combine orders • Can result in bottlenecks • May require second stage to pack orders

(Continued)

TABLE 1.5 Order-picking strategies comparison chart (*Continued*)

Pick method	Typical applications	Benefits	Disadvantages
Batch pick to zero	e-commerce Retail store orders	• Multiple orders picked at the same time • Very effective for e-commerce orders where 100s of orders for single line items are received • Reduced travel • Increased accuracy • Can be used successfully in a cross-dock operation	• Urgent orders cannot be separated easily • Requires system assistance to combine orders • Pick to zero initial pick likely to take longer than pick to line • Requires sortation area and additional staff • Repackaging required
Batch pick by line	e-commerce Retail store orders	• Multiple orders picked at the same time • Increased accuracy • Very effective for e-commerce orders where 100s of orders for single line • Reduced travel	• Urgent orders cannot be separated easily • With pick to line, excess products need to be returned to location • Requires sortation area and additional staff • Repackaging required

TABLE 1.5 Order-picking strategies comparison chart (*Continued*)

Zone pick	Situations where there are large numbers of SKUs and low number of items per order line	• Less travel for operator • Orders can be picked simultaneously or sequentially • Can accommodate different families of items on orders such as hazardous, temperature controlled, ambient etc • Less training if pick to light used	• Normally requires conveyors • Cost of equipment • Normally combined with pick/put to light systems • Can lead to idle time if work is not balanced between zones
Wave pick	When orders are released on a timed basis or to meet departing trucks	• Ability to schedule work efficiently • Orders are picked in time for a production run or vehicle departure	• Urgent orders cannot be separated easily • Requires a WMS to manage the allocation
Goods to picker	High intensity pick operations	• High pick rates • High accuracy • Equipment moves, operators stay in the same place • Reduced space requirement • Product security • Ergonomic workstations • Training is less intensive	• High equipment costs • High energy costs • Potential system failure • High opportunity cost • Standardized unit loads required • Limited to smaller items in the main

Ackerman, K (2000) *Warehousing Profitably*, Ackerman Publications, Columbus, OH

Frazelle, EH (2002) *World Class Warehousing and Materials Handling*, McGraw-Hill, New York

Richards, G (2014) *Warehouse Management*, 2nd edn, Kogan Page, London

Van den Berg, J P (2012) *Highly Competitive Warehouse Management*, Management Outlook Publishing, Utrecht, Netherlands

1.5 Choosing pick technology

Introduction

The picking function in a warehouse can be up to 55 per cent of the operating cost, with travel to, between and from locations being up to 50 per cent of that labour involvement. It is therefore crucial to choose the most appropriate method of picking.

Many warehouses continue to use system-created paper pick lists to pick orders within the warehouse. There are a number of alternatives, the majority requiring some form of technology. Table 1.6 shows the advantages and disadvantages of each method. One thing to point out here is that many warehouses will use a combination of pick methods, depending on requirements such as velocity of movement, lead times and accuracy requirements.

When to use

When looking to improve both productivity and accuracy within the warehouse.

How to use

Table 1.6 compares the different picking systems. A new picking method called 'vision pick' utilizing technology similar to Google glasses has been introduced by a number of companies recently. This is currently in its early stages and therefore not included, but as more companies use the system we will look to update the table.

Further information

There is some excellent content at http://www.inventoryops.com/order_picking.htm

TABLE 1.6 Pick technology comparison chart

	Applications and pick rate	Benefits	Drawbacks
Paper picking	• Most operations • Where there is very little systems support • Low cost areas • <100 lines per hour	• Low cost • Single-stage picking operation although two-stage update operation (key information into system) • Flexible • Quick implementation • Ability to isolate urgent orders • Picker able to decide pick path • Low maintenance • Suitable as part of a contingency plan	• Low pick rate • Not hands free • Low accuracy • Duplicated tasks • Not real time • Training can take some time • Requires manual update of system from written instructions • Requires return to desk for further instructions
Pick by label	• Most operations • Where there is very little systems support • Low cost areas • <100 lines per hour	• Low cost • Reasonably accurate • Single-stage picking operation although two-stage update operation • Flexible • Quick implementation • Low maintenance	• Low pick rate • Not hands free • Duplicated tasks • Need to print labels • Not real time • Training can take some time • Label information may be difficult to read • Can damage product if errors made • Requires return to desk for further instructions

(Continued)

TABLE 1.6   Pick technology comparison chart *(Continued)*

	Applications and pick rate	Benefits	Drawbacks
Barcode scanning with gun	• Most operations • <100 lines per hour	• Improved accuracy* • Paperless • Flexible • Real-time stock update** • Ability to deal with multi-SKU locations	• Low/medium pick rate • Not hands free • Can take longer than paper picking • Cost of hardware • Requires barcode on every product • Issues with international bar code standards • Requires system interface • Requires maintenance • Real time system requires wireless receivers throughout warehouse
Wearable scanners	• Most operations • <150 lines per hour	• Paperless • Flexible • Improved accuracy • Improved productivity • Hands free • Less strain on operators • Damage reduction • Real-time stock update • Ability to deal with multi-SKU locations	• Cost of hardware • Requires bar code on product • Issues with international bar code standards • Requires system interface • Requires maintenance

(Continued)

TABLE 1.6   Pick technology comparison chart (*Continued*)

	Applications and pick rate	Benefits	Drawbacks
Voice picking	• Most operations • Ideal for temperature-controlled areas • Heavy, awkward items • 100–250 lines per hour	• Paperless • Flexible • Fewer processes • Improved accuracy* • Improved productivity • Quick training • Hands free/eyes free • Improved safety • Less strain on operators • Damage reduction • Real-time stock update	• Cost of hardware • Difficult in very noisy environments • Requires system interface • Requires maintenance • Problem with multi-SKU location • Serial number capture is an issue • Accuracy issue if product in incorrect location • Unsure of long-term health issues
Voice picking plus finger scanning	• Most operations • Ideal for temperature-controlled areas • 125–250 lines per hour	• Paperless • High accuracy • Good productivity • Hands free • Less strain on operators • Damage reduction • Real-time stock update • Ability to deal with multi-SKU location	• Cost of hardware and software • Requires bar code • Requires system interface • Issues with international bar code standards • Unsure of long-term health issues

(*Continued*)

TABLE 1.6 Pick technology comparison chart (*Continued*)

	Applications and pick rate	Benefits	Drawbacks
Pick to light	• High no. SKUs high frequency sales per individual item • Mail order/e-commerce • (approx. 250–450 lines per hour)	• High accuracy* • High productivity • High pick rate • Easy to train staff • Staff can choose pick sequence • Real-time stock update • Hands free • Improved safety • Damage reduction • Simultaneous or sequential picking • Can be used for goods-to-person and person-to-goods picking (zone)	• Cost of hardware • Requires system interface • System failure • Cost of maintenance • Low flexibility • Long implementation time • Limited in terms of product types • Problem with multi-SKU locations • Difficulty with batched or clustered orders
Put to light	• Retail store operations	• High accuracy • High productivity • Damage reduction • High pick rate • Easy to train • Real-time stock update • Can be used for goods-to-person picking	• Cost of hardware • System failure • Limited in terms of product types • Cost of maintenance • Two-stage operation

(*Continued*)

TABLE 1.6 Pick technology comparison chart *(Continued)*

	Applications and pick rate	Benefits	Drawbacks
RFID	• High-value goods • Items requiring accurate traceability • 200–300 lines per hour	• Very high accuracy • High productivity • Real-time stock update	• Cost of hardware • Cost of tags • Read distances very short • Requires international standards • Issues with certain types of products – metal and liquids • Requires system interface • Cost of maintenance

* High accuracy is dependent on accurate put-away. Can be supplemented by reading out last four digits of barcode for voice picking.

** Scanning can be real time or information can be downloaded once the tasks are completed.

1.6 Cross-docking

Introduction

Cross-docking is a technique utilized in distribution centres and warehouses to speed up the throughput of products. It eliminates the need to store product by consolidating items during the inbound process and taking them directly to the shipping or despatch area.

Items are likely to remain on site for a maximum of 24 hours, with most leaving in a much shorter time. These can be despatched separately or can be consolidated with product picked from stock. The costs of holding and handling inventory are significantly reduced. Walmart puts some of its success down to cross-docking as much as 85 per cent of its products through working closely with its suppliers and having sophisticated IT systems.

When to use

The pressure on companies to reduce order lead times requires products to move through the supply chain much faster. Cross-docking enables this to happen.

A variant of this is a sequencing centre where parts destined for a production line are consolidated and sorted so that they arrive at the production line only when they are required.

How to use

To operate an efficient cross-dock requires a good information technology system. Advanced shipping notifications (ASNs) are essential and goods need to be identified easily at the inbound stage to enable staff to move them directly to the dispatch or shipping area as opposed to the storage area. To enable this, barcodes have to be aligned across suppliers and customers.

Suppliers can be requested to label the items with information that enables the goods-in team to identify the items quickly. Alternatively, the inbound team are alerted to the fact that a transfer of goods is required by an instruction on the paperwork, a voice message or a message on the barcode scanner. If the company is using scan technology, a message appears on screen as soon as the goods for cross-docking have been identified. Instructions as to where to move the product should also be given at this time.

Ideally a vehicle is already waiting on the loading dock for the items in question. This requires excellent coordination and planning. Alternatively, the pallets or cartons are placed in a section of the dispatch area that is marked out for outbound loads. If space is at a premium in the dispatch area, drive-in racking can be used to hold the products until the outbound vehicle arrives; see Figure 1.3.

The coordination of inbound and outbound movements is key to the system working effectively. An example of this is the hub operation for a parcel or pallet distribution operation where items arrive in time to meet a departing vehicle returning to its geographic area. A vehicle cannot depart until the last vehicle carrying goods destined for its area has arrived.

Finally, warehouse design plays its part in terms of where the inbound and outbound doors are located. If they are situated next to each other as in Figure 1.3, there is a need to ensure that congestion is not an issue. Alternatively, doors can be situated at opposite sides of the building, with

FIGURE 1.3 Example of cross-dock operation

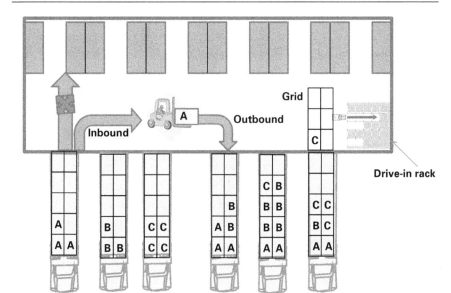

forklift trucks travelling the length of the building to load out the vehicles – less congestion but increased travel distances.

Further information

Further information can be found at http://www.werc.org/store/item. aspx?ItemId=27

1.7 Slotting or item profiling

Introduction

Inventory slotting or profiling is the process of identifying the most efficient placement for each stock item in a warehouse or distribution centre, taking into account item popularity, characteristics and safety aspects. Strategically placing the item in the optimum location allows workers to pick items efficiently, quickly and accurately, and reduces the risk of injuries.

When to use

To enable you to improve the efficiency of your picking operation within the warehouse.

How to use

Slotting can be done manually using standard spreadsheets, database programs or specifically designed slotting software. Slotting is a recent addition to many warehouse management systems (WMS).

There are several ways to increase picking productivity with slotting. Placing fast-moving items close to the dispatch area, conveyors and aisle ends minimizes picker travel time. Using easier-to-pick locations for high-activity items, such as the middle levels of shelving and carton flow racks, also facilitates quicker and more ergonomic picking.

Items that are often sold together should be stored together to reduce travel. This can also help distinguish between similar parts. For example, placing the same size nut and bolt together not only reduces travel but also separates one bolt size from another. Other potential pairings include dry pasta and pasta sauces.

From a safety point of view, frequently picked and moderate-weight items should be placed at a height between an average person's waist and shoulders to minimize the chance of injury to pickers and replenishment staff. In warehouses where there is a mix of heavy and fragile items, the heaviest items should be placed at the beginning of the pick path so that they are loaded at the bottom of a pallet, carton or tote.

Where items appear frequently on orders, these should not only be put close to dispatch but also into multiple locations in this area of the warehouse in order to balance the workload and avoid bottlenecks.

Items can also be grouped within the warehouse based on vendor or product similarities. Vendor groupings can simplify merchandise put-away. Family groups can also be established to cluster items that are often sold together or items with specific storage or handling requirements. Retailers may use family groups to organize the warehouse logically so that the pick mirrors the layout in the stores.

Careful slotting can also ensure that items are placed in properly sized locations. The full cubic capacity of the location should be used, allowing for clearance height requirements. The location should hold a sufficient quantity of inventory to meet the restocking goals for the warehouse, for example a full shift's pick.

How to start

The first step in any inventory slotting project is gathering the necessary information about the items, locations in the warehouse and product sales.

Data may already be stored in the WMS or ERP (enterprise resource planning) system. Otherwise items and cases need to be physically measured. The following information is typically needed for each SKU:

- item length, width, height and weight;
- case quantity and dimensions (length, width, height and weight) for items stored by the case;
- pallet quantity (or cases/tier and tiers/pallet – TiHi) for items stored by the pallet;
- vendor if items are to be stored in vendor groupings;
- family group if items are to be stored by product groupings;
- special storage conditions, if applicable (flammable, refrigeration, high value, etc);
- maximum stacking height or crushability factor, if applicable;
- items that often appear together on an order;
- items that are very similar resulting in miss-picks or that can cause a chemical reaction should not be stored next to each other.

Each pick location in the warehouse needs to be defined. Information typically required for each slot is:

- location number;
- usable size (length, width, height);
- weight capacity;
- proximity to material handling equipment (MHE) and shipping;
- position within the pick path;
- types of items eligible to be stored here (hazard code, vendor or family group, batch code).

Item movement can be captured in terms of the number of times each item was sold (hits), the quantity sold, sales forecast (stocking level) and the on-hand quantity. Hits and quantity sold are most typically used because high-hit items should be placed in the most efficient locations and the optimal size location can be established using the quantity sold and the dimensions.

If items change frequently and do not have any historical movement figures, sales forecasts may be used instead of history. On-hand quantity data are important for warehouses that choose to size locations in slow pick areas to a typical on-hand inventory level, rather than a sales level.

Slotting rules

Once the necessary data have been collected, slotting rules must be established by setting up constraints (rules that cannot be broken) and objectives (goals). Constraints include weight limits, hazardous material areas and vendor/family group areas. Objectives define factors such as the desired stock level, where faster-moving items are placed and how activity will be balanced. Examples of some typical rules include:

- Put the fast-moving items close to the shipping dock and on the lower pallet rack levels. Store slower-moving items on higher levels and further away from the dock.

- In the case pick area, locate taller cases and heavier cases at the beginning of the pick path. Put faster-moving cases on floor/lower levels.

- If using carousels, balance the activity among carousels in pod. Spread faster-moving items among the carousels and put them on the centre shelves.

- Place fast-moving items into carton flow racks, with the very fastest on the centre levels. Balance the workload among the flow rack units.

- Put slower-moving items into shelving, with the faster-moving ones placed closer to the take-away conveyor or end of aisle. Locate heavier items on the centre levels.

Proper slotting takes time to establish, and regular maintenance is required to keep items positioned efficiently; however, slotting software can ease the burden of keeping items in proper locations. Slotting items properly increases picking productivity and makes order selection easier, safer and more accurate.

Trial re-slotting runs should be made to test the rules and refine them so that they will yield the desired results. You can opt to make the profile changes gradually during normal operations, rather than interrupting fulfilment activities to move hundreds of items. You can review item placement on a weekly basis and move items each night to relocate the most badly placed SKUs. Although it will take several months to achieve the optimal profile, picking productivity will increase with each set of moves.

(Reproduced by kind permission of Sedlak Management Consultants, http://www.jasedlak.com)

Further information

Details on specific slotting software can be found at http://www.slot3d.com, http://www.insight-holdings.com/dc-expert-40

1.8   Resource planning

Introduction

Labour is a significant cost within a warehouse operation. Warehouse managers are constantly charged with optimizing the number of staff employed and reducing overall headcount by increasing productivity. Planning work is therefore crucial to the running of a cost-effective warehouse.

Labour management enables warehouse managers to compare productivities between staff and engineered standards, and as a result identify opportunities for further training or possible redeployment. The system can also be used to introduce incentive schemes and be part of an appraisal system.

There are a number of labour management systems (LMSs) available on the market, some of which are listed at the end of this tool. Some WMSs also have a labour management module. However, it is possible to plan the resources required within a warehouse manually through the use of spreadsheets.

When to use

It is our contention that all warehouses should operate with some form of resource plan to ensure that the correct number of staff are deployed each day and therefore it should be part of daily operations. Resource planning enables the warehouse manager to reasonably calculate the number of staff required each day for each section of the warehouse and, when busy, to calculate how many additional staff may be required.

How to use

Table 1.7 details a number of warehouse tasks together with the volume of activity, productivity standards and the expected time to undertake these tasks. Forms such as this can be completed each day based on the activities planned for the coming days and weeks. It requires advanced information in terms of receipts and orders, whether forecast or actual. It also requires staff to undertake time-and-motion studies to calculate the time required to undertake each activity.

The data can be updated with actual figures once the task has been completed: this provides a more accurate picture for future similar work. Table 1.7 details an in-handling operation over the course of one day. Each activity is listed together with the expected volume and this, together with the engineered standards previously estimated, enables the warehouse manager to calculate the number of staff required and the equipment needed. By completing this form, the warehouse manager is able to calculate the number of people and equipment required for that particular day's operation.

Utilizing an electronic LMS enables you to evaluate the productivity of individuals as well as the team as a whole. It measures the performance of each individual for completed tasks against existing labour standards to determine how the time spent performing each task compares with the expected task completion time. The system, if interfacing with voice or radio frequency, can more accurately measure the task in hand, taking into account idle time, delays and bottlenecks. The system is able to assign the operator an overall score. This enables the warehouse manager to compare performance against engineered standards and the operator's peers. The system is a great deal more sophisticated than a spreadsheet and will produce the data much faster. A number of steps are required to set up the system; see (Figure 1.4).

The more sophisticated LMSs can also create a list of tasks for an operator and coordinate tasks. As Obal (2011) says: 'When you start interleaving and measuring people, you are driving out a lot of inefficiencies. You're maximizing your labour that is already there in the warehouse.'

Although many WMSs have LMS as an option or even inbuilt, there are a large number of standalone systems that can be interfaced with both warehouse and transport management systems. A list of suppliers of LMS can be found at the website below.

Further information

http://www.capterra.com/workforce-management-software?gclid=CMaxj8 DF57UCFXDKtAodqxsAYA

Reference

Obal, P (2011) cited in 2011 *Market Trends Report: Warehouse Management Programs*, http://www.warehousemanagementsystemsguide.com/blog/2011-market-trends-report-warehouse-management-systems-1020911/#ixzz2Kzs7qs30

TABLE 1.7 In-handling resource plan

| Activity Description | Daily volume (average) | | Productivity standard (units per hour) | Hours required | MHE Type 1 | MHE Type 2 | MHE Type 3 | Other equipment eg radio frequency scanner |
Inbound operation	Activity (units)	Unit of measure						
Unloading								
Unload palletized trailer	260	Pallets	52	5	PPT			RFS
Unload loose loaded containers & palletize	5000	Cases	200	25				RFS
Stretch-wrap pallets	100	Pallets	40	2.5				
Put-away								
Collect pallets, put away in wide aisle racking	210	Pallets	20	10.5		FLT		RFS
Collect pallets, put away in drive-in racking	124	Pallets	16	7.75		FLT		RFS
Collect pallets, put away in pick locations	26	Pallets	5	5.2	PPT			RFS

(Continued)

TABLE 1.7 In-handling resource plan (Continued)

Activity Description	Daily volume (average)		Productivity standard (units per hour)	Hours required	MHE Type 1	MHE Type 2	MHE Type 3	Other equipment eg radio frequency scanner
Inbound operation	Activity (units)	Unit of measure						
Sub-total				55.95				
Ancillary work (collect paperwork, equipment etc. (15%)				8.39				
Total Hours required				64.34	10.20	18.25		
Available productive hours per person/truck per day				7.2	8	8		
Approx. number of staff required				**8.94**				
Approx. number of equipment required					**1.28**	**2.28**		

FIGURE 1.4 Setting up a labour management system

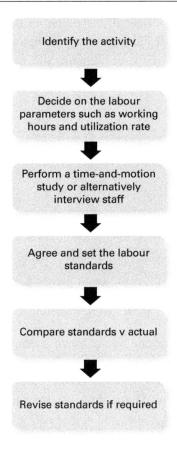

Identify the activity

Decide on the labour parameters such as working hours and utilization rate

Perform a time-and-motion study or alternatively interview staff

Agree and set the labour standards

Compare standards v actual

Revise standards if required

1.9 Task interleaving

Introduction

Minimal movement within a warehouse is key to efficiency and productivity. There are a number of ways of reducing the amount of travel undertaken in a warehouse.

As we have seen in the ABC/Pareto tool (tool 1.3), the notion of placing the most popular items as close to the dispatch area as possible reduces the amount of travel in the warehouse. Another method of movement reduction is task interleaving or dual cycling. Task interleaving is controlled by a WMS that allocates tasks to ensure an operator travels full both ways.

For example, an operator unloading a trailer on inbound and taking the pallet to reserve storage will be tasked with collecting a pallet for replenishment or possibly dispatch depending on the amount of travel required between locations. This can reduce equipment use by up to 30 per cent. The system works well with full pallet movements both inbound and outbound.

When to use

When looking to increase efficiency and reduce travel within the warehouse.

How to use

The idea is to combine work for a forklift truck or powered pallet truck. According to Tomkins (2003), task interleaving is especially good for tasks with the following characteristics:

- The same materials handling equipment can be used to undertake both types of moves.
- The end location for one type of move is relatively close to the collection point for the other move. This means that the operator and truck are utilized both ways rather than two separate single trips, which often happens. This is similar to the back-loading concept used in freight transport.
- The moves are pretty much equal both ways. Ensuring that the tasks are well matched needs an accurate set-up in the WMS.

Although put-away and replenishment may seem a good match, it is likely that interleaving these tasks can cause increased travel and delays for both processes. For task interleaving to be successful, it needs the support of an information technology system. Most modern WMSs have this capability. This also works better when the doors are on the same side of the building and can be used for both inbound and shipping activities. It can also work reasonably well with doors on adjacent sides. It needs operations to be more flexible and not have dedicated inbound and outbound teams. The operators need to be free to undertake both put-away and dispatch activities. As a result, staff need to be able to multitask and move between operations.

Task interleaving will not be successful if inbound activities are undertaken in the morning, dispatch in the afternoon and replenishment overnight, for example. Task interleaving works best at larger facilities where more tasks can be queued up and staff will have continuous work.

The key is to manage the task allocation and not to disrupt urgent operations. The tasks have to be controlled sufficiently well and planned to coincide with other tasks. Releasing tasks too early or too late can have a devastating effect on productivity and on equipment and manpower usage.

Reference

http://www.tompkinsinc.com/task-interleaving/

1.10   Selecting warehouse storage equipment

Introduction

The selection of warehouse storage equipment is best carried out in conjunction with the equipment manufacturers. They are the experts and have experience of different types of warehouse operations. Ensure that you get a number of opinions and, if necessary, use a consultant to sense-check the options.

In this guide we look specifically at storage media. There are a number of different options when it comes to choosing the method of storage. The choice of how to store product will very much depend on the product size, its speed of throughput, the number of pallets per line item and the stock rotation policy (see Table 1.8).

There are, of course, many variables that will impact on the price. The main one is pallet size and type; for example, with drive-in racking there are different design options and alternative support rails available. On double-deep racking it would normally be the use of adjustable pallet racking (APR), but some trucks require a low-level beam to accommodate reach legs, which would increase the price, and very narrow aisle (VNA) operational costs will fluctuate depending on the guidance system used. In terms of special MHE required, we mean anything other than a counterbalance or reach truck.

Figure 1.5 provides an approximate figure in terms of how many pallets can be stored within a specific area utilizing the different types of racking.

TABLE 1.8 Choosing a warehouse racking system

	Use of floor space	Use of cubic space	Speed of throughput	Access to individual pallets	Special MHE required	Rotation of stock	Pallets stored at ground level in 4,636 sq metres (50k sq ft)	Cost per location*
Adjustable pallet racking	**	**	***	****	No	FIFO	1,250	100
Very narrow aisle	***	***	***	****	Yes	FIFO	1,650	100
Drive in racking	*****	***	**	*	No	FILO	2,120	200
Double-deep racking	***	***	**	**	Yes	FILO	1,650	100
Push-back racking	***	***	**	**	No	FILO	1,950	500
Gravity-fed racking	****	***	****	*	No	FIFO	2,500	700
Mobile racking	****	***	*	****	No	FIFO	2,325	400
Satellite racking	*****	****	***	*	Yes	FILO	2,500	500

*The cost column assumes that standard adjustable pallet racking is given a base cost of 100.

SOURCE: Information provided by Nene Ltd

FIGURE 1.5 Pallet rack capacity

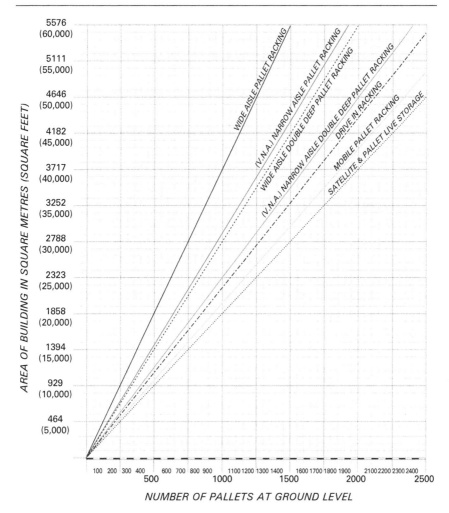

NUMBER OF PALLETS AT GROUND LEVEL

SOURCE: reproduced by kind permission of Constructor Group, http://www.constructor-group.co.uk/

1.11 Warehouse location numbering

Introduction

When you enter the majority of warehouses you are faced with row upon row of storage racks. An interesting aspect from a consultancy viewpoint is how each row or aisle of racking is identified. The following text suggests how to number rows of racking or shelving within a warehouse facility.

When to use

If a company is looking to introduce greater efficiency into its picking operation and reduce travel time, it needs to consider carefully how it numbers its pick locations.

How to do it

In Figure 1.6 we see that each row of racking is given a letter: A, B, C, etc. This results in one-sided picking as denoted by the arrows. The numbers denoted in the boxes are the pallet locations. The shaded area is an order pick location.

In this example the first pick location will have a location identification (ID) of A (row) 06 (bay) 01 (ground floor) – A0601, while the second location will be B0401. The pick list produced for the operator will automatically send him or her to the location in Row A. This can result in large walking distances as the order picker first visits the location on one side of

FIGURE 1.6 Pallet row numbering

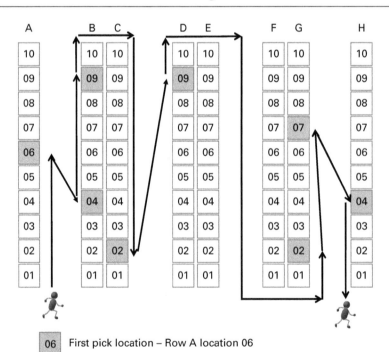

06   First pick location – Row A location 06

SOURCE: adapted from and reproduced by kind permission of JP van den Berg

the aisle and then returns to visit the locations on the other side. This method of identification can be utilized in very wide aisles; however, for narrow aisles and shelving it is more efficient to number the aisles as can be seen in Figure 1.7.

In Figure 1.7 the aisles are given letters, as opposed to each row, which results in the picker traversing the aisle and thus picking from both sides at one pass. This will reduce the amount of travel significantly. In the example the first pick location is A0801 and the second becomes A1101. As a result, the pick travel has reduced significantly. This is referred to as snake path or S-shape picking.

It can also be noted in Figure 1.7 that the location numbers begin at the other end of the aisle for aisle B thus allowing the picker to travel less and in sequence. Care should be taken in terms of which items are at the beginning of the pick sequence: heavier items should be picked first. The section on slotting (tool 1.7) gives further guidance on this subject.

FIGURE 1.7 Aisle numbering

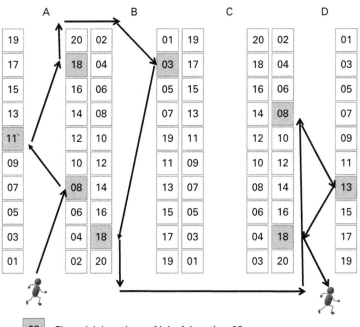

| 08 | First pick location – Aisle A location 08 |

SOURCE: adapted from and reproduced by kind permission of JP van den Berg

1.12   Selecting warehouse material handling equipment (MHE)

Introduction

The choice of MHE within a warehouse is closely linked to the choice of storage medium. It is therefore key to ensure that they are done simultaneously, taking into account the trade-off between additional space capacity and speed of throughput. In choosing the most appropriate equipment we are looking to:

- ensure staff safety;
- lower unit handling costs;
- reduce handling time;
- maximize cubic space utilization;
- reduce energy consumption and emissions.

Table 1.9 compares different truck types working in a racked storage environment. We have taken a warehouse with the following storage area dimensions – 48 metres × 120 metres × 10 metres – to bring out the differences between the trucks. Note the lift height capability of the trucks together with the aisle space required. Also note that the VNA truck requires another truck to transport the product to and from the racked area.

1.13   Warehouse space calculations

Introduction

For those companies that do not have access to warehouse design software there are a number of simple ways to calculate the space required for specific operations. In this tool we have included a calculation for dock space and racked pallet storage.

How to do it

1. Calculation of dock space requirements

The formula for this is relatively simple, as follows:

Dock space = Roundup ((Number of loads received x hours per load) / hours per shift) × (Size of load × pallet dimensions)

(continues on page 47)

TABLE 1.9 Comparison of different MHE

Type of truck	Minimum aisle width (millimetres)	Aisle space v storage space	Maximum lift height (mm)	Maximum weight at maximum lift height (kg)	Put-away rate, pallets per hour	Flexibility – internal and external usage	Additional feed truck required	Approx. total pallets stored
Reach truck BT RRE140-250	2,684 (RRE160) 2,933 (RRE250)	53% / 47% (RRE160)	10,500 (RRE160) 12,500 (RRE250)	800 (RRE160) 800 (RRE250)	28	Yes (O-series)	No	10,584 (RRE160)
Counter balance truck Traigo 48 1.5 – 2.0t 3W 1.6 – 2.0t 4W	3,102 (8FBE15T 3W) 3,438 (8FBM20T 4W)	58% / 42% (8FBE15T)	7,500 (all)	450 (8FBE15T 3W) 950 (8FBM20T 4W)	19	Yes	No	7,840 (8FBE15T)
Counter balance truck ICE Tonero 1.5 – 3.5t	3,600 (8FGF15) 4,185 (8FGJF35)	63% / 37% (8FGF15)	6,500 (all)	570 (8FGF15) 1100 (8FGJF35)	18	Yes	No	5,488 (8FGF15)
Pedestrian or stand-on stacker BT SPE120-200*	2,462 (SPE160)	53% / 47% (SPE160)	6,000 (SPE160)	660 (SPE160)	20	No	No	8,496 (SPE160)

(Continued)

TABLE 1.9 Comparison of different MHE (*Continued*)

Type of truck	Minimum aisle width (millimetres)	Aisle space v storage space	Maximum lift height (mm)	Maximum weight at maximum lift height (kg)	Put-away rate, pallets per hour	Flexibility – internal and external usage	Additional feed truck required	Approx. total pallets stored
Very narrow aisle truck Vector VCE150A	1,760mm	43% / 57%	14,300	1,500kg @ 11,000mm	25	No	Yes	12,936 (VCE150A)
Articulated forklift	2,000	48% / 52%	10,000	800 kg	20	Yes	No	11,088
Double-deep racking with reach truck BT RRE250	2,933	47% / 53%	12,500	800	26	No	No	11,760

Note the lift height capability of the trucks together with the aisle space required. Also note that the VNA truck requires another truck to transport the product from and to the racked area. The table compares different truck types working in a racked storage environment. We have taken a warehouse with the following dimensions to bring out the differences between the trucks: storage area of 48 metres × 120 metres × 10 metres, based on a GKN pallet load (1000 × 1200 × 1200) and each product type working to its respective full height where under 10 metres.

*Stacker figures calculated using Euro pallet as opposed to GKN

Figures provided by Toyota Fork-lift trucks

Data

Receiving 20 loads per day

Each load is 26 pallets

Each pallet is 1 m × 1.2 m

45 minutes per load to unload vehicle

30 minutes per load to stage prior to put-away

8 hours per day work shift

Calculation

Roundup $((20 \times 1.25)/8) \times (26 \times (1.2 \times 1.0))$

$= \text{roundup} (3.125) \times 31.2$

$= 4 \times 31.2$

$= 124.8$ square metres

Dock space $= 124.80$ square metres

Add double the space for working and travel area $= 249.60$ square metres

Total space required $= 374.40$ square metres

2. Pallet storage calculation

This tool enables operators to calculate the number of pallets that can be stored within a particular cubic area. It works on the basis of calculating width, length and height modules within the warehouse.

A module width is calculated as follows:

Module width = Width of aisle + 2 Pallet lengths (short side) + 100 mm

For example, given the following data:

Aisle = 2,500 mm (variable with type of MHE used)

Pallet size = 1,200 mm × 1,000 mm

Two pallets short side = 2 × 1,000 mm = 2,000 mm

Clearance = 100 mm between back-to-back pallets

Therefore:

Width of module
= 4,600 mm (the sequence is pallet–aisle–pallet–clearance)

A module length is calculated as follows:

Module length = Width of upright + Clearance + 2 Pallets (long side)

FIGURE 1.8 Width module calculation

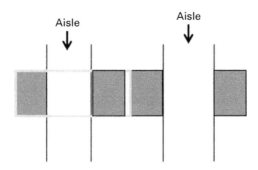

FIGURE 1.9 Length module calculation

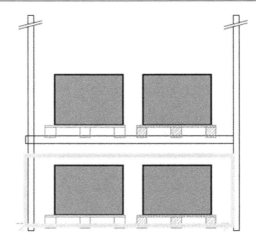

Rack upright plus clearance = 420 mm (120 mm + 3 × 100 mm)

Two pallets (long side) = 2 × 1,200 mm = 2,400 mm

Therefore:

Length of module = 2,820 mm (the sequence is upright–clearance–pallet–clearance–pallet–clearance) (see Figure 1.9).

Module height = Height of pallet + 150 mm

Pallet height = 1,350 mm

Clearance above pallet = 150 mm

APR beam width of 140 mm

Therefore:

Height of module = 1,640 mm (sequence is pallet and goods–clearance–beam height) (see Figure 1.10).

FIGURE 1.10 Height module calculation

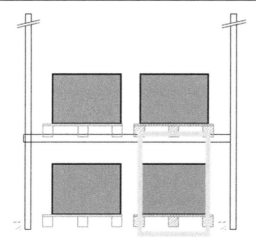

Total pallets stored within cubic capacity of a warehouse section, excluding receiving and dispatch areas, gangways and other areas:

(No. of width modules × pallets in module width) × (No. of length modules × pallets in module length) × (No. of height modules) = No. of pallets into cube volume of warehouse.

So, for a warehouse section with a width of 48 metres, a length of 120 metres and a height of 10 metres:

Width calculation = 48 m/4.6 m = 10 modules

Length calculation = 120 m/2.82 m = 42 modules

Height calculation = 10 m/1.64 m = 6 pallets

Therefore, total number of pallets = (10 × 2) × (42 × 2) × (6) = 10,080 pallet locations in this warehouse storage area.

Further information

There are a number of free resources that can calculate the number of pallets that can be stored within a specific area or volume. These are supplied, in the main, by the material handling and storage equipment companies, for example http://webtools.cisco-eagle.com/rack/

A simple pallet calculation sheet using Excel can be downloaded from http://howtologistics.com

1.14   Warehouse location

Introduction

Locating a warehouse strategically and in the most cost-effective geographic location is one of the most important decisions a company will make. The decision as to whether to operate the warehouse in-house or outsource is covered elsewhere in this book (see tool 5.1).

The selection of a warehouse location requires multiple criteria to be assessed, including both quantitative and qualitative data. Many companies will look at the location and size of customers which, although relevant, are not as important as they would be when locating a retail outlet. Factors to take into account include the following:

- cost of land, rent, rates and local taxation;
- access to transport networks;
- availability of trained labour;
- transport links for staff;
- availability of funding, grants, etc;
- availability of existing buildings;
- availability and cost of utilities, including telecoms;
- availability of finance and resources;
- goods traffic flows;
- proximity to ports, including inland ports and airports;
- location of suppliers and manufacturing points;
- the potential neighbours, eg opportunities for co-loading or, negatively, chemical facilities.

When to use

When the company is looking to locate or relocate a warehouse operation.

How to use

Figure 1.11 provides a list of criteria companies need to take into account when deciding on a new location for their warehouse. Fortunately, this does not have to be a totally manual decision as there are a number of software programs available that will take the majority of these criteria into account and produce a number of viable alternatives.

FIGURE 1.11 Warehouse location criteria

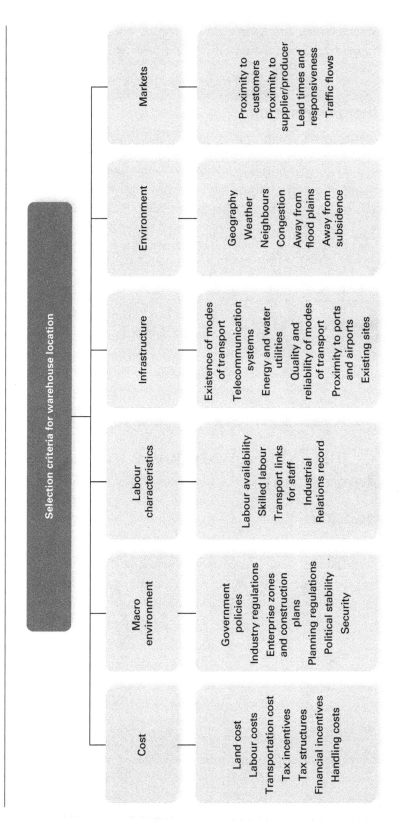

Route planning and optimization software will produce a viable location; however, supply chain optimization tools will further enhance this decision.

Further information

The websites for a number of providers of this software are:

Cirrus Logistics – http://cirruslogistics.com/products/cost2serv-network-strategy/

JDA – http://www.jda.com/solutions/

Llama Soft – www.llamasoft.com

Plan LM – www.solvoyo.com

SCM Globe – https://scmglobe.com/user_sessions/new

References

Demirel, T, Demirel, N Ç and Kahraman, C (2010) Multi-criteria warehouse location selection using Choquet integral, *Expert Systems with Applications,* 37 (5), pp 3943–52

1.15   Justifying a warehouse management system (WMS)

Introduction

A WMS has become essential to the smooth and efficient operation of complex warehousing and distribution environments around the world. Recognizing the need for a WMS is a reasonably straightforward exercise for many warehouse managers. Inaccurate inventories and pressure to continually reduce costs and improve service levels make the investment decision almost intuitive. Investments, however, are rarely made based on intuition. Fortunately, the benefits of a WMS can be identified and, to a great extent, quantified, to provide an accurate basis for justification.

When to use

When contemplating the acquisition of a WMS.

How to use

Red Prairie (now JDA) suggests a five-step plan to justify the introduction of a WMS.

Step 1: Define the problem areas

Four principal benefits can be expected to arise from the implementation of a WMS. These benefits lie in the four areas that cause the majority of efficiency problems in warehouses, including: inventory accuracy, resource management, customer service and visibility. The first step is to identify the main problems currently experienced. Begin by creating a matrix using these four benefits as the primary categories. Next, list the facility's problems under each category.

Common problems occurring under inventory accuracy include excess inventory, lost product, and miss-picks. Under resource management, problems may include wasting time looking for material, inefficient pick paths and no means of measuring performance. Customer service problems include ship errors and delayed shipments. Finally, information management problems may include stock-outs, false stock-outs, transaction update delays of hours and days, and data entry errors.

Step 2: Estimate the costs

Once any warehousing problems have been documented, the next step is to estimate the costs associated with each. This step is critical to understanding the severity of any problems. A variety of equations and industry standards can be used to quickly estimate the costs. Four examples of typical costs are listed in Table 1.10. Having completed a quick estimate of the costs, it becomes easy to identify the most urgent problems – those problems that represent your biggest cost factors. The first example indicates the impact of ship errors. Two calculations are made: one assuming a ship accuracy of 98.5 per cent and one assuming 96 per cent. Ship accuracy above 95 per cent is often thought of as excellent, yet the cost of errors in these two cases is significant – $33,750 and $90,000 respectively.

Step 3: Identify the savings

The savings associated with the reduction of inventory levels may themselves justify investment in a WMS. Many companies have reported reducing inventory levels by as much as 30 per cent. This level of reduction greatly affects carrying costs, which typically equate to 25 to 35 per cent of the cost of inventory (see Table 1.11).

TABLE 1.10 Typical cost penalty if no WMS

	Occurrence (%)	Cost/Occurrence	Total cost
Ship errors	1.5	$45	$33,750
	4.0	$45	$90,000
	(assume 50k orders pa)		
Shrinkage	1.0	.01 × $1m in invoicing	$10,000
		.01 × $7m in invoicing	$70,000
Data entry errors	4.0 (assume 100k transactions pa)	$10	$40,000
Lost product	5.0	$2.50	$31,500
	7.0	(10 minutes searching × $15/ hour)	$43,750
	(assume 50k orders × 5 lines per order)		

TABLE 1.11 Potential cost savings from introducing a WMS

	Potential cost savings (%)
Labour utilization	10–35
Inventory reduction	5–30
Floor space utilization	10–30
Maintenance	0–10
Shrinkage	50–75
Rolling stock	10–20
Increase shipping accuracy to	99+
Increase data entry accuracy to	99+

Realistically, during the few months of implementation cost savings will not be maximized because of 'learning curve' issues such as training and a re-engineered warehouse culture. However, over time, users should expect near-perfection in those areas that were once major problems. Estimated cost savings should take into consideration the fact that year two will return greater savings than year one. Minimizing the learning curve can be accomplished through training (commencing long before implementation) combined with good internal communication (change management).

Step 4: Determine the cost of a WMS

At this point in the process, it will be reasonably clear how much money and time a good WMS product will be able to save. The next step is to determine how much will have to be spent to integrate the system. Although vendors use various pricing models, the components of their pricing proposals usually fall into five categories:

1 licence fees;

2 custom development (if applicable);

3 computer hardware;

4 RF hardware; and

5 services such as design, implementation, training, testing and travel.

Your internal costs to implement the system should also be included when defining the total cost of the implementation, as well as the cost of maintenance over the time period for which you are calculating the ROI.

An alternative pricing and implementation model may also be considered. WMS systems are now available on a SaaS (software as a service) basis. In this model you typically pay a modest upfront implementation fee and then have a single monthly payment (including system and hardware costs and maintenance fees) for a specified period such as three or five years. Add the sum of the payments for the life of the contract and the implementation fee to determine total system costs.

Step 5: Calculate the ROI

See tool 8.3. Once calculated and accepted by the board you can begin the process of supplier selection (see tool 1.16).

Reference

http://www.jda.com/knowledge-center/

1.16 Selecting a warehouse management system (WMS)

Introduction

If I had to choose one tool to operate within a warehouse it would have to be a WMS, closely followed by ABC analysis (see tool 1.3). This tool describes how you should go about choosing a WMS.

A WMS can process data quicker and can coordinate movements within the warehouse. It can produce reports and handle large volumes of transactions, as seen in e-commerce operations. The potential benefits of having a WMS in place include the following:

- efficient and effective labour management;
- improvements in productivity and accuracy;
- stock visibility and traceability;
- accurate stock-takes;
- reduction in picking errors;
- reduction in returns;
- accurate reporting;
- improved responsiveness;
- remote data visibility;
- automatic replenishments;
- improved customer service; and
- minimized paperwork.

To embark on a WMS project you need to be certain that you are going to achieve significant business benefits. Such systems need capital investment, plus there are some running costs involved; however, the main 'cost' is the drive, enthusiasm and commitment needed from the entire warehousing team and senior management to ensure that the system is set up correctly, used properly and regularly optimized. A WMS is not a 'quick fix' option. A WMS is more than a stock control and data collection tool. It is a system that helps you 'automate' your warehousing operations as much as possible.

IT projects arguably should be justified on the same basis as any other business investment. A WMS is very much a tactical 'execution' system and is therefore a lot easier to justify than many IT projects. It forms an important component for strategic business improvement but nevertheless is still tactical.

When to use

When you have decided on the purchase or rental of a WMS.

How to use

Step 1: Undertake a return on investment (ROI) calculation

The justification process (see tool 1.15) is important because it helps you to set a budget for your project and also focus on the functional 'must haves' rather than the 'nice to haves' when selecting suppliers. The key areas to consider are:

- the potential for a WMS to give you improved stock accuracy – by reducing errors, providing real-time information and enabling perpetual inventory counting;
- the potential for increased productivity and cost savings – through improved labour, equipment and space utilization;
- the need for improved traceability – a WMS can give you two-way traceability, almost as a by-product of being in place;
- improved customer and client service – through overall improved warehouse control, improved pick and dispatch accuracy.

The more transactions per day (eg pallet moves, picks) and locations in the warehouse, the greater the potential for payback and the greater the justification. In addition, warehouses use expensive equipment where optimization can bring significant savings – sometimes to such an extent that less equipment needs to be purchased and fewer staff employed.

Understand the cost methods used by WMS vendors. These can be broken up into four main components:

1 *Licences* – the software licence needed to run the system. Typically this is charged by 'user', ie PC user or radio data terminal user, although different models are now being offered, including paying by transaction and/or paying monthly rather than outright purchase of the system.

2 *Professional services* – the costs for project management, training and go-live support.

3 *Development costs* for requirements not catered for in the package, including interfaces to third-party systems.

4 *Support costs* – typically an annual cost based on licence costs and often development costs; the scope of service and cost varies significantly from supplier to supplier.

Ensure that the suppliers you approach give you costs for all of the above. Ask them to indicate which prices are fixed and which are variable. Watch out for hidden costs such as travel costs, travel time and project management time. Summarize all the costs in a spreadsheet, showing the initial cost and then costs for years one to five with accumulated totals. You may be surprised by the results!

In addition, there are the hardware and infrastructure costs. These costs have to be considered in terms of project budget and ROI, of course, but in many cases can be managed as a separate project with interdependencies with the main project.

Step 2: Decide on the process

Modern WMSs are highly configurable, normally by the end user, and should be capable of working in virtually any type of warehousing environment. In the past, the production of large detailed ITTs (tender documents) was an important part of the WMS selection process. This reflected the limited functionality of most systems at that time. A major disadvantage of ITTs is that they cannot hope to take account of a company's future requirements and are often over-prescriptive. The other disadvantage is that many WMS providers will often not respond to ITTs. They consume a vast amount of time, which the vendor might prefer to spend in other directions under its own control.

There are spreadsheet templates that are downloadable from the internet; however, many of these are, or were originally, prepared by WMS vendors and are slanted towards their products. Most WMS vendors therefore view such documents with suspicion.

Step 3. Understand and analyse your existing systems

If your ERP/business system already has a WMS module then you should analyse this in the first place. The same due diligence applies to this selection as to any other system, but normally any small shortfalls in functionality are outweighed by reducing any risks of systems not interfacing with each other reliably and accurately.

Similarly, if your warehouse is highly automated, with cranes, conveyors or sortation systems, you may wish to focus on the WMS provided by the automation systems company. This will typically be known as a warehouse control system or WCS. Again, shortfalls in functionality are often outweighed by the avoidance of an interface to an external WMS. There are many papers available on this subject and some of these are mentioned below.

Step 4: Is there an in-house development capability?

Owing to the 'packaged' nature of the WMS market nowadays, in-house development is very rarely viable as a typical WMS vendor will have perhaps 100+ clients over which it amortizes the continuous development costs; these same 100+ clients serve as a very valuable and thorough proving ground for the product in question. In-house development is sometimes viable if the overall requirements are particularly specialized or require specialized integration with existing in-house systems.

Step 5: Request for information

Prepare a short RFI document (request for information); this should typically be no more than a few pages long. In this document you describe your business, your future business direction, your warehouse and your plans for the warehouse. Then talk in broad terms about what you want to achieve from the WMS.

By this stage you will have completed an operational specification for the warehouse to gain capital approval. The key elements from this specification are an ideal base for the RFI, for example number of loading bays, number and type of reserve locations, number of pick face locations, and pick and pack station details. Of particular relevance is the number of users, ie administrative users, forklift-truck drivers, pickers, packers and so on. Provide a guide to the number of transactions per day (receipts, put-aways, picks, dispatches) and indicate if there are any significant peaks across the day, week or month.

Do not try to describe how the system should work – in fact it can be dangerous to be too specific at this point, as there may be faster, better, cheaper ways of doing things and part of the selection process is to see how potential suppliers can guide you in this regard. You could use the services of a specialist consultant to help you.

Within the RFI, ask the vendor for budget costs and implementation timescales. You should ask for supplier information, including:

- company history;
- financial history and status;
- number of sites using its current WMS product;
- who owns the IP (intellectual property – source code) for the WMS;

- client list;
- daily rates and support charges;
- support cover;
- development plans;
- track record.

We suggest that you send this RFI to six to 10 suppliers initially. Focus on suppliers that have experience in your market – this is particularly the case if you are a third-party logistics provider; WMS vendors with no experience in this sector are unlikely to have the functionality and importantly the expertise to help you. Focus on suppliers that have a track record linking to any business or ERP system you are operating.

At this stage you will need to decide whether to purchase the software and hardware outright or to rent the software and operate it on a third-party server platform. A SaaS (Software as a Service) WMS is an internet-based application that is developed, hosted and maintained by a third-party software provider on secure servers. The vendor rents out the system to a number of different clients. These clients, in turn, will choose the various modules within the software they require and pay for them as they use them. The advantages are:

- lower cost of entry;
- reduced start-up costs;
- instant upgrades;
- user-driven innovation;
- ability to turn on and off as required, eg to run a temporary warehouse operation.

Such a system will be attractive to start-up companies and small and medium-sized enterprises (SMEs), although it could benefit larger companies that are looking for a temporary fix. Potential disadvantages include the possibility of poor internet links between the companies and worries over data security.

Step 6: Short list

Produce a short list of three to five suppliers. Price, of course, is not the main criterion at this stage but can be used to rule out suppliers that will exceed your budget. Get the suppliers to visit you for an informal meeting. This will help you get a feel of their company – how professional they are, how carefully they listen and respond to your needs, how well they answer your questions.

Before you get into the detailed demonstration stage, do a little more checking on each of the suppliers; this will help you to reject unsuitable suppliers at an early stage. A good way of doing this is to telephone-interview at least six reference sites, preferably sites you choose from a longer list. These calls should all be made with the knowledge of the supplier – unless you have contacts with their clients already.

Get the short-listed suppliers to provide you with a tailored demonstration. Get them to focus on what you believe is especially important for your operation – for instance, pick face replenishment, or kitting and assembly. At some time during the selection process you should also get them to give you an overview of their company, products and people and of their strategy – in terms of both company and product.

Visit their head office to get a better understanding of their culture, management and team working. It is very important to get a good 'people' fit with any organization you select. It is always worth asking the suppliers why they think they should be selected for your project.

The reference site visit/s is often the crux of supplier selection. Make sure you are given a choice of sites, not just 'the one', and make sure it is similar in terms of size and processes to yours – or preferably slightly larger and slightly more complex.

If you have identified any gaps in functionality, now is the time to get these specified and costed. The supplier should be asked to provide an accurate project cost, clearly identifying any variable costs. This is where the contacts you have developed with the suppliers' reference sites will pay off, as you can talk to them about how well the supplier worked to budget and time.

Step 7: Final choice

Choose the most appropriate supplier. Utilize a decision matrix, taking into account the criteria mentioned above (see tool 6.2).

Summary

Here are 20 tips for choosing a WMS:

1 Have a clear long-term vision of what your warehouse could look like in the future – this will help you ensure that you choose a solution that is sufficiently scalable, flexible and functional.

2 Ensure complete 'buy-in' from senior management.

3 Keep an open mind about how your WMS will operate – let the WMS vendors listen to your needs and show you different ways of using their solution.

4 Ensure that your processes are working efficiently before introducing a WMS.

5 Look for a supplier that is warehouse and logistics focused; more generalist companies will often change strategy and reduce their focus on warehousing as their fortunes change.

6 Look for a supplier with a strong team of warehousing specialists, otherwise you will be training the supplier in warehousing or at best will be reliant on one or two individuals.

7 Choose a WMS vendor that you get along with – it is about partnership.

8 Make sure that help desk and support cover is available during your working hours – 24/7 if necessary.

9 Look for a WMS that has been specified by warehouse and logistics professionals, rather than by programmers and analysts.

10 Make sure that the product is relatively new but with a sound track record, and uses the latest software technology.

11 Make sure that the product is being developed on an ongoing basis to meet future warehousing and supply chain needs. Historically, WMS vendors have made their money by charging their customers significant amounts of money for development work. This has several major disadvantages: it invariably costs more than functionality provided as a package, it extends the project time and it introduces risk (bespoke software often fails to perform due to both technical issues and differences in interpretation of the specification). A further disadvantage is that custom software often makes software upgrades cumbersome, risky and expensive.

12 Choose a WMS vendor that can demonstrate a significant track record in your type of warehousing operation; get them to take you to customer sites to see the WMS in action, and make sure that you talk to the users and the management team at each site.

13 Look for a WMS that is an end-user-configurable package. Nowadays it is impossible to predict future WMS needs, particularly in a third-party environment, so flexibility is the name of the game.

14 Where small but important changes are needed to make the system meet your very specific needs, ensure that these changes do not compromise the package upgrade route.

15 Look for relevant reference sites. Look for a vendor with a good, active user group, and ensure that this group has real influence on the product strategy and support services.

16 Ensure that the vendor is of the right size – not so small that it has insufficient resource and not so large that you have no influence on product development and service levels.

17 Ensure that the vendor will help and support you in commercial and technical discussions with suppliers, customers and clients.

18 Have an in-depth demonstration of the WMS. Make sure that potential users of the system go along. Ensure that the WMS is easy to use and related closely to your operation.

19 Make sure that you involve your IT team in ensuring that the WMS vendor can work with you to provide solid interfaces with your other business systems. Do not let them dominate the project – a WMS is a tactical, operational solution and, as such, in most cases the project should be managed and run by logistics people.

20 Make sure that you identify a project champion in your organization, build a team around him or her and get the champion to own the WMS implementation.

(This tool is adapted from a white paper written by Stephen Cross and re-produced with his permission. The original paper can be found at http://www.cenglobal.com/atms/wp-content/uploads/2015/04/chapter-12-systems.pdf)

Further information

A comprehensive list of WMSs can be found at http://www.capterra.com/warehouse-management-software

Two examples of WMS RFP templates are https://www.highjump.com/resources/rfp-templates/rfp-1 and http://transportation-warehousing.technologyevaluation.com/

Papers discussing best of breed versus ERP WMSs can be found at http://www.inboundlogistics.com/cms/article/the-million-dollar-question-erp-or-wms/ and http://www.clydebuiltsolutions.com/white-papers/one-stop-vs-vs-best-of-breed/

1.17   How to implement a WMS

Introduction

Once you have decided you really need a WMS, and you have selected a WMS vendor, the hard work begins. There is no substitute for good and robust project management, alongside the selection of a good team. The WMS project must be owned from the top of the organization to the bottom. A project sponsor is an invaluable member of the project team – someone who ensures that the focus is maintained on delivering business benefits with minimal disruption.

A project champion needs to be appointed to effectively take charge of the project and this person will often come from a warehousing rather than an IT background. Crucial to this is having project management experience. IT staff should also be represented on the team, but increasingly IT is seen as a business support function as opposed to the main 'drivers' of a WMS project. Too many projects have failed when the project manager has not been experienced or has not been able to concentrate fully on the project itself.

Use the guidance and support of your WMS vendor as much as possible; a major part of your selection process should have been to identify a vendor that adds value during the implementation process. This guidance needs to be paid for, of course, so make sure that you have budgeted for it.

Methodology before technology is the key reminder for virtually all IT projects, particularly WMS projects. Ensure that your warehouse is running in an optimal manner with tried and tested processes before trying to implement a WMS: otherwise expect failure! That is not to say you cannot introduce new and better processes while implementing a WMS – this is often the case – but if your warehouse is disorganized, tackle that problem before doing anything else. Do not automate a bad process: you just get the wrong result faster.

In the case of a greenfield operation, methodology before technology is not normally possible as timescales are tight. Here it is vital to have a strong and experienced management team with a logistics background. In addition, you may want to use the services of a specialist consultant or an interim manager. Interim management can be a very cost-effective way of providing the extra resource needed in this change management process.

The scope of the project should be documented. The scope is just building on the WMS description you wrote for your RFI, ie what you want the system to do for your business. This need not be an arduous or tedious task but it is important to focus on top-level business requirements and warehouse processes rather than being prescriptive as to how the WMS should function in detail at this stage. This top-level approach is particularly relevant where a well-established packaged solution has been purchased – in the final analysis, such a solution should be highly flexible and configurable.

Interfaces to external systems, including ERP systems, transport management systems, warehouse control and automation systems and parcel carriers all have to be thought about and specified. This is a specialist area and can be one of the riskiest areas of a WMS project if not managed properly.

A project plan should be drawn up – often the WMS vendor will have a template available (see Table 1.12). The plan will detail all the tasks required, responsibilities and timescales. Regular review meetings will monitor progress against the plan and make corrective actions as required. Make sure that there is no project creep: learn to say no! Start as simply as possible and get some quick wins.

The contract

A contract should be drawn up between you and the vendor. This should be done before you commit any major finances, but far enough into the initial stages of the project that you can have it scoped, planned and costed.

Your RFI and scope document form a key part of this contract, as does all documentation received from the vendor. An outline plan should have been produced by this stage, showing key milestones and deliverables. This plan also forms part of the contract.

The contract should as far as possible be in plain English. It does not necessarily need to be produced by a lawyer, but you should get appropriate legal advice. The contract needs to be produced by someone with knowledge of the principles of contract law.

Infrastructures

The IT infrastructure needs to be planned around the WMS. Your internal IT department can help with this, assuming they have the skills and resources. Alternatively, you can contract it out or in certain cases the WMS vendor will take on complete responsibility.

The IT infrastructure will consist of servers to run the applications, PC workstations, network infrastructure and printers. In some cases you will also use radio data terminals (RDTs) or a voice-enabled technology for the system. Both are mini-projects in their own right that need to be planned and specified. Often the WMS vendor can provide the subsystem, or you

TABLE 1.12 Generic project plan

Generic Project Plan – Warehouse Management System Implementation Plan for FZ Company			
Task	**Detail**	**Duration**	**Resource & Responsibility**
Project planning		5 days	
	Internal project kick off		WMSS Projects, WMSS Sales
	Identify project teams & responsibilities		Customer, WMSS Projects
	Identify scope & boundaries		Customer, WMSS Projects
	Identify server & PC requirements		Customer, WMSS Projects
	Identify any additional RF requirement		WMSS Projects, Customer
	Identify printers / print servers requirements		Customer, WMSS Projects
	Understand existing network		WMSS Projects, Customer
	Sourcing server		WMSS Projects
	Source progress		WMSS Projects
Project management		7 weeks	
	Project meetings		WMSS Projects, Customer
	Update meetings		WMSS Projects
	Document and diarize		WMSS Projects
	Action		WMSS Projects, Customer

(Continued)

TABLE 1.12 Generic project plan (*Continued*)

Generic Project Plan – Warehouse Management System Implementation Plan for FZ Company			
Task	**Detail**	**Duration**	**Resource & Responsibility**
Identify RF Hardware		2 days	
	RF survey		Hardware vendor
	Design overall hardware configuration		Customer, WMSS Projects
	Order equipment		Customer
Configuration/ consultancy		3 days	
	Identify existing/ proposed business processes		WMSS Projects, Customer
	Business process document		WMSS Projects, Customer
	Present – process overview		WMSS Projects, Customer
	Acceptance/gap analysis		WMSS Projects, Customer
	Configuration		WMSS Projects
Interface (if any)		2 days	
	Specify & agree interface requirements		WMSS Projects
Installation & commission		7 days	
	Server available		Customer
	Remote access implemented		WMSS Technical/ Customer
	Install progress		WMSS Deployment

(Continued)

TABLE 1.12 Generic project plan (*Continued*)

Task	Detail	Duration	Resource & Responsibility
Generic Project Plan – Warehouse Management System Implementation Plan for FZ Company			
	Deploy standard WMS		WMSS Deployment
	Application, data, menus, scripts		WMSS Deployment
	Shutdown, truncate, back-up etc		WMSS Deployment
	Create deployment document for support		WMSS Deployment
	Data collection sheet		Customer
Interface (if any)		3 days	
	Develop & test interface		WMSS Devt, WMSS Projects
	Install		WMSS Deployment
Training		15 days	
	Training on full system		WMSS Trainer, Customer
	General guides – WMSS & Warehousing		WMSS Projects, Customer
	STP & datahub overview		WMSS Projects, Customer
	Basic data set-up		WMSS Projects, Customer
	Inbound processes		WMSS Projects, Customer
	Outbound processes		WMSS Projects, Customer
	In-house processes		WMSS Projects, Customer

(Continued)

TABLE 1.12   *Generic project plan (Continued)*

Generic Project Plan – Warehouse Management System Implementation Plan for FZ Company			
Task	**Detail**	**Duration**	**Resource & Responsibility**
	Train the users		Customer
	Change management		Customer
Go-live preparation		2 days	
	Create implementation plan		WMSS Projects, Customer
	Resourcing		WMSS Projects, Customer
	Determine & source necessary consumables		WMSS Projects, Customer
Data entry support		10 days	
	Locate and harvest static data		Customer
	Preliminary dynamic data		WMSS Projects, Customer
	Full data take-on		WMSS Projects, Customer
	Stock take pre go live		Customer
Documentation		1 day	
	Document revisions to user manual		WMSS Projects
System live		3 days	
	Go-live support		WMSS Projects
	Project summary meeting		WMSS Projects, Customer
Project review meeting		1 day	WMSS Projects, Customer
Total days		54 days	WMSS Projects

may prefer your IT supplier to provide the wireless network backbone and then the WMS vendor or hardware vendor provides the necessary equipment. Note that if you are considering a SaaS, the software will be run on the vendor's server to which you will have remote access.

Pilot project

Set up a pilot project, either as a conference room pilot or ideally in the warehouse itself. Focus on one customer, one product group or one function, such as receiving. Create a test plan and continue to test to ensure that the system is operating as required and that operatives understand the system and are working optimally.

Start working out how you are going to do a 'data take-on', ie all the data you need to start and run the system, including locations, location maps, product codes, product details, pallet sizes and configurations. A lot of these data can come from your ERP system. You can construct spreadsheet templates to compile them. You also need to start planning the 'rules' within the warehouse, for example put-away rules, replenishment rules, FIFO, LIFO, etc. If you are moving into a warehouse with existing stock, consider how you are going to label and record this stock.

Remember that you are testing for failure as well as testing for success. This is an ideal opportunity to test the interfaces to external systems; interface testing invariably takes longer than planned.

Ensure that you train the trainers or super users and then cascade the training down to the users; this way, you will build your in-house expertise.

Going live

The go-live stage needs to be planned carefully. Go live can be a 'big bang' or can be phased, according to the nature of your operation. You are likely to need extra personnel during this period. Budget very carefully for the on-site support you may need from the WMS vendor; costs can escalate in this area, particularly for out-of-hours, evening and weekend support. It is likely that your performance levels will be low to start with until the operation has moved up the learning curve; for this reason it is best to go live during a quiet period if possible, although ensure that your key personnel are not on holiday at this time.

In summary

As with all system projects, and indeed projects in general, the more you plan and prepare, the better your results will be. Supplier selection is the crux of a successful project along with good project management and good project ownership. Obal (2001) says that during implementation the following have to be avoided:

- establishing an unrealistic implementation schedule;
- buying a low-end system and expecting high-end results;
- failing to track vendor progress;
- failing to develop a contingency plan;
- overselling the system to users;
- lack of system integration training;
- providing the software vendor with faulty, incomplete or out-of-date data;
- thinking a newly integrated WMS will eliminate all inefficiencies within the operation;
- blaming the WMS provider for glitches that occur during the software's initial launch;
- failing to audit the results to see if the system is working as efficiently as possible.

(Adapted from JDA and a white paper written by Stephen Cross and reproduced with his permission.)

Further information

For additional information visit www.JDA.com

Reference

Obal, P (2001) *Selecting Warehouse Software from WMS & ERP*, http://www.cenglobal.com/atms/wp-content/uploads/2015/04/chapter-12-systems.pdf

1.18 Warehouse maturity scan, by Jeroen van den Berg

Introduction

This tool enables companies to assess the maturity of their warehouse operations (an introduction to maturity models is given in tool 4.7). The model comes from *Highly Competitive Warehouse Management* by Jeroen van den Berg (2012). In his book he makes a distinction between four phases of warehouse maturity:

- Phase 1 – *Reactive*. The warehouse is not well structured.
- Phase 2 – *Effective*. Processes are streamlined with more transparency in the operation.
- Phase 3 – *Responsive*. Processes are better planned and controlled by the use of intelligent IT.
- Phase 4 – *Collaborative*. The warehouse is an equal partner in the supply chain and generates more added value.

When to use

The scan can be used to assess the maturity of a distribution centre.

How to use

The assessment requires answers to 18 specific questions about your current warehouse operation. The four answers to each question represent an increasing level of sophistication. If you believe that your operation ranks in between two answers, you should select the lowest answer; for example, if your distribution centre almost meets the requirements of answer c but not completely, then choose answer b.

Example question

Are services and service level agreements (SLAs) formally defined for the distribution centre?

- **a** No, we do not distinguish services and SLAs.
- **b** Somewhat, we do have a few SLAs (response time, accuracy) for some clients/customers.
- **c** Yes, we use a complete list of all available warehouse services and associated service levels for all clients/customers.
- **d** Yes, we use a complete list of all available warehouse services and associated service levels for all clients/customers and charge fees per individual service.

A comprehensive maturity model can be completed online at http://www.jvdbconsulting.com/english/research/46-maturity-model.html

A full supply chain maturity scan can be completed at http://www.jvdb-consulting.com/english/supply-chain-maturity-scan.html

Reference

van den Berg, J P (2012) *Highly Competitive Warehouse Management: An action plan for best-in-class performance*, Management Outlook Publishing, Utrecht, Netherlands

1.19 Warehouse risk assessments

Introduction

Warehouses, like any industrial facility, can be dangerous places to work in, especially with the movement of forklift trucks, the risk of slips and trips, and people working at height. So, to ensure a safe and secure environment, companies need to undertake risk assessments regularly. (A full description of risk assessment is included in tool 4.12.) Note that:

- *a hazard* can be anything – whether work materials, equipment, work methods or practices – that has the potential to cause harm;
- *a risk* is the chance, high or low, that somebody may be harmed by the hazard.

The following are potential risk areas:

- falls from height;
- slips, trips and falls;
- manual handling;
- falling objects;
- operation of MHE;
- operation of other machinery;
- traffic movements;
- portable electrical equipment;
- lighting;
- hazardous substances; and
- fire.

TABLE 1.13 Example risk assessment for the warehouse

Location	Date:			Assessor:		
What are the hazards?	Who might be harmed and how?	What are you already doing?	What further action is necessary?	Action by whom?	Action by when?	Completed?
Falls from height	Staff can suffer severe or even fatal injuries if they fall while climbing racking	All staff are given instructions never to climb racking – monitored by supervisors	Signage put in place to reiterate the point	Warehouse manager	01/03/20–	Yes 01/03/–
	Staff or contractor could suffer severe or fatal injuries falling through fragile roof lights when effecting repairs	No controls in place	• Put up 'fragile roof' signs on each side of the building and at access points	Facilities manager	01/03/20–	Yes 8/02/20–
			• Only trained contractors to access the roof	Facilities manager	02/04/20–	No
			• Full risk assessment to be undertaken by contractor	FM/ Contractor	As required	
Slips, trips and falls	All staff may suffer sprains or fractures if they trip over debris or slip on spillages	• Flooring kept dry and quality maintained	• Suitable absorber to be made available for liquid spills	FM	25/02/20–	24/02/20–
		• All staff trained to maintain good housekeeping standards	• Extra bins provided for waste	FM	25/02/20–	24/02/20–

When to use

To ensure the safety of all visitors to, and staff working in, a warehouse.

How to use

The guiding principles that should be considered throughout the risk assessment process can be broken down into a series of steps:

- Step 1: Identifying hazards and those at risk.
- Step 2: Evaluating and prioritizing risks.
- Step 3: Deciding on preventive action.
- Step 4: Taking action.
- Step 5: Monitoring and reviewing.

As can be seen in the risk assessment form in Table 1.13, it is essential that there is a suitable person responsible for the action to be taken, and that a target date is set for completion. We have completed part of the form as an example. The form can be downloaded from http://howtologistics.com, discount code lsct0104

Further information

- http://osha.europa.eu/topics/riskassessment
- http://www.hse.gov.uk/risk/
- http://www.hse.gov.uk/toolbox/index.htm
- http://www.osha.gov/Publications/3220_Warehouse.pdf

1.20 How to 'green' your warehouse and save energy

Introduction

In recent years environmental issues have come to the fore, both at home and at work, with corporate social responsibility (CSR) initiatives concentrating on the environment, waste, health and safety, and the local community. The introduction of these initiatives does not have to cost the earth. In the majority of cases there are grants and significant opportunities for cost saving as well as the resulting reduction of the company's impact on the environment.

The following list provides warehouse managers with ideas on how to reduce their impact on the environment and thus help companies achieve their CSR targets and save energy:

- Lighting in a non-automated warehouse can be up to 70 per cent of the total energy costs. Ways to reduce lighting costs are as follows:
  - Introduce energy-efficient lighting.
  - Switch off all non-essential lighting out of business hours.
  - Install movement sensors and timers.
  - Introduce and regularly clean skylights and clerestory windows to increase the use of natural light.
  - Switch off lights when daylight is sufficient.
  - Turn off external lights when daylight is sufficient.
  - Switch off office lights on exit or introduce motion sensors.
- Use of alternative energy production methods:
  - solar panels;
  - wind turbines;
  - biomass boilers.
- Heating/air conditioning can make up 15 per cent of a warehouse's energy costs:
  - Use zoned and time-controlled thermostats that are set accurately (a 1 per cent reduction in temperature on the thermostat can reduce heating bills by 8 per cent).
  - Experiment with switch-on times for heating and air conditioning and switch off well before close of business.
  - Ensure hot water supply is sized in relation to site occupancy.
- Install time controls on equipment that is not required after close of business, such as vending machines.
- Use of natural ventilation systems:
  - using ventilation stacks;
  - atria and automatic window openings combined with automatic control systems;
  - passive cooling such as breathable walls;
  - using the effective thermal mass of buildings to reduce cooling and ventilation energy.
- Cooling the warehouse can also increase energy costs:

- Introduce sunlight reflectors.
- Use mobile air handling units.
- Switch off equipment when not in use.
- Ensure all doors have sufficient seals to prevent air and water entry.

- Make better use of resources:
  - Rain water collection for reuse in vehicle washing, toilets, etc.
  - Low water use in sanitary appliances.
  - Check insulation levels and increase where practical.
  - Reuse or recycle where feasible and cost-effective.
  - Move to utilizing plastic totes/bins in place of cardboard.
  - Utilize plastic or aluminium pallets.
  - Use of gas, electric or hybrid forklift trucks.
  - In-rack charging for narrow aisle trucks and shuttle systems.

- Movement reduction within the warehouse to reduce energy consumption:
  - Use of ABC analysis (see tool 1.3) to ensure that popular items are placed close to the dispatch area.

- Kinetic-energy plates positioned on the access road to produce power from vehicles entering and leaving the site.

- Introduce car-sharing schemes for staff.

- Encourage staff to walk or cycle to work or take public transport.

- Introduce training in green initiatives such as fuel-efficient driving.

- Source materials locally, such as packaging, paper, MHE, etc.

- Continually assess the situation by walking around the warehouse at various times during operating hours.

- Plant trees and shrubs to assist with the removal of emissions.

- Finally, ensure that your warehouse is operating effectively – no unnecessary movements, accurate picking and dispatch, and effective utilization of space and packaging materials.

In the UK, the Carbon Trust Implementation Services provides expert support to warehouse and logistics companies that are looking to cut energy costs by implementing new lighting or heating equipment (see Figure 1.12 for its figures on energy usage in an SME warehouse). The new service introduces warehouses to established suppliers of energy-efficient equipment that are accredited by the Carbon Trust. It helps warehouse companies obtain a set of high-quality

FIGURE 1.12 Energy usage in an SME warehouse

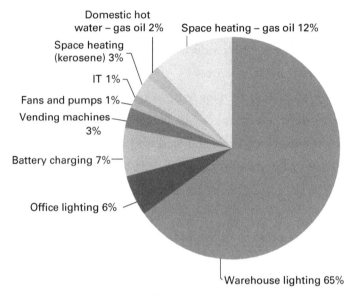

SOURCE: Carbon Trust 2013. Reproduced with permission

proposals and competitive quotes for an energy efficiency project. The Carbon Trust delivers value to warehouses through energy efficiency:

- It helps warehouses develop a compelling business case for an energy efficiency project – demonstrating a proven ROI.

- For no upfront cost, warehouses can obtain high-quality proposals and competitive quotes from established equipment suppliers, accredited by the Carbon Trust.

- In partnership with Siemens Financial Services, the Carbon Trust provides affordable financing packages for new equipment and projects that are designed to pay for themselves.

Further information

Other initiatives include being part of Voluntary Sustainable Building Award schemes such as:

- BREEAM (Building Research Establishment Environmental Assessment) – UK: www.breeam.com

- LEED (Leadership in Energy and Environment Design) – United States: www.usgbc.org

- Greenstar – Australia: http://www.gbca.org.au/green-star/

- CASBEE (Comprehensive Assessment System for Built Environment Efficiency) – Japan: http://www.ibec.or.jp/CASBEE/english/index.htm

References

http://www.carbontrust.com/
www.ukwa.org.uk

1.21 Hazardous packaging and labelling

The consignor/supplier is responsible for ensuring that packaging of hazardous items conforms to the regulations for the product. The packaging can vary from a cardboard box or paper bag for low-risk powders in small quantities to very sophisticated double-skinned stainless steel packages for more complex high-risk products.

To promote the safe storage and transportation of dangerous goods, an international system of classification has been introduced (The UN Classification System). Examples are:

- UN1263: Paint or paint-related materials

- UN1498: Sodium nitrate

- UN1500: Sodium nitrite

The system divides the different types of dangerous goods into classified groups, each group identified by a code marking. There are nine classes, some with divisions, as shown in Table 1.14.

In general, the package needs to be UN approved and compatible with the product. For every UN number there is a list of packaging options available to the packer.

All over the world there are different laws on how to identify the hazardous properties of chemicals (called 'classification') and how information about these hazards is then passed to users (through labels and safety data sheets for workers). This can be confusing because the same chemical can have different hazard descriptions in different countries; for example, a chemical could be labelled as 'toxic' in one country but not in another. This also acts as a barrier to international trade.

Given the expanding international market in chemical substances and mixtures, to help protect people and the environment and to facilitate trade, the United Nations has developed a 'Globally Harmonized System' (GHS) on classification and labelling. The GHS is a single worldwide system for classifying

TABLE 1.14 Hazardous classes

Class	Type of material
1	Explosive substances and articles
2.1	Flammable gas (eg butane)
2.2	Non-flammable and non-toxic gases which could cause asphyxiation (eg nitrogen, helium, carbon dioxide) or oxidizers (eg oxygen)
2.3	Toxic gases (eg chlorine, phosgene)
3	Flammable liquids (eg lighter fluid, petrol)
4.1	Flammable solids, self-reactive substances and solid desensitized explosives
4.2	Substances liable to spontaneous combustion
4.3	Substances which, in contact with water, emit flammable gases
5.1	Oxidizing substances
5.2	Organic peroxides
6.1	Toxic substances
6.2	Infectious substances
7	Radioactive material
8	Corrosive substances
9	Miscellaneous dangerous substances and articles

and communicating the hazardous properties of industrial and consumer chemicals. GHS sits alongside the UN Transport of Dangerous Goods system. The GHS is not a law – it's an international agreement. To make the GHS legally apply, each country or bloc of countries must adopt the GHS through legislation. EU Member States agreed to adopt the GHS across the EU through a direct-acting Regulation, the European Regulation (EC) No 1272/2008 on Classification, Labelling and Packaging of substances and mixtures. This is also known as the 'CLP Regulation' or just 'CLP'. This will finally lead to a reduction in the regulatory burden on manufacturers, which currently have to struggle with many different systems of classification depending on the countries they manufacture in and export to. Figure 1.13 shows the new pictograms.

FIGURE 1.13 GHS pictograms

GHS Pictograms and Hazard Classes		

• Oxidizers	• Flammables • Self Reactives • Pyrophorics • Self-Heating • Emits Flammable Gas • Organic Peroxides	• Explosives • Self Reactives • Organic Peroxides

• Acute toxicity (severe)	• Corrosives	• Gases Under Pressure

• Carcinogen • Respiratory Sensitizer • Reproductive Toxicity • Target Organ Toxicity • Mutagenicity • Aspiration Toxicity	• Environmental Toxicity	• Irritant • Dermal Sensitizer • Acute toxicity (harmful) • Narcotic Effects • Respiratory Tract • Irritation

SOURCE: reproduced from United States Department of Labor (nd)
Reproduced from http://www.osha.gov/dsg/hazcom/ghs.html

Further information

- UK – www.hse.gov.uk/ghs/

- United States – https://www.osha.gov/dsg/hazcom/pictograms/index.html

- EU – http://ec.europa.eu/enterprise/sectors/chemicals/classification/index_en.htm

- Details regarding hazardous goods transportation can be found in tool 2.13.

Reference

United States Department of Labor (nd) [accessed 9 May 2013] *A Guide to The Globally Harmonized System of Classification and Labelling of Chemicals (GHS)*, Occupational Safety and Health Administration, Washington, DC, https://www.osha.gov/dsg/hazcom/ghsguideoct05.pdf

Transport management tools

2.1 Transport audit checklists

This section provides audit checklists for a road freight transport operation; an extract is shown in Table 2.1. The questions are not exhaustive and can be added to by users to mirror their own operations. The audit incorporates questions to ensure compliance with the UK Fleet Operator Recognition scheme (FORS).

Audits should be undertaken by an independent person, either an outside consultant or someone from another department within the company. The purpose of the audit should be explained to the staff. Results should be shared with all staff who should take ownership of the results and the improvements necessary. A timescale should be agreed to undertake the improvements.

A full set of audit forms can be purchased from http://howtologistics.com; discount code: lsct0104.

2.2 Calculating emissions in freight transport

Introduction

Companies worldwide are being encouraged to lessen their impact on the environment and many governments are likely to introduce taxation based on greenhouse gas emissions so as to meet their own targets. This section provides information on how to measure these emissions in a freight transport environment.

TABLE 2.1 Transport audit checklists

Transport Audit (Part 1)				
Carried out by:	Location:			Date:
Item:	No	Yes	N/A	Comments
Transport Yard				
Sufficient space for goods vehicle parking				
Comprehensive signage for drivers in multiple languages				
Comprehensive signage for visitors				
Staff cars parked away from freight vehicles				
Perimeter fencing in good order				
Security gates/barriers in good working order				
External ground in good condition, no potholes etc.				
LPG and diesel kept in suitably safe and secure area				
Vehicle and trailer wash facilities available				

Another reason for transport operators to calculate their emissions is to provide information to their customers. For most transport operators, this will mean calculating their total emissions, and then using an appropriate method to fairly 'allocate' an appropriate share of those emissions to each of their customers.

Greenhouse gases (GHGs) can be measured by recording emissions at source by continuous emissions monitoring or by estimating the amount emitted by multiplying activity data (such as the amount of fuel used) by relevant emissions conversion factors. These conversion factors allow activity data (eg litres of fuel used, number of miles/kilometres driven, tonnes of freight carried, tonnes of waste sent to landfill) to be converted into kilograms of carbon dioxide equivalent (CO_2e). CO_2e is a universal unit of measurement that allows the global warming potential of different GHGs to be compared.

Values for methane (CH_4) and nitrous oxide (N_2O) are presented as carbon dioxide equivalents (CO_2e) using global warming potential (GWP) factors, consistent with reporting under the Kyoto Protocol and the second assessment report of the Intergovernmental Panel on Climate Change (IPCC).

How to use it

The following examples illustrate how to calculate $kgCO_2e$.

Total fuel used by company vehicles per annum = 150,000 litres

UK emission factor for diesel is 2.67 $kgCO_2e$/litre

Therefore total $kgCO_2e$ = 400,500 $kgCO_2e$.

If the company does not have details of fuel consumed it is possible to use the following formula based on DEFRA emission factors:

Total emissions = distance × emission factor

$$= 377,015 \times 0.94353*$$

$$= 355,725 \text{ } kgCO_2e$$

*Note that these emission factors change occasionally. Up-to-date factors can be found at: http://www.ukconversionfactorscarbonsmart.co.uk/

The website shown at the end of the tool provides spreadsheets to enable the user to calculate these figures automatically. For those wishing to use a quick and simple method the following formula provided by the UK Road Haulage Association (RHA) can suffice. The calculation is as follows:

To convert miles per gallon to kilometres per litre, multiply by 0.352.

To obtain litres per kilometre, divide 1 by the kilometre/litre figure above.

To obtain CO_2 in kilograms per kilometre, multiply by 2.63.

To obtain CO_2 in grams per kilometre (the accepted measure), multiply by 1000.

Example: carbon footprint calculation:

Assume a 44-tonne articulated vehicle returning 8 miles per gallon:

8.0 multiplied by 0.352 gives 2.816 kilometres/litre;

1 divided by 2.816 gives 0.355 litre/kilometre;

0.355 multiplied by 2.63 gives 0.93365 kilograms of CO_2/kilometre;

That figure multiplied by 1,000 gives 933.65 g of CO_2/kilometre.

Further information

http://www.ukconversionfactorscarbonsmart.co.uk/

https://www.gov.uk/government/uploads/system/uploads/attachment_data/file/218574/ghg-freight-guide.pdf; http://www.defra.gov.uk/environment/economy/business-efficiency/reporting/; http://www.ghgprotocol.org/standards/corporate-standard

Data reproduced under the Open Government Licence. http://www.nationalarchives.gov.uk/doc/open-government-licence/

http://www.ipcc-nggip.iges.or.jp/public/2006gl/

2.3 Fuel adjustment factor formula

Introduction

Fluctuations in the price of fuel have a significant impact on the rates paid for the transportation of goods. To enable companies to pass on the increase (or decrease) in the cost of fuel to their customers, a mathematical formula can be used to calculate the percentage increase/decrease. Not only does the transport supplier need to understand the mechanism but so does the customer in terms of how it has been computed.

Over recent years the cost of fuel as a percentage of total transport costs for UK hauliers has been in the region of 30 per cent. With the reduction in fuel cost during 2015 this has fallen to 27.5 per cent.

How to use

At the beginning of the contract a base price for the fuel needs to be agreed between both parties. This needs to be written into the contract. The contract should also state the review frequency. If the haulier is undertaking a large number of jobs for the customer and the price of fuel is continually rising or falling, then maybe a weekly adjustment is required. Other contracts can be set up on a quarterly or six-monthly basis.

A further calculation is the cost of fuel as a percentage of the total cost or revenue for the transport company at the time of the fuel increase. Any fuel taxation such as Value Added Tax needs to be excluded from the price of fuel.

Once these figures have been calculated, the formula shown in the examples following can be used to calculate the overall increase/decrease in price for the work undertaken. The figures are illustrative only. Figure 2.1 covers a situation where fuel has increased in price, while Figure 2.2 covers a situation where fuel has gone down in price.

FIGURE 2.1 Fuel increase example – quarterly review

1.	Assume the base buying price on 1 September 2015 was 86.69 pence per litre, excluding VAT.		
2.	Every 1p change in price is therefore 1.15%. (1/86.69%)		
3.	(a)	Revenue for the last 3 months was	£153,750
		Fuel cost for the last 3 months was	£42,281
		Fuel as a percentage of revenue was therefore	27.5%
		It follows that, for every 1p per litre difference in price from 86.69 pence, adjustment should be: 1.15% × 27.5 = 0.32%. Therefore, if on 1 December the haulier is paying 91.69 pence per litre, an average increase in total rate of (91.69 - 86.69) = (5.0 × 0.32%) a 1.6% increase in overall rate is appropriate.		

FIGURE 2.2 Fuel reduction example

1.	Assume the base buying price on 1 September 2015 was 92.8 pence per litre, excluding VAT.		
2.	Every 1p change in price is therefore 1.01%.		
3.	(a)	Revenue for the last 3 months was	£161,000
		Fuel cost for the last 3 months was	£44,275
		Fuel as a percentage of revenue was therefore	27.5%
		It follows that, for every 1p per litre difference in price from 92.8 pence, adjustment should be: 1.01% × 27.5 = 0.28%. Therefore, if on 1 December 2015 the haulier is paying 86.7 pence per litre, an average decrease in rate of (92.8 – 86.7) = – (6.1 × 0.28) = a 1.71% reduction will be appropriate.		

SOURCE: agreement and calculations provided by kind permission of Apprise Consulting Ltd and the UK Road Haulage Association, www.rha.uk.net

2.4 How to improve fuel efficiency

Introduction

Fuel represents approximately 27.5 per cent of transport costs within a distribution operation in the UK today, based on 2015 fuel prices. It is therefore vital that companies look to reduce the amount of fuel consumed and improve metrics such as miles per gallon or kilometres per 100 litres.

The following is a list produced by Goodyear Dunlop on how to improve fuel efficiency. It has been supplemented by further advice from Freight Best Practice.

Driver training

Driver behaviour is the biggest factor affecting fuel consumption. Investing in driver training will therefore quickly pay off and cut costs.

Work with equipment manufacturers

A key aspect of driver training will often be working with the vehicle manufacturers, which can offer advice on how to get the most from their vehicles. This relationship should be extended across all equipment manufacturers. Tyre, trailer and aerodynamics suppliers can advise you on how best to use their equipment and provide ongoing maintenance to ensure fuel consumption stays as low as possible.

Make fuel efficiency a key consideration for vehicle procurement

Truck manufacturers are increasingly offering vehicles with improved fuel efficiency. The upfront cost of investing in these vehicles will be more than outweighed by the future savings from reduced fuel consumption.

Invest in cost-effective tyres

The cheapest tyres are not always the most cost-effective. Tyres should be selected on the basis of what offers best value – this means selecting a tyre that offers optimal safety, longevity and fuel efficiency, even if it may be more expensive upfront. Tyre pressure monitoring systems (TPMS) can also help maximize the cost-effectiveness of tyres in the long term.

Aerodynamic improvement

Investing in aerodynamic improvements to vehicles can pay big dividends. Aerodynamic drag is a major factor in fuel consumption and retro-fitted improvements such as side skirts can offer a quick return on investment (ROI).

Perform regular and thorough maintenance

There is little point in spending money on fuel-efficient trucks, tyres and aerodynamic improvements if this equipment is not well maintained. It is necessary to keep all of this equipment in good condition if it is to deliver the desired savings in fuel consumption.

Improve your logistics

Better route planning and journey organization can cut journey times, avoid congestion and reduce empty running, saving fuel.

Work with your customers

Customers are increasingly asking for more environmental freight services. Cooperating with them can help reduce fuel consumption by making deliveries easier and journeys shorter. Customers can be encouraged to place depots out of urban centres to avoid congestion, to reorganize deliveries to reduce empty running, and to organize distribution to ensure trucks run on full rather than half loads, improving fuel efficiency.

Use telematics to track fuel consumption

Using telematics software can allow fleets to track their fuel consumption. It can be used to identify drivers who are wasting fuel and routes plagued by congestion, allowing fleets to act on these issues. A guide to vehicle telematics systems can be found below.

All of the above

Improving fuel efficiency requires a holistic approach – improving in only one area is not enough and the investment may not be recouped if other areas are neglected. Fleets need to identify a reduction target, devise a fuel management plan that covers all areas and then measure how successful it is. This kind of thorough plan may be more expensive, but it will also save much more money in the long run.

Best-practice advice to drivers

1 Always drive the truck with as low an engine speed as is practicable. This means using as high a gear as possible and monitoring the speedometer to ensure that the needle is always in the green band. Remember, the higher the gear, the lower the engine revs.

2 Make full use of the engine exhaust brake or engine brake, if fitted.

3 Avoid double-declutching on a synchromesh gearbox.

4   Do not use every single gear in the gearbox when shifting up or down. Make use of block changing/forward shift techniques where it is safe to do so, for example: 2–4–6–8. Where a splitter gearbox is fitted, use this facility to your best advantage. Again, do not use it automatically on each gear, but rather in the top range only as a 1/2 gear step. It helps to keep optimum speed up and engine revs down.

5   Safety checks and prompt defect reporting should be carried out before, during and at the end of every shift.

6   Let the engine work for you and 'lug' (ie work within the green band) on gradients. Remember, use maximum engine torque and thus pulling power. Use the engine's 'sweet spot'.

7   Make sure tyre pressures are correct. Incorrect pressure accelerates tyre wear, may jeopardize safety and affects fuel consumption. Fill tyres with nitrogen as opposed to air.

8   Use cruise control, whenever safe and practicable.

9   When filling fuel tanks, take care not to fill to the brim. Never leave a fuel nozzle unattended.

By undertaking a combination of the above, the result will be:

- lower fuel consumption;
- better tractive effort;
- reduced engine and transmission wear;
- reduced wear on brake components;
- reduced tyre wear;
- optimum speeds and journey time;
- reduced environmental impact;
- less driver fatigue;
- safer vehicles on the road;
- fewer road accidents;
- fewer prohibition notices and driver convictions;
- less fuel spillage (both in the depot and on the road).

References

http://fleet-fuel-efficiency.eu/en/fuel-calculator/top-tips-for-fuel-efficiency/ [accessed 5 March 2013]
Top Tips http://www.telematicsguide.com/

2.5 Incoterms® 2010

Introduction

Incoterms® are a set of uniform rules produced by the International Chambers of Commerce for the interpretation of international commercial terms. They define and set out the obligations of both consignors and consignees of goods in relation to the risks and costs that relate to each party during the movement of the goods between the seller's premises and those of the buyer.

Incoterms® are internationally accepted definitions and rules of interpretation for most common commercial terms. Incoterms® rules are recognized by UNCITRAL as the global standard for the interpretation of the most common terms in foreign trade.

A major consideration when selecting the correct Incoterms® rule is that sellers and buyers should *not* use a term that imposes risks and obligations beyond their control. One point to note here is that under an ex-works agreement it is the responsibility of the buyer to load the vehicle, yet in the majority of cases it is the seller's staff who tend to load the vehicle on departure. The question is: 'Who is responsible if the goods are damaged while being loaded?'

Technically the seller should make the goods available but not load the goods on collecting vehicles and the seller is not responsible for clearing them for export. If the seller does load the goods, it does so at the buyer's risk and cost. If the parties want the seller to be responsible for the loading of the goods on departure and to bear the costs and risk of such loading, this must be made clear by adding explicit wording to this effect in the contract of sale and any other specific documentation.

It is imperative that precise delivery points are identified, especially with regard to port or terminal areas. The typical functions and responsibilities identified by Incoterms® 2010 are listed below. It notes who is responsible for:

- packing and marking of the goods (packing in cases, etc for contract and mode of transport – *not* loading items in, or on containers);
- providing and paying for the goods;
- preparing documentation, whether in hard copy or electronically;
- arranging dispatch of the goods to specific delivery points;
- sorting out (and paying for) export and import clearances;
- ensuring import and export licensing is in order;
- ensuring security requirements are met;
- loading and unloading of cargo at the agreed delivery points;

- pre-shipment inspection (always the buyer for UK exports);
- obtaining documents or their equivalent electronic messages (online documentary considerations);
- insuring the goods – this is for additional cargo insurance, *not* carriers' liability insurance;
- paying duties and taxes, usually at the point of import.

According to 512 Sheffield, a UK-based freight forwarder, the way to avoid problems is to do the following:

- ALWAYS quote the specific three-letter abbreviation.
- ALWAYS mention a PRECISE place of delivery.
- ALWAYS add the phrase 'as per Incoterms® 2010' – in the contract, the quotation, order, order confirmation – and on the invoice.
- ALWAYS ensure that all parties understand that they are working to the terms qualified in Incoterms® 2010 and not a perception of what they think a term means.
- ALWAYS ensure that any contractual issues that may cause deviation from Incoterms® 2010 are clarified and resolved before the contract is agreed and signed.

The following is a list of the 11 Incoterms® used:

When transporting goods by any mode of transport, be it air, sea, inland waterways, rail or road:

EXW – ex works – (named place of delivery)

FCA – Free Carrier – (named place of delivery)

CPT – Carriage paid to – (named place of destination)

CIP – Carriage and Insurance paid to (named place of destination)

DAT – Delivered at Terminal (named terminal at port or place of destination)

DAP – Delivered at Place – (named place of destination)

DDP – Delivered Duty Paid – (named place of destination)

When transporting by sea and inland waterways only:

FAS – Free alongside ship (named port of shipment)

FOB – Free on Board (named port of shipment)

CFR – Cost and Freight (named port of destination)

CIF – Cost, insurance and freight (named port of destination)

As can be seen from Table 2.2 (on p. 94), the majority of terms specifically show whether it is the buyer or supplier who is responsible for the cost and risk involved. However, there are situations where risk and cost will be determined by the named place of destination; these are denoted by B/S on the chart. Table 2.2 details the responsible party based on the Incoterms® agreed. The chart is for guidance only. A copy of the newest Incoterms® 2010 can be found at http://www.iccwbo.org/products-and-services/trade-facilitation/incoterms-2010/.

Further information

UK: www.5-1-2.com
United States: http://export.gov/faq/eg_main_023922.asp

2.6 Load and pallet configuration

Introduction

The efficient loading of containers and trailers is crucial in today's environment of rising transport costs. Unused space is inefficient and can cost a company a great deal of money.

Efficient loading of vehicles and containers begins with the initial packaging of the products. Companies need to ensure that the outer packaging of their products is designed to fit perfectly onto the pallets used for both transportation and storage. The ideal is to ensure no overhang whatsoever, with a reduction in unused space.

Pallet loads need to be configured to ensure that product damage is minimized, cubic capacity is fully utilized, load stability is ensured and the configuration is acceptable to the receiving location. Fortunately, there is software available to assist not only with pallet loading but also container and trailer loading. The software can also optimize packing within an individual carton.

The pallet configuration software works on the basis of TiHi (tier × high), which determines how many cartons should be placed on a layer or tier, in which configuration and how many layers in total (see Figure 2.3).

In the figure, on the left there are 12 cartons per layer and four layers, giving a carton total of 48. Utilizing pallet configuration software, Able Plastics was able to increase the number of cartons to 52 by changing the layout of the cartons. This can lead to significant savings in transport costs.

TABLE 2.2 Incoterms® 2010 responsibilities

	EXW		FCA		FAS		FOB		CFR		CIF		CPT		CIP		DAT		DAP		DDP	
	R	C	R	C	R	C	R	C	R	C	R	C	R	C	R	C	R	C	R	C	R	C
Loading onto collection vehicle	B	B	S	S	S	S	S	S	S	S	S	S	S	S	S	S	S	S	S	S	S	S
Export customs formalities	B	B	S	S	S	S	S	S	S	S	S	S	S	S	S	S	S	S	S	S	S	S
Carriage to point/place of export	B	B	B	B	S	S	S	S	S	S	S	S	S/B	S/B	S/B	S/B	S	S	S	S	S	S
Unloading of vehicle at point/place of export	B	B	B	B	S	S	S	S	S	S	S	S	S/B	S/B	S/B	S/B	S	S	S	S	S	S
Loading costs on main mode of transport	B	B	B	B	S	S	S	S	S	S	S	S	S/B	S/B	S/B	S/B	S	S	S	S	S	S
Delivery to point/place of import	B	B	B	B	B	B	B	B	B	S	B	S	B	S	B	S	S	S	S	S	S	S
Unloading charges at point/place of import	B	B	B	B	B	B	B	B	B	B	B	B	S/B	S/B	S/B	S/B	S	S	S	S	S	S
Import customs clearance	B	B	B	B	B	B	B	B	B	B	B	B	S/B	S/B	S/B	S/B	B	B	B	B	S	S
Loading on collection vehicle at point/place of import	B	B	B	B	B	B	B	B	B	B	B	B	S/B	S/B	S/B	S/B	B	B	B	B	S	S
Carriage to named place of destination	B	B	B	B	B	B	B	B	B	B	B	B	S/B	S/B	S/B	S/B	B	B	B	B	S	S
Insurance for cargo in transit	N/O	N/O	N/O	N/O	N/O	N/O	N/O	N/O	N/O	N/O	S	S	N/O	N/O	S	S	N/O	N/O	N/O	N/O	N/O	N/O
Import duties and taxes	B	B	B	B	B	B	B	B	B	B	B	B	B	B	B	B	B	B	B	B	S	S

R – Risk   B – Buyer   N/O – Represents no obligation for the buyer or the seller
C – Cost   S – Seller

FIGURE 2.3 Comparison between manual planning and load configuration software

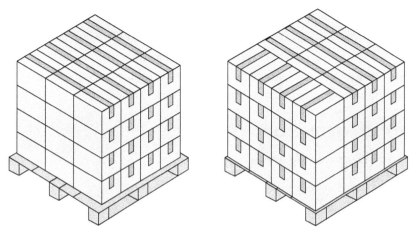

SOURCE: reproduced from http://www.ableplastics.com.au/_blog/Sustainability/page/2/

Many retailers insist on products being delivered in a certain way so that they conform to their storage mediums. For example, a retailer could ask for the goods delivered to its DC to conform to the list shown in Table 2.3. The same can be achieved in terms of efficient container and trailer loading.

TABLE 2.3 Retail DC requirement

Overall pallet height	1,500 mm
Pallet width	1,000 mm
Pallet length	1,200 mm
Cartons per layer	13
Layers per pallet	4
Total number of cartons	52
Total gross weight	780 kg
Weight per carton	15 kg
Type of pallet	Chep/White/Red
Pallet exchange	Yes/No
Special instructions	Product label on all four corners
Ability to block stack	Yes/No
If yes, how high	3

Sophisticated software optimization can not only take into account the cube of the products but also their load-bearing strength and location within the container. This ensures ease of offloading at the receiver, with all the cartons from the same product line being located together. The software also ensures that lighter items are packed on top of the heavier ones.

Many websites provide software to enable operators to calculate the most efficient way of loading containers and trailers and also configuring boxes on different pallet sizes and items within cartons.

Further information

Load configuration websites:

www.onpallet.com

www.cubedesigner.net

www.cubemaster.net

www.exds.co.uk/cubiscan.htm

www.koona.com/qpm/

www.logensolutions.com/vms/CubeDesigner/Palletizing_Package_
Design_Software_Overview.html

www.softtruck.com/

www.topseng.com/TOPS_Pallet_Configuration.html

2.7 ISO containers, weight volume ratios and pallets

Introduction

ISO containers enable companies to ship product via a number of different transport modes, including deep sea, short sea, inland waterways, road and rail. There are several basic types of ISO containers, including flat racks, open-top, dry freight, insulated, refrigerated and tank containers.

ISO 6346 requires a visual identification system for every container, including a unique 11-character serial code used for container tracking that defines the owner (three letters), container category (one letter), a unique owner identifier (six numbers) and a check digit (one number), eg MSCU 123456 7. There are four possible category identifiers:

- U for all freight containers;
- J for detachable freight container-related equipment;

- Z for trailers and chassis;
- R for refrigerated containers.

A further four characters denote the size and type of container:

- Character 1 denotes the length.
- Character 2 denotes the width and height.
- Characters 3 and 4 denote the type.

Table 2.4 provides data regarding the dimensions and capacities of ISO containers in use worldwide. The dimensions will vary between different shipping companies and therefore it is wise to check with them or your freight forwarder before ordering a particular container for collection.

TABLE 2.4 Standard ISO container dimensions

	Length			Width	Height	
Dimensions	6,058 mm	12,192 mm	13,716 mm	2,438 mm	2,591 mm	2,896 mm
	20′	40′	45′	8′6″	8′6″	9′6″ HC
Minimum internal dimensions	5,867 mm	11,998 mm	13,532 mm	2,330 mm	2,350 mm	2,655 mm
	19′3″	39′4⅜″	44′4¾″	7′7¾″	7′8½″	8′8½″
Minimum door opening dimensions	–	–	–	2,286 mm	2,261 mm	2,566 mm
	–	–	–	7′6″	7′5″	8′5″

Other points to note are as follows:

- The floor of a container should be able to carry a forklift truck with a maximum axle load of 5,460 kg providing that the contact area per wheel is at least 142 cm^2.
- The figures quoted are based on ISO 668 and ISO 1496-1, which provide the standard dimensions for ISO containers. Some 10 ft and 30 ft containers remain in use and in the United States containers can also be operated at 48 ft and 53 ft lengths.
- Container capacity tends to be expressed in 20-foot equivalent units (TEU). An equivalent unit is a measure of containerized cargo capacity equal to one standard 20-foot (length) × 8-foot (width) container.

Effective 1 July 2016, any container leaving from any port in the world must be accompanied by a shipping document signed either electronically or in hard copy by the shipper on the bill of lading listing the verified gross mass of a container in order to be loaded onto a ship. The mandate from the International Maritime Organization under the Safety of Life at Sea (SOLAS) convention comes after mis-declared weights contributed to a number of maritime casualties.

Weight/volume ratios

In terms of freight costs shipped by different modes of transport, there are conventions that need to be understood. One of the main conventions is the weight to volume ratio.

The following provides a guide to charging for air, sea and road freight. Weight versus volume charges are based on weight but calculations switch to volume over a certain threshold:

$6 \text{ M}^3 / 1000$ kg = Airfreight

$1 \text{ M}^3 / 1000$ kg = Sea freight

$3 \text{ M}^3 / 1000$ kg = Trailer freight

Pallets

The use of pallets or skids to move and store product is familiar the world over. The only problem is that there is very little uniformity in terms of the sizes and types of pallets. Table 2.5 is a guide to the sizes of pallets used in different countries. Other specialist pallet sizes for the storage and movement of paper, drums, etc also exist.

TABLE 2.5 Pallet sizes (length × width)

Dimensions	Geographic area of use
1219 × 1016 mm (48 × 40 inches)	North America
1000 × 1200 mm (39.37 × 47.24 inches)	Europe, Asia
1165 × 1165 mm (44.88 × 44.88 inches)	Australia
1067 × 1067 mm (42.00 × 42.00 inches)	North America, Europe, Asia
1100 × 1100 mm (43.30 × 43.30 inches)	Asia
800 × 1200 mm (31.50 × 47.24 inches)	Europe

Pallets can be purchased or they can be rented. Both wooden and plastic pallets are available for rental. Pallet rental companies include the following:

www.chep.com

www.ifco.com

www.igps.net

www.ipplogipal.co.uk

www.loscam.com

www.lpr.eu

www.pecopallet.com

Further information

Further information on pallets can be found at: www.napd.co.uk, www. palletcentral.com and www.palletlink.com

Further information on containers can be found at: http://www.iso.org/ iso/home/store/catalogue_tc/catalogue_tc_browse.htm?commid=51156 and http://www.hapag-lloyd.com/downloads/press_and_media/publications/ Brochure_Container_Specification_en.pdf

2.8 Calculating road freight transport charges and rates

Introduction

As a haulier or trucker, one of the most difficult aspects of running a business, alongside keeping costs as low as possible and attracting clients, is calculating charges for freight deliveries. To do this accurately you need to understand the total costs within your business, both fixed and variable.

For each particular delivery or collection you need to fully assess both the time required to complete a job and the number of miles/km covered. You must then apply to the time element the cost per day, including overheads, add any specific bonuses, extra hours, subsistence and sundries (tolls) and miles at the appropriate cost.

This will give you a fair cost for the job for which you are quoting. To this you must add a percentage for profit. In today's market this is extremely difficult because, on many occasions, you will find the costs as properly determined from these notes are greater than the revenue likely to be derived from the rates being charged by your competitors.

Notwithstanding this, you must aim for a reasonable profit margin. In the case of fuel you should always attempt to negotiate a clause into all rate schedules and contracts allowing fuel price increases to be passed on to the customer as they occur (see tool 2.3).

You must then decide whether you can accept a job at less than the rate calculated and, even more crucially, whether you can accept it at less than the true cost of undertaking it. In anything but the shortest run you cannot afford to do the latter, except perhaps for casual or special jobs that fit into the pattern of your overall work.

How to use

The following template allows you to calculate the costs involved and the rates required. Example costs for a 44 tonne gross (6 × 2 + tri-axle trailer) combination are shown in Table 2.6. Note that bonuses, excess hours, subsistence and similar are not included. These should be added to costs as they are incurred, by job (Table 2.7).

TABLE 2.6 Example costs for articulated truck and trailer

Data	Average figures	Enter your figures here
Vehicle price (representative)	£82,880	
Average depreciation period (years)	6	
Typical miles per annum	73,000	
Average days worked per annum	240	
Average miles per gallon	8.0	
Average tyre life (miles)	65,000	
Time-related costs	**Per annum**	
Driver employment costs	£35,380	
Depreciation	£13,815	
Licences (vehicle taxation)	£1,200	
Vehicle insurance	£3,760	
Interest on capital (6%)	£2,490	
Overhead per vehicle	£23,080	
Ownership of one trailer	£2,880	
Total time costs	£82,605	
Time cost per day	**£344.19**	

(Continued)

TABLE 2.6 Example costs for articulated truck and trailer *(Continued)*

Mileage related pence per mile (ppm)	Tractor ppm	Trailer ppm	Tractor ppm	Trailer ppm
Fuel at 88.69 pence per litre (ppl)	49.26			
Tyres	2.05	2.56		
Repairs and maintenance	8.80	3.62		
Total mileage costs	**60.11**	**6.18**		

TABLE 2.7 RHA template for haulage rate quotation

TEMPLATE FOR RATE QUOTATION 1 NAME OF CUSTOMER .... 2 DETAILS OF JOB	
3	Size of truck required
4	Estimated days/hours for job
5	Estimated trip miles/km
6	Details of market competitor (if known) & likely charge
7	Anticipated time cost for job
8	Anticipated distance cost of job
9	Job specific costs Subsistence Bonus Tolls Ferry Other
10	Total cost of job
11	Target profit margin
12	Target revenue
13	Target rate
14	Agreed rate
15	Return load time cost
16	Return load distance cost

(Continued)

TABLE 2.7 RHA template for haulage rate quotation *(Continued)*

	TEMPLATE FOR RATE QUOTATION 1 NAME OF CUSTOMER .... 2 DETAILS OF JOB	
17	Return load specific cost	
18	Total return load costs	
19	Total round trip cost (10 + 18)	
20	Return load revenue	
21	Minimum required outward revenue (19 – 20)	
22	Actual revenue	
23	Actual time costs	
24	Actual mileage cost	
25	Actual specific costs	
26	Actual profit/loss	

Notes:

(a) You will often find that a job will be completed with some hours in the day 'left over'. These hours will be costing you.
  You will need to decide whether you can use them for something else.
  If not, can those hours be charged to the job without making you uncompetitive?

(b) Where a return load is involved, it is important that you cost the whole round trip, allowing for the revenue you are likely to earn for the return and deciding how much to allow against the outward job for which you are quoting.

(c) When you are allocating costs in lines 7, 8, 15, 16, don't forget when using the appropriate figures from the tables, if possible to substitute YOUR costs where they are different.

(d) Rate = time cost + mileage cost + job cost + profit.

Rates and charges – example

You are asked to give a quotation for loading a 26 pallet load weighing 24 tonnes at a shipper's factory, delivering to a nominated address and returning to base with a full load of empty pallets. You are using a 44-tonne gross vehicle weight (gvw) articulated unit and tri-axle trailer.

You decide from your experience that this task will occupy two full working days, and you ascertain that the total distance to be covered will be 480 miles. Referring to the cost tables above, you derive the standard costs and estimate other items as shown in Table 2.8. Substitute your own figures for those shown.

TABLE 2.8 Standard costs

	£	Your figures
2 standard days at £344.19	688.38	
480 miles at 66.29 pence per mile	318.19	
Driver's subsistence	30	
Driver's bonus and any additional overtime	15	
Bridge toll	10	
Total cost	1061.57	
Target margin (say 5%)	53.08	
Desired rate and quotation	1114.65	

If possible, and before submitting this quotation, try to determine what the 'going rate' or market rate for these movements is. Decide whether or to what extent the gap between approximately £1,115 and the market rate can be bridged. Negotiate as strongly as possible to 'educate' the customer about realistic figures.

(© The Road Haulage Association and Apprise Consulting Ltd 2015. Reproduced by kind permission of Brian Fish and the RHA, www.rha.uk.net) (These templates can be downloaded for free from http://howtologistics.com)

2.9 Transport management system (TMS) selection process

Introduction

Many companies continue to utilize whiteboards and spreadsheets and rely on transport planner experience to manage the routing and allocation of their vehicle fleets. This is fine, but there are systems on the market that can optimize transport movements and introduce greater efficiency. This can lead to an improvement in vehicle utilization and a reduction in total cost.

If you are operating your own vehicles there are two routes to implementing a TMS – license the TMS from a software provider and manage the software in-house or get the TMS provider to host the system for you. Own-account operators and third-party logistics companies will have different requirements. The model from Cap Gemini cited below outlines the potential features of a TMS.

When to use

When you are looking to improve both the efficiency and effectiveness of your transport fleet through introducing a TMS.

How to use

First, you have to fully understand your needs and the key business requirements, not only today but some time into the future so that you select the solution that best matches your business objectives. You also need to calculate the ROI on the purchase and ongoing support of the TMS (see tool 8.3).

The choice of a TMS roughly follows the same lines as that of any software acquisition and implementation. To ensure that the system you choose is the right one for your operation, here are some best practice guidelines courtesy of BASDA and Sage:

1 Ensure full commitment from the board of directors and the IT department.

2 Form a project team:

  – Assemble a team of people capable of logical thinking who will decide what your company needs from a TMS and what functionalities it must have and those it will be nice to have. Members of the team should include a member from finance, sales, operations (if applicable), IT and of course the transport department.
  – Ensure the availability of all key staff throughout the project.

3 Define, record, review and improve current processes:

  – Ensure that your processes are working properly before introducing a TMS. Do not make the error of automating poor processes.
  – Understand how the transport department communicates both internally with other departments and externally with customers and suppliers.

4 Create a list of key functions required of the new system:

  – Each project team member needs to compile a list of the key functions required of a system and rank them by importance, for example 1, 2 or 3 or essential, greatly desired or nice to have.

- There are a number of templates that can be downloaded from the internet to help you. A website can be found at the end of this section.

5 Produce a current base cost for the operation.

6 Incorporate any future growth plans in your specification:

- Although difficult to forecast, you need to take into account likely future events when specifying a TMS.

7 List the benefits of a TMS to your company:

- The right TMS can maximize the efficiency of your fleet, the productivity of your labour and aid with network design. All of these need to be quantified and presented alongside the ROI report.

8 Research and approach a select number of vendors and produce a list of companies with experience of providing solutions in your market sector.

9 Visit reference sites to look at operational effectiveness and discuss the benefits the TMS has brought about since implementation:

- This is very important. Try to visit a cross-section of companies and speak to the operators, not just the managers who chose the software in the first place.

10 Produce a ROI report:

- This is vital if you want to convince the board to spend some money (see tool 8.3).

This is not the type of purchase you make through an e-auction. As with many large service offerings such as outsourcing, the likely success of the project will ultimately come down to your relationship with the people at the software vendor. As a previous manager of mine told me, 'people buy people', therefore it is very important to meet the vendors, not only the sales staff but also the operations and support staff.

The main aspects to look for in a partner include the following:

● Look for providers that employ staff with significant operational experience as well as staff with the ability to produce a best-in-class TMS.

● Not only will the operational staff have had input into the TMS but they will also be able to understand your own requirements better. Choose a vendor that listens effectively and understands your organization fully.

- Check how long the company has been in business and what its creditworthiness is like – it will certainly check yours!

- Choose a vendor that emphasizes the benefits of the software, not just the features.

- Choose a provider that has already installed TMS with clients in your industry.

- Ensure that the vendor can supply not only the system but also the installation, training, maintenance and help desk service.

- Verify that your prospective TMS provider is reinvesting significant capital into research and development, and future product enhancements.

- Choose a vendor you are comfortable working with. Try to find a vendor that is culturally similar to yourselves, is professional and well respected in the industry.

- Ask for a large list of customers and visit the customer sites that you choose.

- Choose a partner that has reasonable modification rates and is willing to set up a realistic budget, based on your needs assessment, prior to formalizing the relationship. Alternatively, look to set up an agreement where your own IT staff are able to introduce certain modifications.

- Make sure that the TMS provider can fully support you during the implementation phase.

- Select a partner that has an adequately staffed help desk and that the help desk is available during your company's hours of operation. Time zones can cause innumerable problems if they are not taken into account at the outset.

- Select a partner that has established partnerships with hardware providers.

A final decision is whether to purchase the software and hardware outright or to rent the software and operate it on a third-party server platform (see tool 1.16 on selecting a WMS).

Further information

A comprehensive list of transport management software can be found at: http://www.capterra.com/transportation-management-software/
Example TMS RFP templates: http://www.technologyevaluation.com/store/rfp-template/Transportation-Management-System-TMS-RFI-RFP-Template.html

References

BASDA (2009) *Logistics and Supply Chain Best Practice Handbook*, available at http://www.basda.org/

https://www.capgemini.com/resources/transportation-management-report-2011 [accessed 21 January 2013]

Ruriani, D C (2003) Choosing a warehouse system, Inbound Logistics, April

Sage Software (2005) How to choose a warehouse management system, available at http://www.myadjutant.com/brochures/How_to_Choose_WMS.pdf [accessed 5 March 2013]

2.10 Transport problems – matching customer demand with supplier capacity

Introduction

The allocation of goods between supply locations and a number of customer locations has become very simple with the introduction of optimization software. However, not all companies are able to afford the software so we need some simple models to help us in this process. Where a single commodity or unit load is transported between a number of supply and demand points and where supply equals demand, we can use a number of simple models to calculate which supply locations can economically service the customer locations, taking into account any constraints (see Figure 2.4).

FIGURE 2.4 The transport manager's dilemma

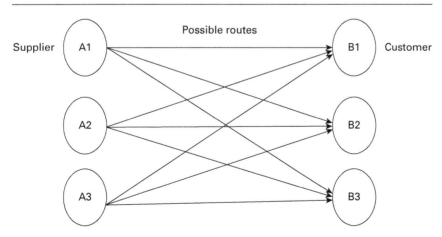

Models include the following:

- North West Method;
- Matrix Minimum Method;
- Vogel's Approximation Method;
- MODI;
- Stepping Stone Algorithm; and
- Linear programming.

At the end of this tool there is a link to a simple Excel spreadsheet to produce the optimum solution.

Example

In this example there are four suppliers and six customers (see Table 2.9). Supply and demand is equal at 180 tonnes. The dollar figures are cost per tonne to deliver between suppliers and customers. If we use a simple method such as the Matrix Minimum method (Table 2.10), we are allocating the highest possible tonnage to the lowest cost per tonne delivery charge. As can be seen in Table 2.10, we allocate 30 tonnes to cell A1/B1. We continue to do this until all the tonnage has been allocated.

TABLE 2.9 The problem

Supplier \ Customer	B1	B2	B3	B4	B5	B6	Tonnes
A1	$5	$10	$15	$8	$9	$7	30t
A2	$14	$13	$10	$9	$20	$21	40t
A3	$15	$11	$13	$25	$8	$12	10t
A4	$9	$19	$12	$8	$6	$13	100t
	50t	20t	10t	35t	15t	50t	

Vogel's Approximation Method (VAM) tackles the problem of finding a good initial solution by taking into account the costs associated with each route alternative. As we can see in Table 2.11, it produces a lower cost than the matrix minimum figure. However, by using the Simplex method of linear programming we can produce an even lower cost (see Table 2.12).

TABLE 2.10　Matrix minimum solution = $1,850

Supplier \ Customer	B1	B2	B3	B4	B5	B6	Tonnes
A1	30	0	0	0	0	0	30
A2	0	10	10	0	0	20	40
A3	0	10	0	0	0	0	10
A4	20	0	0	35	15	30	100
	50	20	10	35	15	50	

TABLE 2.11　Vogel's approximation method solution = $1,680

Supplier \ Customer	B1	B2	B3	B4	B5	B6	Tonnes
A1	0	0	0	0	0	30	30t
A2	0	20	10	10	0	0	40t
A3	0	0	0	0	10	0	10t
A4	50	0	0	25	5	20	100t
	50t	20t	10t	35t	15t	50t	

TABLE 2.12　Utilizing the Simplex method = $1,650

Supplier \ Customer	B1	B2	B3	B4	B5	B6	Tonnes
A1	0	0	0	0	0	30	30t
A2	0	20	10	10	0	0	40t
A3	0	0	0	0	0	10	10t
A4	50	0	0	25	15	10	100t
	50t	20t	10t	35t	15t	50t	

Further information

A full explanation of VAM can be found at http://wps.prenhall.com/wps/
media/objects/9434/9660836/online_tutorials/heizer10e_tut4.pdf
An Excel spreadsheet can be downloaded from http://howtologistics.com

2.11 Vendor assurance of transport logistics service providers

Introduction

When outsourcing logistics and supply chain services, it is vital that companies
understand the risk profile of the suppliers they are using if they are to protect their brand and reputation as well as their service levels. A company
outsourcing its logistics may congratulate itself that it is no longer responsible for the headache of safety and compliance management; however, if
there is a serious accident or breach of health and safety legislation, publicity
will normally focus more on any connection with a branded goods manufacturer or retailer than on the typically less well-known logistics service
provider. Similarly, any interruption in service associated with the loss of a
facility, bankruptcy or loss of key personnel will have a dramatic and serious
impact on the outsourcing company, particularly when the service includes
warehousing or e-commerce activities.

When to use

Outsourcing companies need to include an audit of vendor risk profiles.
Ideally this is done during the tender process and repeated at appropriate
intervals throughout the life of the contract. The frequency and depth of
such audits will depend on the criticality of the service being outsourced.

Where more than one company is audited, or a company is audited more
than once over a period of time, it is best to use a standard list of questions
that reflect the risks that are relevant for that contract, with standardized
scoring for the responses. Scores may then be compared to see relative risk
and to assess progress over time. However, the main value of the audit tool
is to identify and track actions to reduce or mitigate risk.

How to use

The questions shown in Table 2.13 should be asked and the answers recorded and analysed.

TABLE 2.13 Vendor assurance questionnaire

Area	Typical questions
Health and safety	Is the supplier aware of their general safety responsibilities in line with current legislation? What is the supplier's approach to the safety of operations and transport on site? What processes does the supplier have in place?
Compliance (with legal operating requirements)	Can the supplier demonstrate compliance with Operator Licence legislation?
Financial	What is the credit rating of the supplier? Have the supplier's latest published accounts been examined by a financial expert?
Performance	Does the supplier issue a regular performance report to the client and to other clients?
Contractual	Is there a record of the agreement between the client and the supplier? Who has the controlling interest in the supplier and how does this affect the contract (are there parent company guarantees in place)?
Dependency	Is the supplier performance dependent upon one or two key individuals? How dependent is the supplier upon their largest other customer? Could loss of this contract threaten the supplier's viability?
Systems	Does the supplier measure and report on their systems performance, and what is the performance? What steps has the supplier taken to protect against systems failure? Is there a disaster recovery plan in place? How widely used is the main software package?
Food safety or dangerous goods	Is the supplier meeting the specific safety or quality requirements related to the products carried for this contract?

Who should audit?

Auditors should have an operational logistics background and have been trained in national health and safety and professional competency standards for road transport and logistics operations. They should also have received training in quality auditing skills and techniques.

Where is the audit carried out?

Typically an audit will be carried out at the premises where the contract is operated from or at a similar site for such services. Health and safety, training and monitoring records should be available to the auditor on request.

Output and follow-up

At the end of the visit the supplier is given a score out of 10 for each area (see Figure 2.5 for an example of a graphical representation of the results), with any significant risks being highlighted. A report is written for each audit, with details of all the areas audited and suggested actions to improve performance. The outsourcing company should then put in place checks to ensure that the actions are carried out by the next audit at least, preferably earlier, depending on the risk attached to non-compliance.

FIGURE 2.5 Example of radar chart summarizing how well the supplier meets the criteria

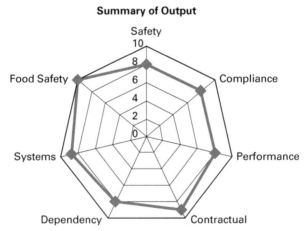

SOURCE: reproduced with permission from Labyrinth Logistics Consulting

(This tool provided by Labyrinth Logistics Consulting Limited, www. labyrinthsolutions.co.uk)

2.12 Drivers' hours regulations, EU and United States

Introduction

This tool looks at the freight drivers' regulations for drivers' hours for both the EU and the United States. This is a quick guide only, with official websites included at the end of the section for more comprehensive information.

The EU and UK

Table 2.14 provides details of current (2013) drivers' hours regulations for the EU and UK. These rules apply if the maximum permissible weight of

TABLE 2.14 Drivers' hours regulations, EU

Working week	Limited to an average of 48 hours over 4-month period, or 6 months if agreed. Excludes breaks and waiting time. 30-min break if working 6–9 hours, 45-min break if working > 9 hours. Maximum of 60 hours per week
Maximum driving period without break	4.5 hours
Break period	45 minutes or combinations of 15/30-minute breaks during the driving period. The second break period must be at least 30 minutes
Daily driving limit	9 hours can be extended to 10 hours twice per week
Maximum weekly driving period	56 hours
Maximum driving time over 2 weeks	90 hours
Daily rest period in 24 hours	11 hours' continuous rest*
Weekly rest period	45 hours

(Continued)

TABLE 2.14 Drivers' hours regulations, EU *(Continued)*

Night working (anyone working between midnight and 4 am)	Limited to 10 hours in any 24-hour period, can be extended to 12 hours
Entitlements	20 days' paid holiday. Night workers get free health assessment

*You may reduce your daily rest period to no fewer than nine continuous hours, with no need to make up for this. However, you can do this no more than three times between any two weekly rest periods. You can take your daily rest in a vehicle, if it has suitable sleeping facilities and is stationary.

your vehicle/vehicle combination is more than 3.5 tonnes. There will be some exemptions which can be found on the website at the end of this section. The fixed week always starts at 00.00 on Monday and ends at 23.59 on the following Sunday.

Driver breaks

The EU drivers' hours rules set out minimum requirements for taking breaks from driving. The rules say that you should not drive for more than 4.5 hours. After this, you must take an uninterrupted break of at least 45 minutes, unless you take a rest within the driving period.

According to the rules, during a 'break' a driver may not drive or do any other work, and must use this time only to rest. You may take a break in a moving vehicle, provided that you do no other work.

Alternatively, instead of taking a full 45-minute break every 4.5 hours, you can take two breaks within a 4.5-hour period. The first must be at least 15 minutes, followed by another of at least 30 minutes.

Weekly rest periods

You must take a weekly rest period within six days of the end of the last weekly rest period. A regular weekly rest period is a period of at least 45 consecutive hours. A reduced weekly rest period must be a minimum of 24 consecutive hours.

United States – summary of Hours-of-Service (HOS) Regulations

These regulations (see Table 2.15) apply to vehicles that weigh 10,001 pounds or more and have a gross vehicle weight rating or gross combination weight rating of 10,001 pounds or more.

TABLE 2.15 Hours-of-service (HOS) regulations, United States

Driving limits	May drive a maximum of 11 hours after 10 consecutive hours off duty
Driving limits	May not drive beyond the 14th consecutive hour after coming on duty, following 10 consecutive hours off duty. Off-duty time does not extend the 14-hour period
On duty time	May not drive after 60/70 hours on duty in 7/8 consecutive days. A driver may restart a 7/8 consecutive day period after taking 34 or more consecutive hours off duty
Rest period	Drivers using the sleeper berth provision must take at least 8 consecutive hours in the sleeper berth, plus a separate 2 consecutive hours either in the sleeper berth, off duty, or any combination of the two
Rest breaks	May drive only if 8 hours or less have passed since end of driver's last off-duty period of at least 30 minutes. [HM 397.5 mandatory 'in attendance' time may be included in break if no other duties performed]
Limitations on minimum '34-hour restarts'	(1) Must include two periods between 1 am and 5 am home terminal time (2) May only be used once per week
On-duty time	Does not include any time resting in a parked vehicle (also applies to passenger-carrying drivers). In a moving property-carrying CMV, does not include up to 2 hours in passenger seat immediately before or after 8 consecutive hours in sleeper berth

(Data reproduced under the Open Government Licence: http://www.nationalarchives.gov.uk/doc/open-government-licence/)

Further information

UK/EU: https://www.gov.uk/drivers-hours
United States: http://www.fmcsa.dot.gov/rules-regulations/topics/hos/index.htm

2.13 Transportation of hazardous products

In terms of the movement of hazardous goods the carrier's duties are far less complicated than the consignor's duties in that there is far less need for interpretation. The following is expected of the carrier:

- The carrier must decide, from the information provided by the consignor's dangerous goods note, as to whether it has a dangerous goods load under the carriage of dangerous goods by road regulations.

- The carrier's obligations have thresholds at which the regulations become relevant and these thresholds are based on the packing group of the goods to be carried.

- The carrier must appoint a DGSA (dangerous goods safety adviser).

- The carrier must ensure the vehicle is roadworthy and not overloaded.

- Drivers must hold vocational training certificates and be trained in emergency action procedures.

- Drivers must carry a photographic identification card.

- Drivers must not carry matches or lighters, or smoke in close vicinity of the load.

Additional requirements include the completion of a security plan that all participants are made aware of. Note that different regulations apply to the different modes of transport utilized. Note also that there are certain hazardous items that cannot be transported together. Each mode of transport will have a dangerous goods segregation chart detailing what can and cannot be transported together.

The carriage of dangerous goods by sea is governed by the International Maritime Dangerous Goods Regulations (IMDG): http://www.imo.org/Publications/IMDGCode/Pages/Default.aspx. The IMDG Code, 2014 Edition came into force on 1 January 2016.

Transporting goods around the globe, by air, is governed by two sets of Regulations: International Civil Aviation Organization (ICAO) and International Air Transport Association (IATA) Dangerous Goods Regulations (http://www.iata.org/publications/dgr/Pages/index.aspx).

In the UK, the Carriage of Dangerous Goods and Use of Transportable Pressure Equipment Regulations (CDG) and the European agreement 'Accord européen relatif au transport international des marchandises dangereuses *par route' (ADR)* together regulate the carriage of dangerous goods by road (http://www.hse.gov.uk/cdg/index.htm).

Other countries will have their own specific regulations. For example, in the United States it is covered by the Federal Motor Carrier Safety Administration (FMCSA) (http://www.fmcsa.dot.gov/safety-security/hazmat/complyhmregs.htm).

Separate pictograms are to be used for labelling hazardous goods in transport. As these are colour coded we have not included them here but they can be accessed on http://www.unece.org/fileadmin/DAM/trans/danger/publi/adr/adr2015/ADR2015e_WEB.pdf, where there is also further information.

Inventory management tools

3.1 Inventory management audit

Introduction

This audit aims to measure the extent to which the inventory is managed against known best practices. It is not an exhaustive list of questions and should be tailored to individual companies, sectors or environments. Nevertheless it will give you a good start in understanding where improvement could be made and will enable you to compare operations at different sites.

When to use

This is a good tool to use when you want to improve inventory management in your business, start a supply chain implementation project or when taking up a new job to understand how well inventory is managed in your new company.

How to use

Table 3.1 shows the first two sections of the audit. The full audit can be purchased from howtologistics.com; discount code: lsct0104.

The full audit contains over 50 questions arranged into nine sections (inventory analysis, inventory reporting, inventory management parameters, inventory accuracy, data management, demand management, supply management, operating efficiency and process management).

TABLE 3.1 Inventory management audit

Inventory Management Audit				
Carried out by:		Location:		
Date:				
Item	**No**	**Yes**	**N/A***	**Comments**
Inventory analysis				
Are inventory families identified?				
Is ABC/Pareto analysis using average usage value carried out by family?				
Is ABC/Pareto analysis using average usage value carried out by item?				
Is ABC/Pareto analysis using average usage rate carried out by family (to identify fast/medium/slow movers)				
Is ABC/Pareto analysis using average usage rate carried out by item (to identify fast/medium/slow movers)				
Is the number of ABC/Pareto classes appropriate for the inventory? (Maybe 4, 5 or 6 classes would be more suitable)				
Are stock-outs systematically recorded and investigated?				
Is demand variation measured using statistical methods?				
Is stock cover calculated and reviewed regularly by item and family?				
Is stock turn calculated and reviewed regularly by item and family?				
Is a non-mover analysis carried out?				
Is a back order analysis carried out?				
Are 'special' items (one-off purchases, not to be re-ordered) clearly identified?				

(Continued)

TABLE 3.1 Inventory management audit (*Continued*)

Inventory Management Audit				
Carried out by:		Location:		
Date:				
Item	**No**	**Yes**	**N/A***	**Comments**
Are non-standard stock (eg, seasonal items, check before re-ordering) items clearly identified?				
Inventory reporting				
Is the inventory value recalculated daily/weekly/monthly? (Choose appropriate time period)				
Is a variety of customer service measures employed?				
Is the level of immediate availability of all items measured daily/weekly/monthly?				
Is the fill rate measured daily/weekly/monthly?				
Is the percentage of orders delivered on time and in full measured?				
Is an inventory performance report issued daily/weekly/monthly?				
Is the number of backorders days/weeks overdue monitored closely to ensure fulfilment as soon as possible (and to prevent 'unreal' back orders when customers forget to cancel)?				
Inventory management parameters				
Is an inventory management strategy (replenishment method) identified for each item/family/class?				

(Continued)

TABLE 3.1 Inventory management audit (*Continued*)

Inventory Management Audit				
Carried out by:		Location:		
Date:				
Item	**No**	**Yes**	**N/A***	**Comments**
Is somebody responsible for setting inventory management parameters for each replenishment method? (reorder points, safety stock levels, reorder quantities,etc)				
Are inventory parameters reviewed at regular intervals?				
Are replenishment lead times checked and adjusted at appropriate regular intervals?				
Is stock cover reviewed at appropriate intervals?				
Does a disposal policy group exist, including representatives of users, finance, warehousing, procurement and inventory management functions?				
Does a disposal policy exist?				
Is the disposal policy clearly described and workable?				
Are candidate items for disposal reviewed regularly?				
Is Kanban used for fast-moving, medium or high value items?				
Is VMI/CMI (vendor managed inventory/ co-managed inventory) used for high usage/low value items?				
Are safety stock levels reviewed at appropriate regular intervals?				
Are stock cover targets set for each family/item?				

(Continued)

TABLE 3.1 Inventory management audit (*Continued*)

Inventory Management Audit				
Carried out by:			Location:	
Date:				
Item	**No**	**Yes**	**N/A***	**Comments**
Inventory accuracy				
Is quantity accuracy measured regularly?				
Is cycle or perpetual counting used?				
Is location accuracy measured regularly?				
Is condition/quality measured regularly?				
Is labelling accuracy measured regularly?				
Is a full stock count carried out at least once per year?				
Are random audits carried out in between formal counting?				
Data management				
Is the ability to change inventory management parameters restricted to a specific individual/group? (i.e. restricted access)				
Is there a procedure for creating new items/codes (to prevent duplicate identities for the same item)?				
Is the new item procedure followed?				
Is the coding system for new items logical and intuitive?				
When adding a new item to the system, is it easy to check if similar items exist already?				
* N/A = not applicable				

3.2 ABC Pareto analysis for inventory management

Introduction

ABC analysis or Pareto analysis has been described as a general tool for distinguishing 'the important few from the insignificant many'. This is especially useful in inventory management. Because of the high cost of holding inventory, it is critical to know which items are capable of generating the greatest holding cost so that we can focus our effort on managing the most important items. ABC analysis for inventory management and procurement depends on item 'usage value', where usage value is the product of usage over a period of time and some indicative item value. By ranking usage value from highest to lowest, the few most important items can be identified. This calculation is essential because there may be a small number of very expensive items that must still be managed carefully, or there could be very high usage of low-value items, eg fasteners, to which it may not be worth dedicating a lot of our precious management effort (see VMI, tool 3.17).

We tend to calculate 'usage value' over a year but it could be calculated over other time periods, eg a week or a month. Usage value has several other applications in inventory management, including setting the limits of the ABC classes, in order to find an appropriate balance between administrative effort (to raise orders and plan replenishment) and replenishment quantity (which influences the average level of cycle stock and hence the average level of inventory and inventory holding costs).

When to use

Item values and quantities consumed change over time and so it is useful to repeat the ABC analysis periodically to ensure that the class allocations are still appropriate, for example every six or 12 months.

The Pareto class of an item is used in inventory management to allocate the most appropriate inventory replenishment method, eg Kanban, MRP or classical inventory management methods for dependent items, or to understand the strategic importance of the item when applying the Kraljic matrix in procurement (see tool 4.6).

How to use

Most inventory management systems have an ABC analysis function. If this is not the case, the data can be downloaded into Excel and manipulated using the data 'sort' function. There are five main steps:

1 Calculate the annual usage value for each item under consideration (formula 1), using some indicative item value (eg most recent price, or average item value):

Annual usage value = annual quantity sold or used × indicative item value (1)

2 Rank the annual usage values from highest to lowest.

3 Starting with the highest usage value, calculate the cumulative usage value.

4 Express the cumulative usage value as a percentage of the total annual usage value.

5 Identify the ABC class of each item.

Note that according to the data, it may be more appropriate to change the class limits, or even have more than three classes. Typical limits for a three-class system are:

A Up to and including 80% of total annual usage value ($x \leq 80.0$)

B Greater than 80% and up to and including 95% ($80.0 < x \leq 95.0$)

C Greater than 95% of total annual usage value ($95.0 < x \leq 100.0$)

Where there are a very large number of B or C items, some companies have identified four or five classes, by splitting B items into B1 and B2, C items into C1 and C2, or introducing a D class to have more precise control.

Example

This example uses just 10 items to demonstrate the method. Clearly, there will be thousands of items in practice! Table 3.2 shows the starting data of average annual usage and indicative unit cost.

The items are then ranked in order of annual usage value (AUV), starting with the highest AUV. Cumulative AUV is then found and this is expressed as a percentage of the total (see Table 3.3). The class of each item can then be identified, using the limits stated earlier.

This example can be downloaded for free from http://howtologistics.com

Further information

Relph, G J and Milner, C Z (2015) *Inventory Management: Advanced methods for managing inventory within business systems*, Kogan Page, London

Wild, T (2005) *Best Practice in Inventory Management*, 2nd edn, Butterworth-Heinemann, Oxford

TABLE 3.2 Calculating the annual usage value

Item no.	Average annual usage	Unit cost (£)	Annual usage value (£)
1	10	295.00	2,950.00
2	5270	0.40	2,108.00
3	22	18.00	396.00
4	185	320.00	59,200.00
5	43	118.00	5,074.00
6	780	12.80	9,984.00
7	550	0.50	275.00
8	365	0.50	182.50
9	150	13.25	1,987.50
10	225	10.35	2,328.75
		Total	84,485.75

3.3 Ballou's inventory-throughput curve

Introduction

Ronald Ballou is one of the early writers who integrated inventory, warehousing, transport and location into a coherent and modern concept of customer service-oriented logistics management. His research has contributed greatly to the development of the field over the years. One of the many tools that he developed from empirical research is a method for using current and historical data to understand the relationship between the level of business carried out by a warehouse and the overall level of inventory required to support that level of business.

Ballou makes the point that warehouses are often planned to have a certain number of stock turns per year. Although this may be the target, it is worth analysing data on existing activities to find out the actual relationship.

TABLE 3.3 Calculating the cumulative percentage annual usage value

Item number	Annual usage quantity	Unit cost (£)	Annual usage value (AUV) in £	Cumulative annual usage value (£)	Cumulative percentage of annual usage value (%)	ABC class	
4	185	320	59,200.00	59,200.00	70.07	A	≤80.0%
6	780	12.8	9,984.00	69,184.00	81.89	B	
5	43	118	5,074.00	74,258.00	87.89	B	
1	10	295	2,950.00	77,208.00	91.39	B	
10	225	10.35	2,328.75	79,536.75	91.14	B	
2	5,270	0.4	2,108.00	81,644.75	96.64	C	>95.0%
9	150	13.25	1,987.50	83,632.25	98.99	C	
3	22	18	396.00	84,028.25	99.46	C	
7	550	0.5	275.00	84,303.25	99.78	C	
8	365	0.5	182.50	84,485.75	100.00	C	

When to use

Periodically, owing to changes in law such as the drivers' hours regulations or changes in markets and demand, it is necessary to review the structure of the distribution network. This review includes the location and size of warehouses and distribution centres relative to the customers and markets they are serving. Alternatively, a new warehouse may be planned to serve a new market. Ballou's inventory-throughput curve gives a first approximation of the total amount of inventory required to support a certain level of business.

How to use

The aim is to plot a graph of the value of the average inventory level against the value of annual throughput or sales. Most warehouses produce a weekly or monthly report of value of inventory and value of shipments made. The average value of inventory can be found by averaging the month-end inventory values from a number of reports. The annual value of shipments can be found by summing shipments across the last 12 months or extrapolating values from the last three or six months.

If this data is plotted for each warehouse in the network, a graph can be built up (see Figure 3.1). The best fit curve is found. If it is proposed to reorganize the network or to open a warehouse in a new market with an estimated volume of business, the total amount of inventory required for a given level of business can be found (Figure 3.1).

FIGURE 3.1 Inventory-throughput curve

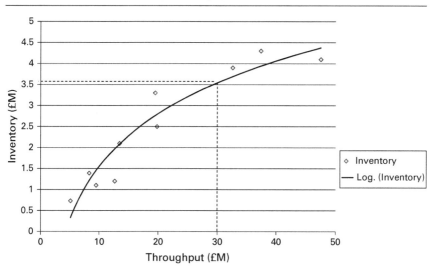

Example

A distribution network expanded from four to six warehouses between 2010 and 2011. Throughput and inventory data are shown in Table 3.4. All of these points can be used and are plotted on a graph (see Figure 3.1). The best curve has been fitted. This can be done in Excel by selecting scatter plot, and then adding the best fit logarithmic curve. A new warehouse is being planned, which is expected to have a throughput of around £30 million. It can be seen from the graph that following previous practice it can be expected that inventory with a value of approximately £3.6 million will be required to support this level of business.

TABLE 3.4 Network data

Year	Warehouse	Throughput (£m)	Inventory (£m)
2010	1	32.6	3.9
	2	8.3	1.39
	3	12.6	1.2
	4	19.5	3.3
2011	1	37.4	4.3
	2	9.5	1.1
	3	13.4	2.1
	4	19.8	2.5
	5	5.1	0.73
	6	47.5	4.1

Note that the method assumes that systems and working practices in the new warehouse will be the same as in the other warehouses, but this may not necessarily be the case. (This example can be downloaded for free from http://howtologistics.com)

Further information

See Ronald Ballou's *Business Logistics Management* or his 1981 paper that described the origins of this curve.

References

Ballou, R H (1981) Estimating and auditing aggregate inventory levels at multiple stocking points, *Journal of Operations Management*, **1** (3), February, pp 143–53

Ballou, R H (2000) Evaluating inventory management performance using a turnover curve, *International Journal of Physical Distribution and Logistics Management*, **30** (1), pp 72–85

Ballou, R H (2004) *Business Logistics Management: Planning, organizing, and controlling the supply chain*, 5th edn, Prentice Hall, Upper Saddle River, NJ

3.4 Consignment stock

Introduction

The term comes from the old phrase 'on consignment', where something is supplied to a customer before payment on the basis that the customer will only pay for what has been sold on or used and can return any unsold stock. Consignment stock therefore refers to inventory that has been delivered to your warehouse, but for which you have not yet paid or even issued a purchase order. When that material is taken out of stock for use, a purchase order is sent to the supplier and payment is made. Ownership of the, as yet, unused material still in the warehouse rests with the supplier and is transferred to the customer at the moment of withdrawal for use. The consignment agreement should specify:

- responsibility for any damage before use;
- the grounds under which either the customer can return the product or the supplier can reclaim the product;
- who pays for the return transport; and
- whose insurance covers its presence in the warehouse.

It is common for a period of time to be specified, after which the goods are returned to the supplier.

There is a particular application of consignment stock in the retail sector where the supplier may use a consignment agreement to propose new products to a retailer, or high-end products the retailer would not normally stock. By this means the associated financial risk is shared between both parties and sales are equally beneficial to both.

Consignment stock can be part of an ongoing VMI/CMI arrangement where ownership of the stock rests with the supplier, and the customer pays only for what has been used (see tool 3.17). The advantages and disadvantages for each party are summarized in Table 3.5.

TABLE 3.5 Advantages and disadvantages of consignment stock for each party

	Advantages	Disadvantages
Supplier	Customer will choose your material over a competitor's material because it is available Can plan your deliveries such that you anticipate future requirements and may be able to reduce the number of deliveries Shared financial risk for products that might not have been ordered otherwise	This material is no longer available to send to another customer who may have an unplanned urgent requirement There may be a long wait before payment Risk of damage in the customer's warehouse Increased inventory in the supply chain
Customer	Can obtain favourable financial terms in a buyer's market Payment terms can be advantageous for the customer since payment is due at some time after use, rather than some period after delivery Material is available if there is a sudden increase in demand Ability to offer/use products that might not have been stocked otherwise	Stockholding cost of items supplied which do not have immediate use Increased space requirement for stock and associated stockholding cost Increased inventory in the supply chain

When to use

Although consignment stock looks financially attractive to the customer, it must be remembered that the customer is holding this stock until the time of use. If this time is not imminent, the stock is simply adding to the inventory that must be managed (allocated space, counted, looked after, etc). In general, supply chain thinking states that we do not want extra inventory at any point in the chain, and that any stock on consignment, rather than delivered against a production or supply schedule, is causing a delay in the flow through the chain.

Consignment stock as part of a VMI agreement is more acceptable since the VMI agreement will have taken into account the stock profile of the different items and set up maximum and minimum stock levels using historical data and a plan of future requirements.

In summary, consignment stock without VMI should only be used for fast-moving items likely to be used in the very short term. In this instance, the flow is hardly limited, the financial effect is primarily a delay to payment, and the customer has received what it was going to order anyway.

How to use

Draw up an agreement taking into account the range of items concerned, methods/timing of supply, payment terms, maximum stock levels, returns at the request of the supplier or customer, return transport cost, insurance and damage. Specify the liabilities and responsibilities of each party.

Check the VAT rules. The application of VAT to consignment stocks depends as much on 'control' (who has the right to withdraw stock) as ownership and it is therefore worth checking liabilities with the accounting function before setting up any agreement, particularly if material is being supplied across borders.

Example

A manufacturer is developing a new product and is refining the specification through trialling various thicknesses of polymer sheeting. Market research has been very positive and the supplier has been engaged to supply material as required on consignment, essentially sharing some of the financial risk of the development process, on condition that its product(s) will be specified for a minimum of the first 100,000 units of production, or one year, whichever event occurs first.

Further information

Wild, T (2005) *Best Practice in Inventory Management*, 2nd edn, Butterworth-Heinemann, Oxford

3.5 Cycle counting or perpetual inventory counting

Introduction

In order to have usable inventory data, it is vital to maintain the integrity of the stock records. This requires user discipline but also a good counting discipline. The primary purpose of stock checking is to count the items and check the quantities found against the quantities recorded in the inventory management system. Sometimes it is useful to take advantage of the stock-checking process to check the location of each item, that it is labelled correctly and is still in usable condition. The traditional approach to stock checking is to set up an annual stock count, usually at the beginning of January, or near the end of the company's tax year. This requires hiring temporary personnel or using existing personnel, which may halt activities or prevent sales while the count takes place.

Another approach is to count a proportion of items regularly throughout the year using normal stores or warehouse personnel. This is known as cycle counting or, sometimes, perpetual inventory counting. There are two approaches to cycle counting: 1) count each item at least once during each replenishment cycle (where the replenishment cycle time is the average time between replenishments); and 2) use ABC analysis to set up a counting plan (sometimes called a periodic counting plan).

When to use

Cycle counting or perpetual inventory counting is used as an efficient alternative to the annual stock count by spreading the counting effort through the year, counting higher-value items and fast movers more often than lower-value or slower-moving items.

How to use

1. Counting each item at least once during the replenishment cycle

The most efficient way to do this is to count the number of items just as the replenishment arrives, ie count the amount remaining just before the new stock is added. At this point, one might expect there to be the least stock to count. Since Pareto class A items should be replenished more frequently than B items, this will result in counting A items more frequently. However, some weeks may see more deliveries than others, so the counting workload could see peaks and troughs.

2. Setting up a periodic counting plan

An alternative to counting just before replenishment is to count a certain number of items every week and thus spread the counting workload evenly across the year (although there may be more stock to count at times since the count will not necessarily take place when the stock level is lowest). For example, if the business works 52 weeks of the year and there are 1,560 different items in inventory, we would plan to count 1,560/52 = 30 different items each week. Clearly we could count more than 1/52 of all items each week if we wanted to count the stock more than once per year. For example, we could count 60 items each week if we thought it necessary to count all items twice per year.

Let us say that we are planning to count all the items once per year and this means counting 30 items each week. How should we choose what to count each week? One method is to choose these 30 items at random from the stock list, and allocate them to week 1, remove those items from the list of items waiting to be allocated, choose another 30 items at random and allocate them to week 2, and so on. This ensures that the person(s) counting will visit the whole of the stores area and may spot any other problems as they carry out the count. Another method is to choose 30 items that are co-located since there is more chance of finding any misplaced items in this way, and the area can be left well organized after counting.

Data about the 30 chosen items are then transferred to a list, either on paper or on a handheld terminal. The data required are:

- item code;
- item description;
- item location.

The person carrying out the stock count would normally be somebody familiar with the stock, for example a person who usually works in the stores. It is important to estimate how long counting takes each week so that enough stores people are employed and that this task is not forgotten in the daily list of tasks and other priorities. In some large warehouses, automotive spare parts for example, some people are employed full-time as stock checkers.

Example

A good approach is to use ABC analysis to determine the frequency of counting. First, decide the frequency at which you wish to count each category of item; for example, to count A items four times per year, B items twice per year, and C items once per year. Table 3.6 shows how to determine what proportion of the total items will appear on the weekly list. Using the frequencies proposed, a weekly list of 1/13 of all A items, 1/26 of all B items and 1/52 of all C items would be created.

TABLE 3.6 Derivation of ABC cycle counting frequencies

ABC class	Desired number of counts (cycles or periods) per year	Fraction of items to be counted in each period	Period of counting	Proportion of items on the weekly list
A	4	¼	¼ × 12 months = 3 months = 13 weeks	1/13
B	2	½	½ × 12 months = 6 months = 26 weeks	1/26
C	1	1/1 = All	1 × 12 months = 12 months = 52 weeks	1/52

Further information

If you are having a problem with inventory accuracy, you may find it helpful to read David Piasecki's 2003 book, which contains a wealth of experience on improving inventory management: *Inventory Accuracy: People, processes, and technology*, OPS Publishing, Kenosha, WI.

References

Relph, G J and Milner, C Z (2015), *Inventory Management: Advanced methods for managing inventory within business systems*, Kogan Page, London

3.6 Maister's rule or the square root rule

Introduction

Deciding upon the number of warehouses to operate within a supply chain is very difficult. We need to take into account the cost of infrastructure, labour and equipment, transport and inventory. The more warehouses we have, the more stock we are going to need to hold. It is unlikely, however, that if we reduce our operation down from two warehouses to one we will be able to halve our stockholding. We therefore need to be able to calculate by how much we will increase or reduce our stockholding when we change the number of warehouses operated.

The square root rule was first introduced by David Maister in 1976. Maister's rule enables companies to quickly calculate the reduction or increase in safety stock required when the number of warehouses is changed. It states that the total safety stock in a supply chain is proportional to the square root of the number of locations at which a product is stored.

When to use

When looking to calculate the amount of safety stock required to be held, based on the number of warehouses operated.

How to use

If we take the example of a firm that operates out of 20 locations and decides to reduce to three locations, according to the square root rule it can theoretically reduce its safety inventory by 61 per cent. The formula is as follows:

Reduction in stock-holding (%) = $[1 - (\sqrt{x} / \sqrt{y})] \times 100$

Where y is the original number of warehouses and x is the proposed number of warehouses.

This calculation cannot be used in isolation. Other factors such as supplier and customer lead times, the product itself (different types of electrical plug, for example), transport costs and distribution centre costs also have to be taken into account.

The rule is based on the assumption that the amount of safety stock in each warehouse in the system is approximately the same. The calculations for a number of different options are shown in Table 3.7, which also shows the likely percentage stock increase if the number of depots is increased.

When the amount of inventory can vary between different warehouses in the network, the throughput-demand curve (see tool 3.3) can be a useful method for determining how much inventory is required for a given level of business.

TABLE 3.7 Square root rule in relation to a change in the number of warehouse operations

Original number of warehouses	Percentage extra stock or reduced stock for change in no of warehouses New number of warehouses							
	1	2	3	4	5	10	15	20
1	0%	41%	73%	100%	124%	216%	287%	347%
2	-29%	0%	22%	41%	58%	124%	174%	216%
3	-42%	-18%	0%	15%	29%	83%	124%	158%
4	-50%	-29%	-13%	0%	12%	58%	94%	124%
5	-55%	-37%	-23%	-11%	0%	41%	73%	100%
10	-68%	-55%	-45%	-37%	-29%	0%	22%	41%
15	-74%	-63%	-55%	-48%	-42%	-18%	0%	15%
20	-78%	-68%	-61%	-55%	-50%	-29%	-13%	0%

Reference

Maister, DH (1976) Centralization of inventories and the 'Square Root Law', *International Journal of Physical Distribution & Logistics Management*, **6** (3), pp 124–34

3.7 Measuring demand variation

Introduction

Coping with variation in supply and demand is one of the inventory manager's biggest challenges. As deliveries from suppliers become gradually more reliable due to improvements in on-time delivery performance, the spotlight is shifting to the demand side. While we try to obtain better forecasts from customers and better demand data (such as point of sale data), many companies are still forced to manage finished goods inventory using historical data only.

It is therefore important to be able to measure variation in historical demand so as to set safety stock levels (see tool 3.14) to meet future demand with a certain level of confidence. We shall consider two methods of measuring variation in demand: mean absolute deviation and standard deviation.

When to use

A measure of demand variation is necessary to be able to set safety stock levels for a given level of availability of finished goods stock (see tool 3.14).

How to use

Method 1: Mean absolute deviation (MAD)

The MAD is defined as:

$$MAD = (\Sigma |x - x'|) / n \tag{1}$$

where x' is the mean demand, x is the demand in a particular time period and n is the number of time periods being taken into account.

Method 2: Standard deviation (SD)

The standard deviation is found from:

$$SD = \sqrt{\left[\Sigma (x - x')^2 / (n - 1) \right]} \tag{2}$$

where x' is the mean demand, x is the demand in a particular time period, n is the number of time periods being taken into account, and Σ means 'sum of'.

Example

Let us consider the demand data for just one item as shown in Table 3.8. The final column shows that total demand is 500 units over the 10-week period. Hence we can say that the average weekly demand is 50 units per week (500/10 = 50). In preparation for calculating both MAD and SD, data are entered into Table 3.9.

TABLE 3.8 Weekly demand for blocks of soap from weeks 20 to 29

Week	20	21	22	23	24	25	26	27	28	29	Total
Demand	48	54	57	49	51	50	46	47	53	45	500

TABLE 3.9 Calculations for weekly demand for bars of soap

1 Week	2 Demand	3 $|x-x'|$	4 $|x-x'|^2$
20	48	2	4
21	54	4	16
22	57	7	49
23	49	1	1
24	51	1	1
25	50	0	0
26	46	4	16
27	47	3	9
28	53	3	9
29	45	5	25
		30	130

Method 1: MAD

Column 3 in Table 3.9 shows the absolute differences between the weekly demand and the average weekly demand (which we know is 50 per week). For example, the demand in week 20 is 48. The difference between 48 and the mean demand of 50 is 2. Thus we see the value 2 in column 3. The two vertical lines either side of $x - x'$ mean 'magnitude'. This means that it does not matter if the actual demand is two units higher or two units lower than the average. We are simply interested in how far apart the two figures are. The sum (symbol Σ) of all these differences over the 10 weeks is found to be 30, shown at the bottom of column 3.

The final stage of the calculation is to divide 30 by the number of weeks being considered, which is 10. We conclude that MAD for blocks of soap from weeks 20 to 29 is 30/10 = 3.

The bigger the variability in demand, the bigger is the MAD. We therefore now have a means of measuring and expressing variability in demand.

Method 2: SD

Standard deviation of demand is a more accurate measure but is a bit more difficult to calculate. In column 4 in Table 3.9, we can see that the absolute difference between demand and mean demand found in the MAD calculation has been squared. To find the standard deviation, we sum all the figures in column 4, divide by $n - 1$ ($10 - 1 = 9$) and then find the square root. The bigger the value found for SD, the bigger is the variation in demand.

$$SD = \sqrt{\left[\Sigma(x - x')^2 / (n - 1) \right]} = \sqrt{[130 / 9]} = 3.8$$

It is worthwhile mentioning that there is a rough relationship between MAD and SD where SD is approximately 1.25 times the MAD value. For example, for blocks of soap, we found that SD is 3.8 and MAD is 3.0, so here SD is 1.27 times the value of MAD. Although SD is more complicated to calculate, it is a more accurate measure of spread than MAD and should be used if possible.

This example can be downloaded for free from http://howtologistics. com.

Further information

Any introductory statistics textbook will provide a thorough explanation of the two methods. See also: Relph, G J and Milner, C Z (2015) *Inventory Management: Advanced methods for managing inventory within business systems,* Kogan Page, London

3.8 Periodic review inventory management system

Introduction

The specific characteristic of a periodic review system is that the level of inventory is checked at regular intervals and it is decided at the moment of review whether to place a replenishment order or not. This is in contrast to the reorder point system where the time between successive orders can vary.

Figure 3.2 shows the idea. A target stock level (TSL) has been set, made up of safety stock plus cycle stock. The cycle stock is the amount of stock that is used and replenished under normal circumstances, that is, the amount of stock between the level of safety stock and the TSL. The stock level is reviewed at regular intervals (indicated by small arrows on the horizontal axis in Figure 3.2). At each review, a quantity is ordered that takes the actual stock level back up to the TSL (dotted line). An order is placed and the replenishment quantity arrives in due course (indicated by the solid vertical lines). The horizontal distance between the vertical dotted line and the vertical solid line is the delivery lead time (reliable in this example). During this lead time the stock is still available for use and so the stock level will fall during the delivery lead time.

FIGURE 3.2 Periodic review system

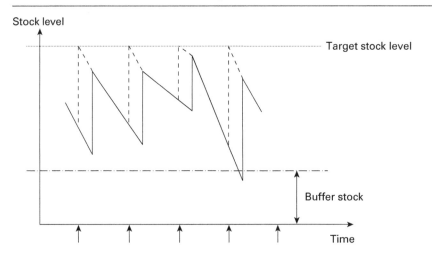

Clearly this type of method suits computerized inventory management systems, where the computer program checks the stock level of every item in the system against its TSL and generates a group of orders, grouping items together on the same purchase order where they come from the same supplier. A computer system can thus review the inventory status for thousands of items very quickly. This is rather difficult to handle in a manual system. Where inventory is managed using a manual system, it is possible to get the same benefits from grouping together items from the same supplier, by reviewing all the items from the same supplier at the same time, and spreading the suppliers over different days of the week, for example all items from supplier P on Monday, all items from supplier Q on Tuesday, and so on.

When to use

This is another method for managing inventory of items subject to independent demand, that is, items that are sold from finished goods inventory. It may also be used for C items, subject to dependent demand, that are used regularly. This method also forms the basis of a family of related inventory management systems.

In a typical supermarket, the computerized inventory management system reviews the stock levels at the end of each afternoon and sends an order to the distribution centre for delivery during the night or early morning.

How to use

This type of system is characterized by regular review intervals and a variable order quantity. The key parameters required to set up the system are the review period (R), ie time between successive reviews, and the TSL.

The time between successive reviews can be any convenient period depending on the location of the supplier and the ease of delivering regularly. Although we saw above that a supermarket typically receives deliveries every 24 hours, the delivery frequency can vary enormously in a manufacturing company. Usually A items are delivered more frequently and so the review period for these items may be daily or weekly. Vendor-managed inventories also use this system (see tool 3.17). A TSL is agreed between the customer and the supplier and the vendor makes deliveries at a convenient time to 'top up' the stock. This might be weekly when delivering fasteners to a manufacturing company or every two hours when delivering freshly made sandwiches to the shop at a petrol station.

The review period is taken into account when calculating the TSL. Longer time intervals between reviews means that a higher TSL will be required. The TSL must allow for enough stock to support the users until the next review period and until the following delivery arrives. Consider the case where the review period is one week and the lead time is two days. A replenishment order will be placed to take the inventory back up to the TSL and this will arrive in two days' time. This stock must be capable of supplying demand until the next review period (one week from now) *and* until the order placed then arrives (two days after that). Hence we need to take into account the average demand (Dav) over this extended time period (formula 1):

$$TSL = (Dav \times [\text{review period} + \text{lead time}])$$
$$+ \text{safety stock level} = (Dav \times [R + L]) + Sb \qquad (1)$$

If the delivery lead time L is reliable, then the level of the safety stock Sb is calculated in exactly the same way as for the reorder point system. Note that it is critical to ensure that all elements use the same unit of time, eg average weekly demand with review period and lead time expressed in weeks.

The quantity to be ordered is calculated from the TSL (formula 2). Let Sc represent current stock level and Qopen be the quantity of items on any outstanding orders (orders already placed for this item but which have not arrived yet):

$$Oq = TSL - \text{current stock level} - \text{any open orders}$$
$$= TSL - Sc - Qopen \qquad (2)$$

Example

Example 1: Find the TSL

Item Z has the following characteristics:

$$\text{Lead time} = 2\,\text{weeks}$$
$$\text{Review period} = 1\,\text{week}$$
$$\text{Average demand} = 60\,per\,\text{week}$$
$$\text{Safety stock} = 20\,\text{units}$$

The TSL is found by applying formula 1:

$$TSL = (Dav \times [R + L]) + Sb = (60 \times [1 + 2]) + 20 = 200$$

Example 2: Find the order quantity

The TSL for item V is 120. At the time of the periodic review, it is found that the current stock level is 42. There are no open orders.

Applying formula 2:

$Oq = TSL$ – current stock level – any open orders
$= TSL - Sc - Qopen = 120 - 42 - 0 = 78$

An order should be placed for 78 units of item V.

Further information

See Wild, T (2005) *Best Practice in Inventory Management*, 2nd edn, Butterworth-Heinemann, Oxford

3.9 Reorder point inventory management system

Introduction

The reorder point system is based on the idea that when the inventory level falls to or below a certain level, the reorder point, we place an order for more, for a predetermined quantity. Figure 3.3 shows what happens under ideal conditions. The reorder point (sometimes called the reorder level), shown as a dotted line in Figure 3.3, is one of the defining parameters of this type of system and is set in advance. The reorder quantity (Oq) is also set in advance.

FIGURE 3.3 Reorder point system

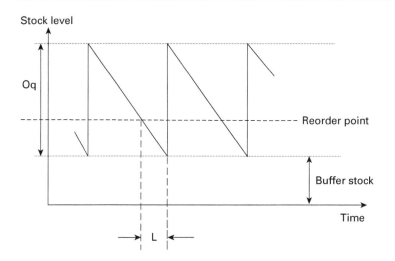

It can be seen from Figure 3.3 that the reorder point has two components. The first is the quantity between the level of safety stock and the reorder point. The reorder point must be set high enough to meet the expected *average* demand during the delivery lead time (L) ie while waiting for the replenishment quantity to arrive. If there is a safety stock, the reorder point must also take into account that we do not expect to use the safety stock under average conditions. The emphasis has been placed on 'average' here because we only expect to use the safety stock under conditions that are not average, eg lateness in delivery or unexpected demand.

So the reorder point is the sum of the quantity of safety stock, Sb, and the quantity that is expected to be used during the delivery lead time, L. The quantity that is expected to be used during the delivery lead time is easily found by multiplying the average rate of demand, Dav, by the lead time, L (see formula 1):

$$ROP = (L \times Dav) + Sb \tag{1}$$

After each transaction, the residual inventory level is checked against the safety stock. If the inventory level is at or below the reorder point (taking into account any existing open orders), a replenishment order is created. This is therefore a continuous review method, with fixed order quantity. According to the rate of demand, replenishment orders are raised as and when required, and the time between raising successive replenishment orders can vary. This means that a number of different orders could be raised on the same supplier during the day, where a vendor supplies a number of different items. This may not be the most efficient method for minimizing transport costs.

Note that it is critical to express all data in the same time units, usually days or weeks.

When to use

This is a method that is suitable for items subject to independent demand, that is, sales from finished product stock. It can also be used for regularly used C items subject to dependent demand (ie materials and components required for a production schedule). There are many different inventory management systems for managing inventory subject to independent demand and this method is one of the building blocks for many other methods.

Historically, when inventory was managed using manual records, it was an advantage to raise orders continuously so as to spread the administrative load. Today, using computer systems, and trying to group as many items as possible to as few suppliers as possible, periodic review systems are more prevalent, particularly in retail distribution.

How to use

To set up a system like this, the following steps must be taken for each item:

1 Analyse demand to obtain an average level of demand per time unit, Dav, say average demand per week.

2 Obtain an indicative lead time, L, for each item and express this in terms of the same time unit, say weeks.

3 Set the inventory parameters – Oq and Sb. For guidance, see the section on replenishment quantities (tool 3.10) and setting safety stock levels (tool 3.14).

4 Determine the reorder point, ROP, from the data above.

5 Monitor the average demand and lead time. If they differ significantly from the quantities used previously to calculate the reorder point, the reorder point should be updated.

Example

Example 1: Setting the reorder point

A new item has been added to the inventory management system of a warehouse and so the reorder point must be calculated. It is expected that about 20 boxes of this item will be sold per week and it has been decided that there should be a safety stock of 10 boxes. Using a delivery lead time of three weeks, we now have all the data required to set the reorder point:

$$Dav = 20\,units\,per\,week$$
$$L = 3\,weeks$$
$$Sb = 10$$
$$ROP = (L \times Dav) + Sb = (3 \times 20) + 10 = 70$$

After each transaction, the residual inventory level is checked against the reorder point, taking into account any open orders (formula 2):

$$If\,(stock\,balance + quantity\,on\,outstanding\,orders)$$
$$\leq ROP,\,then\,place\,an\,order. \qquad (2)$$

Example 2: Raising a replenishment order

An order has just been received in a warehouse for 10 boxes of plastic gloves. The inventory record shows that there are 69 boxes in stock. The reorder point is 60. The reorder quantity is 200. There are no open orders.

Should a replenishment order be raised? Remember that this system is a continuous review system and we review the stock level after each transaction.

New stock balance = opening stock − quantity issued = 69 − 10 = 59.

Then we apply formula 2:

Stock balance + quantity on outstanding orders = 59 + 0 = 59
If (stock balance + quantity on outstanding orders)
    ≤ ROP, then place an order

We can see that 59 is less than the reorder point of 60, so an order is raised.

Let us say that later the same day another order for boxes of plastic gloves is received. This time the order is for two boxes. We make the issue as before and the new stock balance reduces to 57. Should we order more? We apply formula 2 again, but this time we have an open order:

Stock balance + quantity on outstanding orders = 57 + 200 = 257

The stock balance is greater than the reorder point, so another order will not be placed.

Further information

Tony Wild's book is highly recommended for learning more about inventory
    management: Wild, T (2005) *Best Practice in Inventory Management,* 2nd edn,
    Butterworth-Heinemann, Oxford.
For those who wish to explore inventory management in even more detail, see:
    Relph, G J and Milner, C Z (2015) *Inventory Management: Advanced methods
    for managing inventory within business systems,* Kogan Page, London, and
    Silver, E and Peterson, R (1985) *Decision Systems for Inventory Management
    and Production Planning,* 2nd edn, Wiley, New York.

3.10 Replenishment order quantities

Introduction

A replenishment order is raised to trigger purchase or production of more units of an existing inventory item to replace what has been used or sold. If the replenishment order is to be produced (rather than purchased), the order quantity will have a major impact on the level of work in progress, the number of setups and the overall lead time. The size of the reorder quantity also has a major impact on the average level of finished goods stock that is held. We can see this from the traditional 'saw tooth' inventory model shown in Figure 3.4.

FIGURE 3.4 Saw tooth theoretical inventory model

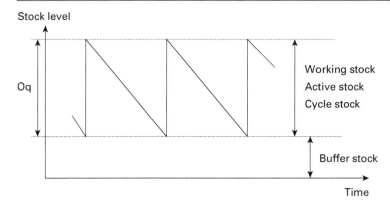

The model shows that the average inventory level is given by the buffer stock level plus the *average* level of cycle stock (formula 1). In this simple model, the *average* level of cycle stock is *half* the total amount of cycle stock:

$$\text{Average level of inventory} = \text{buffer stock} + \tfrac{1}{2}(\text{cycle stock}) \qquad (1)$$

We know that if we place a lot of small orders (where Oq, the order quantity, is small), the cost of administration and delivery for those small orders will be high. Similarly, if we order in large quantities, the cost of administration and delivery will be low but the average level of stock (formula 1) will be high. Many years ago, these two conflicting factors were encapsulated into another theoretical model, called the 'economic order quantity' (EOQ) (tool 3.11), and it was used in some industries for a number of years. These days, however, we prefer to use this model to understand where improvement should be sought but use other methods to calculate the actual quantity to be ordered. In short, we need to find the smallest order quantity that is practicable. There are many more reasons for ordering the smallest quantity possible:

- less buffer stock required;
- more frequent deliveries, which leads to greater reactivity to changing demand;
- lower stock levels, which requires less storage space;
- less chance of obsolescence, damage and other shrinkage;

- easier to count;
- easier to introduce new items.

It can be seen that it is the 'soft' costs, or hidden costs associated with inventory, that are reduced by ordering in smaller quantities and so it often takes more effort to justify this method financially. Methods for reducing the administration and delivery costs associated with small orders include:

- using local vendors where possible;
- using milk rounds to collect supplies from vendors;
- purchasing as many items as possible from the same vendor to render frequent deliveries of small amounts of each item economic;
- raising a blanket order and calling off deliveries against it;
- using 'soft' forms or ordering by internet;
- using VMI;
- using Kanbans.

In production, it is necessary to continue to keep reducing set-up times in order to minimize the penalty for switching production from one product to another, and thus enable smaller and smaller production quantities to be economic.

When to use

Sometimes we have little control over the size of the replenishment quantity. The supplier insists on a minimum order quantity (or value) or supplies only in multiples, eg boxes of 100. The factory insists on a certain run time or a production tank holds only a certain volume. However, when you can buy or make exactly what you want, how much should you buy or make?

How to use

If you are in the fortunate position of being able to set any replenishment quantity you wish, a good starting point is to consider what delivery frequency is ideal and then try to figure out how this can be sensibly achieved. A useful guide for doing this is, once again, ABC analysis. The delivery frequency will differ according to the sector. Some examples are given below.

Example

An ABC delivery schedule for replenishment quantities will be developed for three different sectors (see Table 3.10).

TABLE 3.10 Typical delivery intervals for ABC items in different sectors

Pareto class	Automotive	Engineering	Retail
A	2 hours	Weekly	Daily
B	½ day	Monthly	2–3 days
C	Weekly	Quarterly	Weekly

Automotive assembly lines work at a certain speed or rhythm, and to a sequenced schedule made up of customer and stock orders. The consumption rate of parts and assemblies, and the sequence in which they should be delivered, is therefore known. Ideally, parts should be delivered at the last possible moment (to minimize storage space required) and, ideally, to the lineside without any unreturnable packaging.

Typical engineering companies do not consume the same volume of parts and assemblies as automotive assembly lines and are also usually subject to greater variation in demand. Although this means that buffer stocks are likely to be higher, it also means that deliveries will be necessarily less frequent.

In the retail sector, supermarkets are supplied with fresh goods and fast movers every 24 hours, while dry goods and household items may be replenished every two to three days.

Further information

See Wild, T (2005) *Best Practice in Inventory Management*, 2nd edn Butterworth-Heinemann, Oxford, and Relph, G J and Milner, C Z (2015) *Inventory Management: Advanced methods for managing inventory within business systems,* Kogan Page, London.

3.11 Economic Order Quantity (EOQ), by Geoff Relph

Introduction

Ford W Harris, while working for Ford Motors in Michigan in 1913, derived a method of establishing an economic order value. It is based on the principle that there is a balance between the cost of ordering and the cost of holding stock. Figure 3.5 shows this relationship graphically.

FIGURE 3.5 Economic Order Quantity

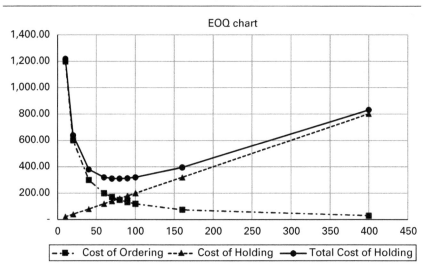

The essence of the formula is that the cost of holding inventory is expressed as the cost of:

- Owning/renting the warehouse.
- Staff to secure and run the warehouse.
- Losses of stock through waste, obsolescence and shrinkage.
- Lost opportunity of the money tied up in the stock.

It is expressed as the formula Quantity Ordered x Unit Cost x Cost of Holding/2.

This is then balanced against the cost of ordering inventory, which is expressed as the cost of:

- Placing order with supplier.
- Transport to warehouse.
- Receiving and putting to stock.

It is expressed as the formula Demand x Cost of ordering/Quantity Ordered

Figure 3.5 shows that the two costs reach a balance point – this is the economic order quantity (Q_{OPT}). It can be expressed as a formula, whose derivation is shown in Figure 3.6. Figure 3.7 shows how the formula works and the data needed to calculate the value.

FIGURE 3.6 Deriving the EOQ

TC = Total annual cost
D = Demand
P = Part Cost per unit
Q = Order quantity
C = Cost of placing an order or set-up cost
i   = inventory carrying rate %

$$\text{Inventory Management Cost} = \underset{\text{Purchase}}{\text{Cost of}} + \underset{\text{Ordering}}{\text{Cost of}} + \underset{\text{Holding}}{\text{Cost of}}$$

$$TC = DP + \frac{D}{Q}C + \frac{Q}{2}iP$$

Cost is at a minimum when Cost of ordering equals the Cost of holding

$$\frac{D}{Q}C = \frac{Q}{2}iP$$

By manipulating the formula you get

$$Q_{OPT} = \sqrt{\frac{2DC}{iP}} = \sqrt{\frac{2(\text{Annual Demand})(\text{Order or Set-up cost})}{(\text{Unit Cost})(\text{inventory carrying rate})}}$$

Based on Chase *et al* 'Production and Operations Management', 1998, p. 588

FIGURE 3.7 EOQ formula for item 9 in Table 3.2

D = Demand	150	
C = Cost of Ordering/Set-up	£80.00	
P = Unit Cost	£13.25	
I = inventory holding rate as %	30%	
W = working days in a year	250	
Economic Order Quantity	$Q = \sqrt{\dfrac{2*D*C}{P*i}}$ $Q = \sqrt{\dfrac{2*150*80.0}{£13.25*30\%}}$	77.70

There has always been a lively debate as to the effectiveness and suitability of the EOQ, the key being the difficulty in determining the true values of the cost of ordering and the cost of holding inventory. However, it highlights the essential relationship that needs to be considered when determining the most effective order size, which balances these two costs. The issues of not being able to evaluate these costs are addressed in the next section.

When to use

All too often when suppliers are asked to give a suggested minimum order quantity (MOQ), their motivation is to minimize their production cost and thus maximize their profit. Often a supplier may incentivize larger batches by offering discounts for the larger quantities. The buyers typically have 'cost down objectives' so will find this attractive, however the planners/operations team will suffer as a result of higher inventories.

How to use

EOQ is useful when testing to see if the discount is really worthwhile, given that you have a reasonable estimate of the cost of ordering and cost of holding stock. It is easy to test the offer made by the supplier by calculating the EOQ for the two costs offered by the supplier and then seeing how close to the calculated EOQ the MOQ requirements are.

Example

Let's say that our supplier for item 9 in Table 3.2 (tool 3.2) is offering a discount of 5 per cent if we increase the MOQ to 150 units. We had asked for an MOQ of 75 based on our calculations.

Table 3.11 shows the EOQ calculated for a range of different costs/discount percentages from 5 to 75 per cent. It is clear from this analysis that the 5 per cent discount does not justify the increase to a MOQ of 150 as the equivalent EOQ for 5 per cent discount or unit cost of 12.59 is only 79.72. To achieve an equivalent EOQ to the offered 150, the discount would need to be just below 75 per cent, which would give an EOQ of 155.41.

TABLE 3.11 Showing EOQ varying with supplier discount

Annual Demand	Unit Cost	Annual Usage Value	EOQ	% discount
150.00	13.25	1,987.50	77.70	
150.00	12.59	1,888.13	79.72	5
150.00	11.93	1,788.75	81.91	10
150.00	10.60	1,590.00	86.87	20
150.00	7.95	1,192.50	100.31	40
150.00	3.31	496.88	155.41	75

Note: Assuming cost of ordering is £80.00 and cost of holding is 30%

TABLE 3.12 Analysis of total inventory management cost to review MOQ discount

MOQ	Unit Cost	Cost of Ordering	Cost of Holding	Cost of Managing	Annual Cost of Purchase	Total Inventory Costs
75	13.25	160.00	149.06	309.06	1987.50	2296.56
150	12.59	80.00	283.22	363.22	1888.13	2251.35

Table 3.12 shows that if only the Cost of Managing inventory is considered then the MOQ of 75 is cheaper, even with the 5 per cent discount on the Unit Cost. However, when the Cost of Purchase is also taken into account, giving the Total Inventory Cost, the larger MOQ is cheaper. This is because, based on the same annual demand, the savings from the Cost of Purchase more than offset the higher Cost of Holding.

This simple financial analysis would therefore suggest that a higher MOQ was acceptable. However, in this case additional considerations will need to be taken into account. For example, the MOQ will be buying 12 months stock: is there a risk that the demand may change in the 12 months, or the stock may deteriorate or become obsolete? Overall the benefit is only 2 per cent rather than the 5 per cent offered by the supplier, with any increased costs and risks moved from the supplier to the business.

Further information

See Harris, F W (1915) *Operations Cost, Factory Management Series*, Shaw, Chicago, IL; Relph, G J and Milner, C Z (2015) *Inventory Management: Advanced methods for managing inventory within business systems*, Kogan Page, London; Relph, G J and Newton, M (2014) Both Pareto and EOQ have limitations: combining them delivers a powerful management tool for MRP and beyond. *International Journal of Production Economics*, **157** (C), pp 24–30.

3.12 Combining Pareto with EOQ to enhance group analysis, by Geoff Relph

In tool 3.2 we looked at Pareto and tool 3.11 looked at EOQ as two techniques for the management of inventory groupings and determining the optimum batch size. In tool 3.10, Table 3.10 gives suggested order periods based on industry types. If our business does not exactly fit one of the three categories described, the answer may be to use the EOQ.

When to use

If we are unsure of where we are in relation to the industries shown in Table 3.10, we may want to compare the EOQ with the recommended delivery intervals. The EOQ is a quantity and the values in Table 3.10 are time intervals. We can convert the EOQ to a time interval, known as the economic order period (EOP). We can calculate the EOP for each item and list them against the recommended Pareto Class calculated in Table 3.3.

How to use

If we use the formula from Figure 3.6 and the items in Table 3.2 we can calculate EOQs for the 10 items, as shown in Table 3.13. What is clear is that there is no specific relationship between the annual usage, unit cost or annual usage value of the product to the recommended EOQ. However items 3, 4 and 5 have similar EOQ in spite of having entirely different Pareto positions. The typically used order periods shown in Table 3.10 may not necessarily be the best ones.

However, we can easily convert EOQ to Economic Order Period (EOP), which would allow us to evaluate the 'days of cover' discussed in tool 3.9. Figure 3.8 shows how to extend EOQ to EOP – or the optimum period represented as number of days of stock rather than the absolute quantity.

We now add the EOP calculation to Table 3.3 and create Table 3.14. Looking at the annual usage values, we can see the higher the annual usage value, the lower the EOP days. What is obvious in Table 3.14 is that there is a direct relationship between EOP and the position of a part in the Pareto list, with item 4 being the top ranked part having the lowest EOP of 25 days, item 5 a B class part with an EOP of 85 days, and item 3 a C class part with 290 days. We can compare the average EOP for each class and compare to the industry types shown in Table 3.10.

TABLE 3.13 Items listed in Table 3.2 with EOQ values

Item	Average Annual Usage	Unit Cost	Annual Usage Value	EOQ
4	185.00	320.00	59200.00	17.56
6	780.00	12.80	9984.00	180.28
5	43.00	118.00	5074.00	13.94
1	10.00	295.00	2950.00	4.25
10	225.00	10.35	2328.75	107.68
2	5720.00	0.40	2288.00	2761.64
9	150.00	13.25	1987.50	77.70
3	22.00	18.00	396.00	25.53
7	550.00	0.50	275.00	765.94
8	365.00	0.50	182.50	623.97

EOQ calculations based on (i=30% and Co = 80.00)

FIGURE 3.8 Extending EOQ formula to represent the EOP

D = Demand	150	
C = Cost of Ordering/Set-up	£80.00	
P = Unit Cost	£13.25	
I = inventory holding rate as %	30%	
W = working days in a year	250	

Economic Order Quantity (EOQ)	$Q = \sqrt{\dfrac{2*D*C}{P*i}}$	$Q = \sqrt{\dfrac{2*150*80.0}{£13.25*30\%}}$	77.70
Economic Order Period (EOP)	EOQ/D (EOQ/D)* W		77.7/150 0.518 years 129.50 days
Economic Order Period (EOP)	$\left(\dfrac{EOQ}{D}\right)*W$	$EOP = \left(\dfrac{77.70}{150}\right)*250$	77.7/150 0.518 years 129.50 days

TABLE 3.14 Items from Table 3.3 with EOP values added

Item	Average Annual Usage	Unit Cost	Annual Usage value	Cumulative Usage Value	Cumulative Percentage of Annual Usage value (%)	ABC Class	EOP days
4	185.00	320.00	59,200.00	59,200.00	70.07	A	23.73
6	780.00	12.80	9,984.00	69,184.00	81.89	B	57.78
5	43.00	118.00	5,074.00	74,258.00	87.89	B	81.05
1	10.00	295.00	2,950.00	77,208.00	91.39	B	106.30
10	225.00	10.35	2,328.75	79,536.75	94.14	B	119.64
2	5,270.00	0.40	2,108.00	81,644.75	96.64	C	125.75
9	150.00	13.25	1,987.50	83,632.25	98.99	C	129.50
3	22.00	18.00	396.00	84,028.25	99.46	C	290.13
7	550.00	0.50	275.00	84,303.25	99.78	C	348.16
8	365.00	0.50	182.50	84,485.75	100.00	C	427.37

based on i=30%, Co = 80.00 and W=250 working days in a year

Example

In Table 3.14 we can see that for the items in Table 3.3 an appropriate class A frequency might be monthly, for the B class quarterly and the C class would be annually.

3.13 K-curve (exchange curve inventory planning), by Geoff Relph

In today's environment we have to manage large numbers of stock-keeping units (SKU) or part numbers with very little time. K-curve is an approach that addresses the problems of managing and optimizing a large group of SKU/parts. The strength of Pareto is its simplicity as it relies on dividing the parts being managed into three groups. If, however, you are looking to manage, say, 10,000 parts, then we will apply the Pareto rules for A, B, C to 2,000, 3,000 and 5,000 parts respectively based on the 80:20 rule.

It is now common to further subdivide the ABC classes into 'super A class' and subdivide C by adding a very low-value class D. In theory this provides more granularity to the classes – meaning that rather than step from five days of cycle inventory for class A to 20 days for class B, we have five days for super class A, 10 days for class A and 20 days for class B. The problem with this is that we now have to make a decision about where to draw the additional boundaries. We can see that EOP has a relationship with Pareto and can assist us in specifying the values in each Pareto class. K-curve goes one stage further and helps define between four and nine groups based on the logical group values of weekly, fortnightly, monthly, etc. It creates an optimum curve that draws the link between the number of deliveries and the value of inventory based on the orders placed.

When to use

If you are being challenged to reduce your inventory levels you will need to decide which parts need to have their cycle stocks reduced. Pareto and EOQ can only advise what they should be for a certain condition. K-curve shows the relationship for the group of parts being managed and lets you see what effect reducing the inventory has on the number of deliveries that will result. To understand, consider this illustration.

An item is delivered once a month. This results in an average inventory of two weeks and 12 deliveries. Now, if we were to increase the delivery frequency to once a week, we would get an average inventory of ½ week but our number of deliveries would rise to 52. So although we gain 1½ weeks of inventory, we have increased the number of deliveries by 40, from 12 to 52. In summary we exchange inventory for increased numbers of deliveries.

How to use

A k-curve can be constructed from the same data that is required to draw a Pareto. (It is beyond the scope of this book to explain in detail how k-curves are constructed but they are clearly explained in Relph and Milner, 2015.) The k-curve algorithm is applied to the data and a range of values of k are tested. This draws an optimum inventory curve, as shown in Figure 3.9.

FIGURE 3.9 Typical k-curve (Inventory Exchange Curve)

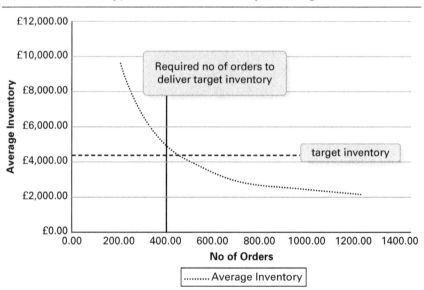

This simply shows the key relationship between the cycle inventory and the number of orders. The set target can then be tested against the required number of deliveries. If this is acceptable, the value of k that gives that point in the curve is then used to provide a table, like the one in Table 3.15, giving the class boundaries (similar to Pareto) which, when applied, will deliver the target inventory level.

TABLE 3.15 Class boundaries derived from k-curve

Work Days	250	
K Value	50	
Value Class	Cycle Days	Class Limit
1	5	£62,500
2	10	£15,625
3	20	£3,906
4	40	£977
5	80	£244
6	160	£0

Example

Table 3.16 shows the results of taking the Pareto items in Table 3.2 and applying the class boundaries from Figure 3.9. What we can see is that the items in Table 3.2 that were divided into three Pareto classes are now divided into six k-curve based value classes with a recommended number of order days for each group/item. It is interesting to note that, in this case, the k-curve classing approach has not allocated items into all classes, unlike Pareto which allocates by percentage. The k-curve approach also avoids the need to evaluate the cost of ordering and cost of holding inventory used to calculate EOQ/EOP as it sets the k value based on the inventory target.

Further reading

Handley, R (1999) *Inventory management*, Control, March, pp 24–6

Harris, F W (1915) *Operations Cost*, Factory Management Series, Shaw, Chicago, IL

Relph, G J (2006) *Inventory Management in Business Systems*, PhD Thesis: Manchester University

Relph, G J and Milner, C Z (2015) *Inventory Management: Advanced methods for managing inventory within business systems*, Kogan Page, London

Relph, G J and Newton, M (2014) Both Pareto and EOQ have limitations: combining them delivers a powerful management tool for MRP and beyond, *International Journal of Production Economics*, **157** (C), pp 24–30

Shah, S (1992) *Setting parameters in MRP for the effective management of bought-out inventory in a JIT assembly environment*, PhD Thesis, Aston University

TABLE 3.16 K-curve classing rules applied to Table 3.2

Item	Average Annual Usage	Unit Cost	Annual Usage value	Cumulative Usage Value	Cumulative Percentage of Annual Usage value (%)	ABC Class	Class days	Order days
4	185.00	320.00	59200.00	59200.00	70.07	A	1	5
6	780.00	12.80	9984.00	69184.00	81.89	B	3	20
5	43.00	118.00	5074.00	74258.00	87.89	B	3	20
1	10.00	295.00	2950.00	77208.00	91.39	B	4	40
10	225.00	10.35	2328.75	79536.75	94.14	B	4	40
2	5270.00	0.40	2108.00	81644.75	96.64	C	4	40
9	150.00	13.25	1987.50	83632.25	98.99	C	4	40
3	22.00	18.00	396.00	84028.25	99.46	C	5	80
7	550.00	0.50	275.00	84303.25	99.78	C	5	80
8	365.00	0.50	182.50	84485.75	100.00	C	6	160

3.14 Safety stock calculation

Introduction

Safety stock is sometimes also called buffer stock or security stock. If we examine the consumption patterns over the same 10-week period of the two items A and B in Table 3.17, we can see that they both have an average demand of 50 units per week. Now look for the maximum and minimum values in each column. It can be seen that item B has much greater variability in demand, ranging from 12 to 89.

TABLE 3.17 Demand data for two different items

Week number	Demand for item A	Demand for item B
20	48	47
21	54	72
22	57	12
23	49	25
24	51	54
25	50	89
26	46	36
27	47	68
28	53	23
29	45	74
Total:	500	500
Average demand:	50 per week	50 per week

Let's say that we replenish the stock of both items once per week. Since item B has a very high variability in demand, a lot of extra stock, or safety stock, will be required to ensure that we can supply during the weeks of high demand. This is stock that is held over and above the amount of stock required to meet *average* demand. A key question to examine is just how important a stockout is to you. If a stockout means losing a contract or a customer, a life or death situation (hospital, aircraft, pharmaceuticals, for example), you will be prepared to invest more in safety stock. If the items are easily substitutable (different colour, make, package size), you may not be prepared to finance a significant amount of safety stock.

So we need to be able to measure this variability to determine how much safety stock is required for a given level of customer service or 'protection level' (protection against stockouts). If you are familiar with statistics, you will know that standard deviation is used to measure variability in data. The standard deviation of demand for item A is 3.8 and for B is 25.7, reflecting the greater variability in demand for item B.

Standard deviation is the preferred method for setting safety stock levels but there are other methods for those who are not familiar with statistical methods. Two easier methods are 'time buffer' and using historical data. In the time buffer method we add safety stock to cover average demand for a certain period of time, for example two days or a week, according to how safe you want to be. Using the historical data method, we look back at demand over previous periods and identify the few times when demand was very much higher than average. A common-sense decision must then be made about whether to cover these occasional high demands and therefore how much safety stock to keep.

The 'How to use' section will present all three methods. We will focus mainly on covering variability in demand rather than variability in lead time.

When to use

Safety stock is required whenever you want to meet demand that is greater than average and/or if the replenishment lead time is highly variable. Longer than average lead times can result in failure to meet demand and so safety stock can be used to compensate for this.

How to use

Method 1

Formula 1 shows how to calculate standard deviation:

$$SD = \sqrt{(\Sigma(x - x')2/(n-1))} \qquad (1)$$

Where: n = number of weeks (10 in Table 3.17)
x' = mean demand (500 in Table 3.17)
x = data item (actual demand in Table 3.17)

The normal distribution is used to determine the 'protection level' required, ie the proportion of time that demand can be met. In our example, adding safety stock equivalent to one standard deviation of demand would yield a protection level of 84.1 per cent (50 per cent + 34.1 per cent), since this is the proportion of the population under the normal distribution curve (Figure 3.10) from minus infinity up to the mean plus 1 standard deviation of demand.

FIGURE 3.10 Normal distribution

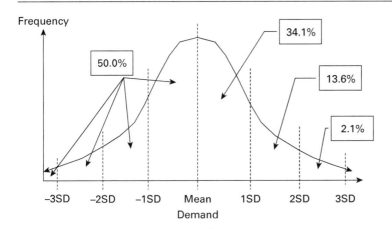

Method 2

In the time buffer method, we add enough safety stock to cover demand for a certain time period. For example, a particular supplier is often one week late in delivering but rarely more, and so we may decide to add safety stock equivalent to one week of demand for that item.

Method 3

In the historical demand method, we look at historical data. Consider the demand for item B in Table 3.17 once again. If these 10 weeks are indicative of demand over the year, we can see that in 10 per cent of the weeks, demand is over 80; and in 30 per cent of the weeks, demand is over 70. Using 50 weeks per year for simplicity, we might decide that it is acceptable to have stockouts in five weeks of the year (10 per cent), but unacceptable to be out of stock during 15 weeks of the year (30 per cent). We would then keep a safety stock of 30 units (remembering that 50 is the rate of average demand and safety stock is used to cover demand that is greater than average). Data for more weeks will give a more accurate picture of demand variation and result in a more accurate estimate of the safety stock required.

Example

Let us say that we are looking for a 90 per cent protection level for item B in Table 3.17, ie we want to meet demand for 90 per cent of the time:

- Using method 1, normal distribution tables show us that 90 per cent protection level requires safety stock equivalent to 1.28 standard deviations of average weekly demand, so $1.28 \times 25.7 = 33$ units.

- Using method 2, we may estimate that we need about three days of safety stock, or half a week's demand, so a proportion of 3/5 or 2.5/5 of average weekly demand (assuming five trading days per week), which would be 25 or 30 units of stock.

- Using method 3, and assuming that these 10 weeks are indicative of the year's weekly demand pattern, it was shown earlier that 30 units of safety stock would give a protection level of approximately 90 per cent.

This example can be downloaded for free from http://howtologistics.com

Further information

For those who are unfamiliar with statistical methods, it is highly recommended that logistic managers get some training in this area. Many books and general training courses are available.

Those who are familiar with statistics may be interested in looking at Stock and Lambert (2001), which gives a formula for safety stock that takes the standard deviation of lead time into account in setting safety stock levels as well as the standard deviation of demand: Stock, J and Lambert, D (2001) *Strategic Logistics Management*, 4th edn, McGraw-Hill/Irwin, New York. Further information can be found in: Relph, G J and Milner, C Z (2015) *Inventory Management: Advanced methods for managing inventory within business systems,* Kogan Page, London.

3.15 Stock counting

Introduction

To have confidence in the inventory management system it is vital to count stock regularly and ensure that the quantities shown in the inventory management system are actually present in stock. In this section, we consider the nitty-gritty of looking for explanations of any differences.

When to use

All companies should count their stock at least once per year for the purpose of preparing the annual accounts. In the section on cycle counting (tool 3.5), it is explained that it is often beneficial to count fast movers and higher-value items more than once per year in order to maintain close control and high availability.

How to use

If there is a significant amount of stock to check it may be necessary to close the business while counting takes place. It may be carried out by the company's employees only, over a weekend or during a shutdown, and temporary staff may be hired to supplement existing staff and speed up the process.

1. General process

- Plan the stock count well in advance and train the staff who will be carrying it out.
- Specify the area to be checked and ensure that each zone and location is clearly identified (to prevent omissions and duplications in counting).
- Produce a list of what is expected to be found in each zone or sub-area, including identity, description and location, listed in the order in which it is expected that the items will be found. Do not include the actual quantity. This list may be either in hard copy or accessed electronically by a handheld device.
- The stock checker moves systematically along each zone, up and down each rack or shelf, according to the layout and height of the storage area, identifying and counting items found.
- Note that two staff will more than likely be required to count stock at height.
- It is important that there is ready and adequate means of recording any anomalies or deviations from the list. For example, an item may be found earlier or later than its stated location (and the new location must be recorded), an item may be found damaged or missing an identity label, etc, and all this must be carefully recorded.

Great care should be taken over the unit of measure for each item. For example, should a box of 50 items be recorded as 50 items or as one box? Normally the list of items should show the unit quantity of each item clearly or the stock checker should make clear what has been counted.

Some special equipment may be required, eg weigh scales for loose items, dipsticks for fluids, measuring tapes, gauges, reel measuring devices, cages for lifting personnel, etc. Sometimes it is necessary to open a box or crate. Materials must be provided for closing and resealing. Sometimes opening such packages may damage the contents, eg for some aircraft parts, and therefore information on the external labelling will have to suffice.

2. Resolving differences

A procedure must be followed to identify the source of each difference, be that quantity, location or condition. If the difference cannot be found, the data in the system must be adjusted.

First we look at differences in quantity. Before making any adjustments to the system data, consider the following questions:

- Were any issues or receipts of the item in question made while the stock check was being carried out?
- If a manual system is being operated, have any arithmetic errors been made in the receipts and issues calculations since the last stock check?
- Was it difficult to count these items? If so, go back and recount them.
- If using a paper-based system, are the figures recorded by the staff legible? Could a 1 look like a 7, for example?
- Is it possible that the items are stored in more than one place? If so, consult the stores person or the inventory management system to find other locations.
- Is it possible that the count itself is not very accurate (for example, weighing a bottle of a chemical fluid to estimate how much remains, or measuring a length of tubing to estimate how much remains)? If the difference is less than x per cent, then make no adjustment. The value of x depends on the accuracy of the measuring system and the desired accuracy of the stock count.
- If more was found than expected, does this difference tally with a recent loss of stock at the last count? For example, the material could have been put in the wrong place and then somebody found it and restored it to the right place.

- Are there any unfulfilled orders in the warehouse or could there have been a short shipment recently?

- If there is less than expected, have any unauthorized personnel been in the storage area since the last count? Has somebody removed the item without recording the issue?

- If there is less than expected, is this item of use outside the business? Might somebody have an interest in stealing it? (In general, look for system errors first before thinking about theft. There are so many opportunities for system errors and they are the cause of the difference in most cases.)

Next we consider differences in location. We have already seen that items may be stored in more than one location. The fifth point above indicates that we did not find enough stock at a certain location and that we should look for more locations of stock for this item. Secondly, we may find stock of an item in an unexpected location. It is important that the location data are correct so that the stores people can find a required item quickly and efficiently. Any differences in location should be discussed with the stores personnel so that a decision can be made about which are the 'correct locations' and then the data records can be updated accordingly.

Finally, the stock checker may notice that some items are damaged or dirty or otherwise not in good condition. Each case should be examined and a decision made on the future of the stock, for example whether the stock is usable or must be removed and replaced. This can also be a good time to identify stock that has been in the warehouse for an excessive time period and is unlikely to be used in future.

3. How to improve future accuracy

Stock data accuracy must become part of company culture, requiring a high level of operator discipline:

- New employees should be well trained in company procedures and be told exactly what is expected of them, including use of computer systems, counting practices, etc.

- All stock should be protected by access control measures such as card readers, or closed circuit television cameras.

- All items and locations should be clearly identified. Procedures should be accessible to all personnel, maybe via a shared area on the company network, or printed in a folder in a common area.

- There should be easy feedback mechanisms for any comments, observations, etc with a clear point of contact. A responsible 'help' point should be available 24 hours a day, seven days a week.

Example

A new set of materials-recording processes had been implemented by consultants into a medium-sized manufacturing company. It appeared that the set of processes was either incomplete or erroneous since the company was obliged to count stock every quarter and effectively write off around 25 per cent of material that was believed to be on site! In view of the nature and size of the materials involved, theft was not the source of the problem.

All raw materials issues, production records, semi-finished product processing records, finished product inspection records and finished product stock records were examined for a period of eight weeks in order to understand the flow of material through the factory from suppliers to customers, and many system and discipline errors were found. To correct the problems, it was necessary to:

- explain to personnel the importance of system discipline and ensure that each person was familiar with the recording processes and was properly trained;
- create procedures for special products that had been ignored in the original system;
- clarify the production routes and recording points for each product type, including in particular handling of withdrawals from finished stock for further processing;
- clarify how to record problems, eg rejection at inspection, re-work.

In consequence, the stock check became an annual event, carried out by personnel over a weekend, saving 10–12 production days per year. Inventory accuracy increased to over 95 per cent in the first year after implementation of the changes.

Further information

For further information about sources of error and methods of correction, David Piasecki (2003) has summarized years of experience: Piasecki, D (2003) *Inventory Accuracy: People, processes, and technology*, OPS Publishing, Kenosha, WI.

3.16 Stock turn

Introduction

One of the easiest measures of inventory performance to implement and to understand is 'stock turn'. Crudely, this means how often the stock turns over during the year. In other words, how many times on average does the material flow in and out of the storage area? For the same level of availability, a higher number of stock turns indicates better management of inventory.

In practice, of course, we know that different items will have very different levels of stock turn. Some items may not be issued at all (non-movers or stock turn of zero). Some may be used and replenished every week. Hence it is useful to consider the overall stock turn for the whole inventory (formula 1) and also stock turn for each individual item (formula 2); stock turn for one item can also be calculated using values instead of quantities.

$$\text{Overall stock turn} = \frac{\text{Cost of total annual issues}(\pounds)}{\text{Value of average inventory level}(\pounds)} \quad (1)$$

$$\text{Stock turn for item } i = \frac{\text{Quantity of item } i \text{ issued during the year}}{\text{Average stock level of item } i} \quad (2)$$

Sometimes it is not possible to obtain the cost of total annual issues and it is easier to obtain the monthly value of stock purchases. This will work just as well so long as the data are consistent for the year.

When to use

Warehouses and distribution centres measure overall stock turn as part of a daily, weekly or monthly inventory performance report. In manufacturing, monthly or even six-monthly measures suffice.

When stock turn is calculated for individual items, we can identify the 'fast movers' (those with the highest stock turn) and the slow movers (those with the lowest stock turn). Non-movers in a period will have a stock turn of zero.

How to use

The average inventory level can be found from the inventory management system or by averaging the end-of-month inventory level figures over a period of time. As mentioned above, either total monthly issues or total monthly purchases can be used to indicate throughput, so long as only one type of data is used for the whole period under review.

Examples

Example of stock turn calculation for one item. We are going to calculate the number of stock turns for safety boots over the year. Table 3.18 shows the issues and end-of-month stock by month for one year. Note that a delivery of 50 pairs of boots was received in June.

First we need to find the average stock level. To do this we find that the average of all the month-end figures is 37.2 (take the sum of all the end-of-month stock levels and divide by 12).

Secondly, we find the total number of pairs of boots issued over the year. From Table 3.18, we see that 68 pairs of safety boots were issued over the year.

TABLE 3.18 Issues and end-of-month stock for safety boots

	Issues	End-of-month stock
Jan	6	42
Feb	1	41
Mar	8	33
Apr	15	18
May	3	15
Jun	4	61
Jul	6	55
Aug	9	46
Sep	8	38
Oct	4	34
Nov	1	33
Dec	3	30
Total	68	

Using formula 2, we can now calculate the stock turn for the year:

$$\text{Stock turn for safety boots} \frac{\text{Quantity of item } i \text{ issued during the year}}{\text{Average stock level of item } i} = \frac{68}{37.2} = 1.8$$

We conclude that stock turn for safety boots for the year was just under 2.

Example of overall inventory stock turn. Over the last 12 months, the cost of total sales from a warehouse amounted to £5,000,000 and the average cost of goods stored in the warehouse was £500,000.

Using formula 1, we can now calculate the overall stock turn for the year:

$$\text{Overall stock turn} = \frac{\text{Cost of total annual sales}(£)}{\text{Average cost of goods stored}(£)} = \frac{£5,000,000}{£500,000} = 10$$

Further information

See Relph, G J and Milner, C Z (2015), *Inventory Management: Advanced methods for managing inventory within business systems,* Kogan Page, London; Waters, C D J (2003) *Inventory Control and Management*, 2nd edn, Wiley, New York.

3.17 Vendor-managed inventory (and co-managed inventory)

Introduction

VMI brings efficiency through grouping more items to each supplier order, having fewer suppliers and combining these with a regular 'milk round' delivery by the vendor.

On perhaps a daily or weekly basis the vendor visits the customer's premises, checks the level of physical stock and adds sufficient replenishment items to take the stock level back up to the desired target stock level (TSL), keeping a record of what has been supplied. The customer is then invoiced, perhaps weekly or monthly. In some cases, the vendor has remote access to the inventory management system to identify the quantities issued of each item and is thus able to prepare the replenishment stock in advance of the visit. Clearly, the ability to operate VMI correctly depends on the level of stock issue discipline being operated by the customer.

Lack of discipline in some cases has given vendors considerable problems and this is an area that must be addressed before setting up VMI. If the customer is not disciplined, there will be unexpected stockouts that have nothing to do with the vendor's activity or efficiency. On the other side, some customers have been concerned that the vendors have been keeping too much stock on site (thus taking up too much space in their warehouse) or they have experienced too many stockouts due to poor estimates of inventory parameters by the vendors. Thus VMI in many cases has been superseded by co-managed inventory (CMI) to reflect the fact that it is often better to set the inventory management parameters jointly. Maximum and minimum stock levels are agreed together, as are replenishment criteria and performance measures. If the customer anticipates extra demand, the vendor should be warned in advance. If the vendor foresees any supply problems, the customer should be notified, and so on.

The main advantages of VMI/CMI are that the administrative costs of the client company are much reduced, including the costs of setting up purchase contracts, placing purchase orders, receiving replenishment quantities, managing the stock, keeping inventory records, making issues and paying supplier invoices. This can take up a disproportionate amount of time compared to the value of the items concerned. For example, if 500 different types of fastener can be supplied from one source, with one invoice per month, there could be considerable cost savings compared with the cost of carrying out purchase and delivery arrangements with perhaps over 20 suppliers, each on different ordering and delivery cycles.

When to use

In the retail sector, VMI/CMI is used increasingly in shops of various sizes. For example, a battery manufacturer directly replenishes batteries in supermarkets. A sandwich maker delivers more sandwiches to augment the stock in petrol stations every two hours, thus ensuring that the product is fresh and that the most popular fillings do not run out.

PepsiCo delivers a whole range of products directly to many small city-centre stores in the United States, puts the stock on the shelves and invoices the customer for the quantities delivered. This saves stockroom space and staff shelf-filling time but also has been found to prevent stockouts and increase sales for both the retailer and PepsiCo.

In industry, VMI/CMI is being used more and more for C class items (low value and/or low usage quantities), typically fasteners, connectors and other non-critical items such as production consumables, office supplies, safety equipment and lubricants. In recent years, higher-value items such as spare parts have been under vendor management, stored at the hub of an express parcel company where it then becomes relatively economic for the express delivery company to deliver parts over a wide area very quickly.

How to use

First, the group of items to be supplied by a particular vendor is agreed with that vendor. It is in the interests of the customer to obtain as many items from the vendor as is possible to minimize transport and administrative costs. Sometimes the vendor is willing to add items to its stock list for a particular customer.

It is important to give the vendor appropriate historical data about item usage and the best possible forecast for future usage. If these cannot be supplied or are considered to be unreliable, larger buffer stocks must be used (ie higher minimum stock levels).

The general conditions of setting up an operation will be discussed and agreed, including:

- frequency of visits, for example to fit in with the vendor's other clients in the area so that transport is economic;
- maximum and minimum limits for the stock of each item, calculated by the vendor (VMI) or agreed together (CMI);
- frequency of invoicing;
- taking inventory of existing stock and any outstanding orders, so that the vendor can take over management of replenishment.

Example

A customer and vendor are setting parameters for the stock of high-visibility jackets in a factory. Issues over the last three years appear to be reasonably stable (see Table 3.19). However, further analysis shows that the monthly issue quantity can vary enormously (Table 3.20). Further questioning reveals that a party of visitors made one large withdrawal in April (which was not returned) and on induction a group of apprentices required another batch of jackets to be issued (and these jackets were then kept by the apprentices).

TABLE 3.19 Total issues during the last three years

High-visibility jackets	Year 1	Year 2	Year 3
Quantity issued over the year	35	31	38

TABLE 3.20 Monthly issues during the last 12 months (year 3 in Table 3.19)

Jan	Feb	Mar	Apr	May	Jun	Jul	Aug	Sep	Oct	Nov	Dec
5	1	0	14	2	0	5	1	9	0	1	0

Although the annual rate of usage is quite small, issue quantities can be highly variable and so it was decided to have a large buffer stock since a stockout could have safety implications. It was agreed to hold a buffer stock of 15 jackets. Apart from the visitors and apprentices, average monthly consumption is approximately two. The minimum level was therefore set at 17 to be safe, and a maximum level of 20. Fortunately, this vendor supplies a wide range of other items so the jackets were added to the list of stock item levels to be checked on the weekly visit. In practice, this means that the vendor checks the stock level weekly and adds enough jackets to take the stock level back up to 20 jackets. Since this is a new item for VMI, and a safety requirement, both sides agree to monitor the situation carefully. Electronic access to the company's inventory management system is being discussed.

Further information

See Winters, J and Lunn, T (1996) *The effective implementation of co-managed inventory, Logistics Focus*, September, pp 2–7. This article describes a trial between the retailer Somerfield and a number of major suppliers.

3.18 Identification and disposal of surplus stock

Introduction

Inventory must be managed actively or it will just grow. Whether you have taken over an inventory that has not been managed properly for a while, or you are already actively managing your inventory, you need to identify stock that is in excess, obsolete or time-expired and you need an agreed policy for disposing of it. It is not always easy to set up a disposal policy since some accountants are reluctant to dispose of stock at less than book value. Some kind of discount is usually necessary for disposal. Nevertheless, it is important to identify and dispose of surplus stock, otherwise it just ties up operating capital and storage space, both of which can be used for more profitable activities.

When to use

Some businesses review their raw materials stock or finished goods stock at regular intervals, perhaps once or twice per year. Other companies use events to trigger a stock review, for example, reviewing spare parts inventory for a machine that has just been sold or scrapped, or the need to create space for a new range of products.

How to use

Two separate elements are required: 1) identification of surplus stock, ie excess, obsolete or time-expired; 2) creation and application of a disposal policy.

1. Identify surplus stock

'Excess' means that you have more stock of an item than is necessary and can usually be identified using stock cover, calculated as:

Stock cover (days) = Current stock level/average rate of usage

If the stock cover seems excessive, this may be a candidate for disposal. Investigate why the stock cover is so high. Was the demand forecast too optimistic? Is it a slow mover? Can this item only be made or obtained in large quantities? Is there a minimum production or purchase quantity? Did somebody buy too much so as to qualify for a quantity discount?

'Obsolete' means that there is no further demand for this item. These items can be identified by looking for non-movers over a time period. 'Non-mover' means that no stock of this item was issued during that period (see Figure 3.11). The time period depends on the nature of the stock and the industry. For example, fast-moving consumer goods companies are interested in stock movements over recent weeks. Managers of spare parts inventories look at non-movers over the last few years. Again, each suspected obsolete item must be investigated before being identified as a candidate for disposal. If they have not been flagged up by the inventory management system already, time-expired items are identified by searching inventory records for their time of arrival and date of expiration.

2. Disposal policy

The disposal policy must be created and agreed by a group of representatives from the departments responsible for inventory management, warehousing, accounting and purchasing (for their experience of searching supply markets). It covers the identification of items that are considered to be redundant, deciding how to dispose of them, their removal from the inventory management

FIGURE 3.11 Non-mover analysis

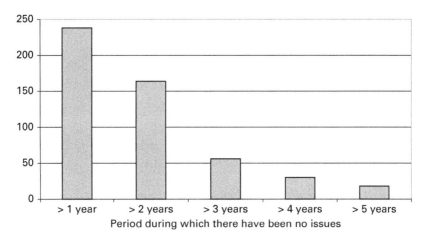

Number
of items

Period during which there have been no issues

system and final disposal. Before creating the procedure, it is useful to brainstorm all possible disposal methods. These may include:

- Destruction, or adding to normal company waste.

- Adding pages to a company website indicating the items that are
available for sale, with or without a suggested price, and details of
who to contact for more information.

- Approaching the original vendor in case these items may be of
interest. This can work well for spare parts, as the vendor may know
of other companies still using the same type of equipment that may
be interested in purchasing a job lot of spare parts.

- Advertising in specialist magazines or websites indicating the type of
items available and who to contact for more information.

- Placing the items for sale through internet sales portals, either general
sales sites or specialized sites for the sector.

- Sub-contracting the advertising and sales process to a company
specializing in surplus inventory disposal, usually for a percentage of
the sales value realized.

- Inviting a company specializing in surplus inventory to come and
remove the items for some nominal value, or for a fee.

- Charitable donation, which can be tax-efficient.

The main elements of the policy are as follows:

1 Identify potential stock for disposal. For example, annually create a list of surplus stock, non-movers and expired items. Apply the methods described above.

2 Inform the users. Circulate this list to their main users (eg production, maintenance, projects, engineering, transport, warehouse) for comments to be returned before a certain date. Do the users envisage any future use for these items?

3 Agree the final list for disposal. Each user department discusses the list of proposed items for disposal and either agrees to disposal of the item or makes a brief justification for retaining the stock. A list of items signed off for disposal is returned to the inventory manager.

4 The items for disposal are physically removed from the main stock to a separate area 'awaiting disposal'. Their location in the inventory management system is changed to this new location and their status is also changed to 'awaiting disposal'. The user departments are informed that this has been done.

5 The 'book price' of each item is given by the accounting department and the disposal group agrees the best method of disposal for each item.

6 When disposal occurs, the items are issued from the 'awaiting disposal' area. The items are deducted from the inventory management system and the item record is closed when all stock has been disposed of.

7 Finally, the accounting department writes off any difference between the book value and the realized value.

Example

Many companies manage production materials very well (raw materials, work in progress, finished product) but some do not apply the same level of inventory control to stocks of spare parts. A new manager to a company in the oil and gas sector in India identified a stock of obsolete parts worth several millions of dollars that he thought could still be useful to oil and gas companies in other parts of the world. The company set up a website that listed the items available, their prices and conditions of sale. Over a period of 12 months it managed to dispose of about three-quarters of the stock value to North Africa, South America and other exploration and production areas.

Further information

An internet search using the terms 'inventory disposal' will bring up a myriad of example procedures from specific organizations as well as companies that specialize in this sector.

3.19 Managing spare parts inventory

Introduction

Inventory is generally managed using forecasts and historical data (for items subject to unknown demand) and by stocking items for planned future needs (expected demand). This is also true of spare parts inventory where some spare parts are stocked for regular maintenance or projects (expected demand) and others for breakdowns (unknown demand).

There are now many options for managing spare parts inventory including:

- Using suppliers that have placed stocks of strategic items at carrier hubs for rapid delivery.
- Holding spare parts on consignment (see tool 3.4) or 'use or return' agreements (eg for planned maintenance interventions).
- Using 3D printing for certain parts.
- Sharing visibility of stocks with a sister or neighbouring company.
- Accessing a network of users of similar equipment.
- Joint planning of major maintenance activities in a group of companies to take place at different times so that 'might be required' inventory can be moved to the next site that may need it.
- Centralizing inventory as much as possible so as to minimize safety stock.
- Increasing the proportion of planned maintenance so as to reduce the number of spares to be stocked for breakdowns.
- Using more sophisticated software and modelling for analysing breakdowns and anticipating future failures.
- Outsourcing some maintenance.
- Using asset condition monitoring to anticipate failures.

When to use

It is worth reviewing the total value of the spare parts inventory against the level of service on an annual basis taking into account the events that have occurred over the year, eg new equipment to maintain, equipment that has been sold, new tools, materials, supplier agreements, particular problems that occurred as well as projects for the next year, eg refurbishment, new equipment, modifications or higher/lower reliability requirements.

In industries with continuous production eg oil and gas, any downtime means loss of revenue. A downtime cost per minute can be calculated.

At this point, consider whether the spare parts inventory strategy should be revised.

A non-mover analysis (see tool 3.18) should be carried out annually. A large number of non-movers could also trigger a review.

How to use

Spare parts inventory management must be linked to the management of the maintenance, repair and overhaul (MRO) activity for which the spare parts are being used. For planned maintenance, a list of parts required and the time of requirement must be supplied from the maintenance planning system to the inventory manager to enable existing stock to be checked (eg for items left over from the previous requirement) and allow new stock to be purchased in time.

Whether items are stocked for expected or unexpected demand, it is critical to carry out ABC analysis and identify each item's class, in terms of usage value (see tool 3.2), and also usage rate (see tool 1.3). To distinguish usage rate classes from usage value classes, we shall call them XYZ, where X represents fast movers and Z the slowest movers.

Items that are stocked in case of breakdowns are far more difficult to manage and the stock will depend on a number of key questions:

- How likely is it that the item will be required in the next year (1–10)? (1 = unlikely, 10 = certain).

- How critical is a stock out of each item? Can we substitute another size/material, etc? Give each item a criticality rating from 1 to 10 (1 = unimportant, 10 = absolutely critical).

- How rapidly can each item be obtained in time of crisis? Give each item a rapidity rating from 1 to 10 (1= fast, 10 = long lead time).

- What is the minimum quantity that must be bought?
- Is there a 'use or return' (consignment stock) agreement with the supplier?
- What was the average annual requirement for this item over the last five years?
- What maximum annual requirement was seen in the last five years?
- What minimum annual requirement was seen in the last five years?

The last three questions aim to understand the level of demand (1 per year? 100 per year?) and the variation in demand (eg 0 some years, 10 or 15 others?). Clearly, these questions are most critical for the A items. It is much cheaper to hold a bigger safety stock of a C item than an A item. More imaginative solutions, such as some of those in the introduction to this tool, will have to be employed for some of the A and B items.

Ultimately, the total number of different items and their stock levels will depend on the total budget available for inventory and the desired level of service to the MRO operation. The 'best guess' of future needs will come from an analysis of past needs for the same or similar equipment, obtained from your company's own records, the manufacturer or other users of this type of equipment. Sometimes there are user groups that are willing to share this information.

When managing spare parts inventory, it is particularly important to record:

- all failures to supply an item immediately (to determine level of service) and reason for non-immediate supply (eg stock out due to late delivery, unusually large demand, dearth in supply market);
- the time required to supply items that were not supplied immediately, from time of demand to time of issue;
- all returns to stores and reasons for non-use;
- cost of any movement from one site to another (for the 'move or buy' decision).

Finally, it is important that the users of the inventory take a disciplined approach. In the heat of the moment, when responding to a breakdown, it is easy for the issue to go unrecorded. If, as in many cases, the spare parts stores are unmanned, security cameras or access control records must be used regularly to check that all issues have been recorded.

TABLE 3.21 Key data for a selection of spare parts

Item code	Pareto ABC	Pareto XYZ	Demand E/U/B	Likelihood of need (1-10)	Crit. (1-10)	Diff. to obtain (1-10)	Min. purch. qty	Use or return?	Ave. ann. use	Min. ann. use	Max. ann. use	Policy decision
PX3494	A	Z	U	3	10	10	1	N	0	0	1	Hold 1 in stock
KT5228	A	Y	U	8	6	2	1	N	5	2	6	ROP = 0, ROQ = 1
HT3446	A	X	B	10	10	2	10	N	30	25	40	ROP = 5, ROQ = 1
CF7889	A	X	U	10	10	3	50	Y	33	10	50	VMI if possible, else ROP
CR9045	A	X	U	10	8	5	10	N	10	2	15	VMI if possible, else ROP
SG5786	B	Y	E	10	8	10	1	N	10	8	12	Buy ahead of planned use

(Continued)

TABLE 3.21 Key data for a selection of spare parts (*Continued*)

Item code	Pareto ABC	Pareto XYZ	Demand E/U/B	Likelihood of need (1-10)	Crit. (1-10)	Diff. to obtain (1-10)	Min. purch. qty	Use or return?	Ave. ann. use	Min. ann. use	Max. ann. use	Policy decision
MC2596	B	Z	B	10	10	5	1	N	1	0	1	ROP = 0, ROQ = 1
AV5489	C	Z	U	10	5	10	1	?	3	1	3	Aim for consignment
MT3214	C	Z	B	10	8	10	1	N	1	0	1	Aim for consignment

Note:
PX3494 is a very high value highly critical item that is rarely required but difficult to obtain because it is customized e.g. a furnace lining

Key:
E/U/B = Expected, unexpected, both
TSL = target stock level
ROP = reorder point
ROQ = reorder quantity

Example

Table 3.21 shows a selection of items from a spare parts stock and the data used to decide how each item should be managed.

Further information

A wealth of software is available for managing spare parts inventory: some of the packages are free and some are part of a computerized maintenance management system, some of which are also free.

Search for INFORMS/MAS Tutorial Managing Spare Parts if you are interested in finding out about the different statistical approaches that have been developed.

Further useful web-based resources are: http://en.slideshare.net/Logio_official/omaintec-spare-parts-workshop-part-2-8-rules, and http://sparepartsknowhow.com/inventory-management/#.VpkPajbSkdU

Supply chain management tools

4.1 Supply chain management audit

Introduction

Many companies have still not integrated their logistics functions (customer order processing, transport, warehousing and storage, inventory management, planning and scheduling, distribution) into a seamless supply chain operation capable of interacting smoothly with their suppliers, customers and service providers. This audit aims to highlight some of the elements of a seamless operation in order to give companies that wish to implement supply chain management some idea of what has been achieved already and what, if anything, remains to be done.

The fact that we talk about a supply *chain* indicates the linkage necessary between the different stages of movement of a product and the different parties involved to achieve this rather than a simple series of transactions which is logistics management. Table 4.1 shows an extract from the full supply chain management audit. The complete audit can be downloaded for a small charge from http://howtologistics.com; the discount code for readers is lsct0104.

TABLE 4.1 Template for supply chain management audit

Supply Chain Management Audit				
Carried out by:		Location:		
Date:				
Item	**No**	**Yes**	**N/A**	**Comments**
Logistic customer service				
Is there a range of defined logistic customer service measures for each sales channel ?				
Is the % of perfect orders measured?				
Are customer complaints systematically logged and investigated?				
Are supply chain analytics used to investigate demand and performance statistics?				
Strategic procurement				
Have you carried out Pareto analysis to classify items/families?				
Do you use Pareto classification in setting procurement policy for items/families?				
Do you use Kraljic matrix (or some other purchasing portfolio method) in setting procurement policy for items/families?				
Do you use category management?				
Are suppliers classified according to their importance and performance?				
Do you consciously apply a range of supplier relationships according to supplier importance?				
Is supplier performance included in vendor selection?				

(Continued)

TABLE 4.1 Template for supply chain management audit *(Cont.)*

Supply Chain Management Audit				
Carried out by:			Location:	
Date:				
Item	**No**	**Yes**	**N/A**	**Comments**
Is a clear and coherent set of supplier performance measures included in the supply contract?				
Are key suppliers involved in Kaizen or joint problem-solving when necessary?				
Are suppliers involved in new product development?				
Supplier management				
Do suppliers have access to a platform or Extranet (for orders, performance, demand forecasts, etc)?				
Do suppliers have access to demand forecasts?				
Do suppliers have access to order history?				
Are suppliers given regular feedback regarding delivery: OTIF, accuracy, quality,etc?				
Has there been an effort to reduce the total number of suppliers?				
Is collaborative planning and forecasting carried out with key suppliers?				
Do key suppliers have longer contracts than other suppliers?				
Inbound transport				
Is factory gate pricing used to determine the best means of inbound transport?				

(Continued)

TABLE 4.1 Template for supply chain management audit (*Cont.*)

Supply Chain Management Audit				
Carried out by:		Location:		
Date:				
Item	**No**	**Yes**	**N/A**	**Comments**
Is there a variety of inbound transport options according to the location of the supplier and volumes to be moved?				
Is there a milk round for local suppliers/customers?				
3PLs				
Has there been a 'buy or manage' review in the last 5 years for transport services?				
Has there been a 'buy or manage' review in the last 5 years for warehousing services?				
Do 3PLs have access to Extranet, platform or portal to see future activity levels?				
Is there direct system linkage to the 3PLs?				
Does each service provider have a clear SLA?				
Is performance against the SLA measured for each service provider?				
Is service provider performance fed back to the provider on a regular basis?				
Is there frequent communication with each service provider regarding current performance and future plans?				
S&OP				
Is there a well-defined S&OP process?				

(Continued)

TABLE 4.1 Template for supply chain management audit *(Cont.)*

Supply Chain Management Audit				
Carried out by:			Location:	
Date:				
Item	**No**	**Yes**	**N/A**	**Comments**
Does S&OP have a horizon of at least 18 months?				
Is S&OP reviewed monthly on a rolling basis?				
Do all functions involved take an active part in S&OP?				
Is S&OP viewed as a positive process for the whole business?				
Production planning and scheduling				
Can customers find out in one phone call the status of their orders?				
Do key customers have access to Extranet, platform or portal to see the status of their orders?				
Is % schedule achievement measured?				
Is % schedule achievement increasing as daily/weekly performance is investigated?				
Are key customers engaged in some form of CPFR?				
Do key customers provide demand forecasts?				
Have clear horizons been set for production order changes, as fixed, modifiable within stated limits, completely modifiable?				

4.2 Collaborative, Planning, Forecasting and Replenishment (CPFR®)

Introduction

(CPFR® is a registered trademark of VICS.)

We know from supply chain research that the more information that is exchanged between suppliers and customers in the supply chain about demand, the less inventory we need in the chain to maintain stock availability to the final consumer and in the chain in total. In the mid-1990s, the Voluntary Inter-industry Commerce Standards (VICS) Association agreed to support an initiative to enable manufacturers and retailers to forecast demand jointly and subsequently plan together the supply of certain items traded between them. This involved not only delivery planning but also exchanging information about forthcoming promotions and other commercial activities, usually regarded as confidential. Since this required communication between information systems, some major software houses were involved as well. The overall results reduced the number of stockouts, reduced inventory levels, increased stock turns and increased sales, by ensuring that the pattern of supply met the pattern of demand more closely. Protocols and other operating methods were established.

Owing to advances in computer systems, and in the exchange of data between companies in particular, more and more companies are undertaking some kind of joint planning and forecasting with key suppliers and customers to achieve these benefits, even though it may not be through membership of GS1 US (which merged with VICS in 2012).

When to use

A lot of attention has been paid to improving on-time delivery in the last few years and this has enabled incoming inventories to be reduced. Further reductions to overall inventory levels can only be made by improving information about demand and this is proving more difficult to achieve. Any company that wishes to improve information flow regarding demand would benefit from closer communication with key customers and by exchanging information about their respective commercial actions (eg promotions, new products) for the forthcoming months. Some companies simply have too many products to track in this manner and so the items generating 80 per cent of sales would be an obvious focus to start. Although the manufacturer–retailer relationship has been most publicized, the supplier–manufacturer link can also benefit.

How to use

Although CPFR® represented a specific agreement between companies under the aegis of VICS, many companies can carry out some form of joint planning and replenishment in other ways. Many companies do this by simply exchanging Excel spreadsheets. Many of these simple business tools are sent via the internet, are undocumented and are clearly open to abuse or problems if one of the parties suffers illness or worse. If a supplier and customer find that this kind of exchange is beneficial to them, it should be worth investing in a more formal process to increase security and ensure business continuity.

A visit to a major supplier or customer to discuss how this could operate and the benefits that it could bring is a good way to start. It is critical that both parties are in agreement about the objectives and methods of data exchange. It is useful to set up a workshop for the main personnel from each party to discuss their business processes, planning tools and decision timing. It may require two or three days to agree the most efficient way to work together. Process maps or flowcharts (see tool 6.4) are a useful tool for this.

The main process steps are:

1 Supplier first creates a top-level forecast from historical records.

2 Customer updates this forecast to include any extra information it has, eg more/fewer shops, expanding/contracting business, and adds information regarding commercial actions.

3 Supplier adds information regarding promotions, product launches, etc.

4 Supplier proposes replenishment plan.

5 Customer agrees or modifies and sets up replenishment orders.

Example

One CPFR® case study that really grabs the attention was the cooperation between Henkel and Eroski. Henkel is a large multinational manufacturer of over 10,000 items with headquarters in Germany. Eroski is a retail chain of supermarkets and hypermarkets mainly based in Spain. A CPFR® pilot study was introduced for nearly 2,000 items supplied by Henkel to Eroski. Overall results included an increase in customer service level while also reducing inventory in the Eroski warehouse, significantly improving the reliability of forecasting, increasing truck and pallet fill and reducing the number of urgent orders.

Another example concerns a supplier to the automotive aftermarket and a major customer who wanted to carry out joint planning and replenishment, rather than formal CPFR®. A team of three or four people from each organization spent several days together in a Kaizen workshop to discuss their processes for replenishment planning and how they could work together in the most efficient way. The overall objective was to reduce the 'soft' costs associated with replenishment planning and ordering while minimizing the level of stock and maximizing availability of product. The outcomes of the workshop included harmonized timing of decision making, an agreed format of data in an Excel worksheet, and clear processes and responsibilities.

Further information

URLs for the Henkel-Eroski case study keep changing but it is well worth the effort to look for it. The search terms 'Henkel Eroski CPFR Case Study' will usually find a document or slide show summary pretty quickly.

Simply using the search terms 'CPFR case study' will find many more cases of interest. See http://www.gs1us.org/ for a wealth of information on supply chain data standards.

4.3 Demand forecasting

Introduction

Many companies do not produce good forecasts, if any. This can be understood to a certain extent since the mathematics can rapidly become complicated. This tool will not enable you to make forecasts but it is hoped that you will be inspired to think about how better forecasting can help your business, and then take steps to implement an improved forecasting process.

In essence, forecasting uses historical data to identify patterns that are likely to continue, enabling us to predict what may happen in future. The safest way to handle forecasts is to remember that 'All forecasts are wrong!' but some are better than others. It is worth making the effort to improve forecasting. Companies that have a better idea of what the future may bring are usually better prepared for that future.

Demand forecasting is particularly critical in supply chain management. The more information we can get about future demand, the less likely we are to suffer from excess inventory or shortages.

When to use

Forecasts are important for planning and decision making. We use sales forecasts to ensure that we have enough capacity for production and enough orders placed with suppliers for goods and services. The sales forecast is the basis for the procurement budget, which in turn must be financed. Similarly, the sales forecast will determine the capacity plan, which must be resourced in terms of space, equipment and labour.

Depending on the purpose of the forecast and the sector, the frequency of forecasting can vary from a rolling 20-year plan for equipment investment in the heavy engineering sector to a daily sales forecast for fast-moving consumer products in the retail sector.

How to use

It is beyond the scope of this short introduction to describe forecasting methods in any detail but we can consider the major elements of forecasting to see what is involved. The overall process has three steps:

1 Collect data on historical demand, by product family or individual items.

2 Use a mathematical method to create the forecast.

3 Use market-specific knowledge to add any other factors that may have a bearing on the situation and determine whether the forecast is pessimistic or optimistic and whether some 'tweaking' is required.

1. Collect data

This information can be extracted from an inventory management system to identify sales or usage of an item on a daily, weekly or monthly basis.

2. Use a mathematical method to analyse the data

The first method to look at is 'time series analysis' where the historical data can be considered to be a 'time series', ie a data item that is changing over time. A time series has four major components that can be separated out:

a Overall trend – is the level of sales increasing, decreasing or remaining stable over time?

b Seasonality – is there an effect of changing demand at different times of the year, for example increased sales of chocolate at Christmas and Easter?

c Cyclic change – are there other factors that increase demand on a regular basis, for example increased sales of DIY products at the weekend?

d Random variation or 'noise' – if the effects of trend, seasonality and cyclic change are removed from the time series, some random variation will remain.

Any demand forecast will have to take account of trend, seasonality and cyclic change. Our next stage is to consider how to create the forecast. There are many methods, ranging from simple moving averages to exponential or regression models, and others.

A certain amount can be done by hand but the use of forecasting software is highly recommended, either as part of the business management software that you are using already, or as a separate package. It is worthwhile identifying somebody in your organization who has an appropriate mathematical background or capability and who would be willing to undertake a short course in forecasting, or learn to use a forecasting package.

Finally, it is worth mentioning that there are several methods for measuring the accuracy of the forecast and this is an essential part of generating confidence in the forecasting process. As data quality and forecasting methods improve, there should be an equivalent improvement in forecasting accuracy, measured and observed.

Example

The Henkel and Eroski case study used to illustrate CPFR® (see tool 4.2) is an excellent example of how forecast accuracy can be improved and the benefits this can bring. The majority of demand forecasts were more than 50 per cent wrong at the beginning of the project period but within 12 weeks 80 per cent of the product forecasts were less than 20 per cent wrong. This was achieved by improving the quality of data being used by both companies for forecasting.

In summary, it is possible and highly desirable to improve the quality of forecasts used in your business but it does take some mathematical effort and interest to do so.

Further information

Many standard texts on operations management give a good introduction to forecasting. For those who really want to study the subject, Makridakis *et al* (1998) explain the many different approaches clearly: Makridakis, S, Wheelwright, S C and Hyndman, R (1998) *Forecasting: Methods and applications*, 3rd edn, Wiley, New York.

Use search terms 'Henkel Eroski CPFR Case Study' to find a document or slide show on this case study.

4.4 Factory gate pricing (FGP)

Introduction

FGP was introduced into the UK in the early 2000s by UK retailers to reduce their overall transport costs, reduce inventory holding in their distribution centres (DCs) and stores, and increase efficiency by reducing the number of vehicles delivering to site and improving throughput through improved co-ordination and consolidation. The introduction of lean principles into the retail supply chain (known as quick response) led to smaller, more frequent deliveries, which increased the pressure on the DCs.

Previously this system would have been described as supplier collection and – to a certain degree – nominated carrier schemes. The principle is very similar to an ex-works situation (see tool 2.5) whereby the consignee collects from the consignor and is liable for all the costs entailed. From a retailer viewpoint, vehicles delivering to stores from the distribution centres are able to call back in to suppliers on their return journeys and collect product destined for the DC. This can be full or part loads or a number of collections from multiple suppliers. This will ultimately depend on the capacity available on the truck and the time available for the driver.

This will result in an increase in on-time delivery at the DCs and greater visibility within the supply chain. Studies have shown (Potter *et al* 2007; Le Blanc *et al* 2004) that logistics related costs can be reduced by between 5 and 8 per cent. Potter *et al* (2007) describe FGP as 'the use of an ex-works price for a product plus the organization and optimization of transport by the purchaser to the point of delivery'.

When to use

When companies are looking to reduce costs and improve visibility within the supply chain. In reality, any company with a fleet of vehicles making deliveries to customers that has suppliers in close proximity can use this system. This can include the collection of raw materials, provided that the vehicles are suitable for both inward and outward journeys.

If vehicles are continually running back empty to base and have sufficient time available to collect goods from local suppliers, then, provided that an agreement on cost can be arrived at with the supplier and a regular pattern of collections set up, there is no reason why it cannot be instigated. Daily fixed transport costs are now shared across two deliveries rather than one. This also reduces the amount of empty running that takes place on today's roads.

However, there can be issues for the suppliers who may well have optimized their fleet and achieved transport efficiency when including these deliveries to the customer. Any reduction in delivery volume will have an effect on the cost per delivery and the overall efficiency of that operation. This is also the case where suppliers have contracted with a local haulier or 3PL to undertake their deliveries, with FGP resulting in less volume being transported by these companies.

In fact, suppliers need to address the following, according to LCP Consulting:

- How much discount can they afford to allow the retailers for collecting their product?
- How do they deal with the different pace of change adopted by the various retailers who will introduce FGP at different speeds?
- How do they deal with their existing infrastructure and logistics contracts as volume is transferred to retail control – making it less cost-effective?
- What commercial, pricing and 'terms of trade' policies and structures are appropriate in this new era?
- Finally, how will FGP affect their own fleet operations if volumes are going to reduce significantly?

There needs to be a workable agreement between supplier and buyer and if the supply chain as a whole is going to gain, the two parties need to work together on this initiative. It can be seen as very one-sided.

How to use

The first step is to identify which suppliers can be incorporated into the scheme. This will be based on location, volume, frequency of delivery, outbound vehicle delivery schedules and current cost of outbound and inbound delivery (if this can be extrapolated from the product cost).

Where it is not cost-effective to change from supplier delivery to FGP, the situation with those particular suppliers will remain as is. However, there are instances where suppliers are now collecting from DCs and delivering to stores on their route back to their facility.

The buyer will need to invest in an IT system that can manage this whole process. There are many transport management and supply chain optimization systems on the market; many of these can be found from tool 2.9.

Compatibility of product is a factor in terms of which supplier collections can be consolidated. This can include cube, weight, temperature requirements, fragility and whether hazardous or not. Scale is also important here, as is the availability of a good information technology system to manage the movements.

Finally, there needs to be an understanding on behalf of the buyer's logistics team of the suppliers' warehousing operation. This needs to include hours of operation and means of loading vehicles. The increasing use of double-deck trailers by retailers for store delivery can cause issues at supplier locations if their loading bays are not capable of receiving such vehicles.

FIGURE 4.1 Example of supplier collections on return from DC to store delivery

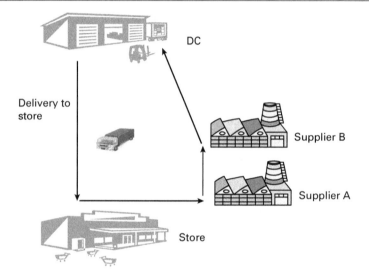

Communication between the inventory and logistics team is vital, as is the relationship with the suppliers to ensure a smooth and accurate flow of information between parties.

References

LCP Factory Gate Pricing – An opportunity to focus on cost and relationships [online] http://www.lcpconsulting.com/news-and-thinking/

Le Blanc *et al* (2004) *Factory Gate Pricing: An analysis of the Dutch retail distribution*, Center for Applied Research Discussion Paper No. 2004-35, Tilburg University, Netherlands

Potter, A, Mason, R and Lalwani, C (2007) Analysis of factory gate pricing in the UK grocery supply chain, *International Journal of Retail and Distribution Management*, **35** (10), pp 821–34

4.5 Kanban

Introduction

Kanban is the Japanese word for signboard or card (Japanese Management Association, 1986) and is just one element of the Toyota Production System that has been generalized into 'Lean' production. Here, we are looking at how Kanbans are used as a method of replenishment.

There are different types of Kanban signals and Kanban systems, but for our purposes we will just consider a simple circuit where Kanbans are used to pull parts from a previous stage in the supply chain. These parts could be coming from a previous production stage or an external supplier.

When to use

This is particularly useful for supplying to production lines parts of high value or parts that are frequently used. It can be used for parts that are supplied nearly all the time (runners), or regularly (repeaters), but is not appropriate for parts that are rarely supplied again (strangers). It is an excellent method for reducing cycle stock of parts from external suppliers (particularly if they are local) or for minimizing work in progress for parts from internal suppliers.

How to use

Figure 4.2 shows the Kanban circuit. It can be seen that a full box of parts is sent to the customer, internal or external. Once all the parts are used, the empty box is returned to the previous production stage or to the supplier to be refilled. If the supplier is external, the supplier collects the empty boxes when the next delivery is made, whether that is by the supplier's own vehicle or milk-round vehicle, or other transporter.

There are three essential elements to setting up and running a successful Kanban system. The first is the nature of the containers that move the parts and the second concerns the number of containers or boxes in the system. The third element is system discipline.

Parts are moved in boxes, where a known and fixed number of parts are allowed in the box. Although boxes are used most frequently, the 'container' may be anything that holds a certain number of parts safely and can be moved easily. This could be, for example, a hanging rail, tube, crate or trolley;

FIGURE 4.2 Kanban circuit

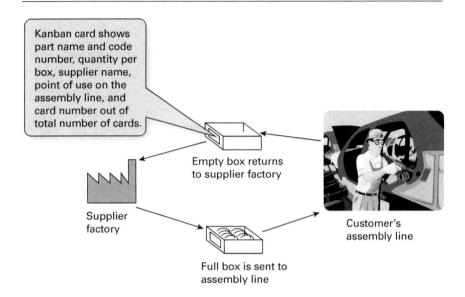

Kanban card shows part name and code number, quantity per box, supplier name, point of use on the assembly line, and card number out of total number of cards.

Empty box returns to supplier factory

Supplier factory

Full box is sent to assembly line

Customer's assembly line

'box' is used here for simplicity. Normally, 'inserts' (formed packaging with shaped spaces for the parts) in the box ensure that only that type of part can be put into the box, and only a certain quantity of parts. The ideal quantity and therefore size for a box is about one hour's work or a box that will hold a weight that can be easily lifted. This varies enormously according to the size and weight of the part. Usually a Kanban card is attached to the box and the Kanban identifies the part name, part number, quantity to be held in the box, source of the part, destination of the part, and the sequence number of the box against the total number of boxes for that part type.

The total number of cards for that part type in circulation controls the overall level of inventory that is allowed for that part type. The more cards that exist, the greater the amount of inventory there will be, with all its associated holding costs and tied-up operating capital. The number of cards and boxes required, however, depends on all the elements that control the flow of parts in terms of capability to supply and rate of consumption of boxes.

The number of boxes is calculated from formula 1, on page 199. It can be seen that a longer lead time to supply will result in more cards being required. Similarly, if there is high hourly demand or if a greater safety stock is required, a greater number of cards are necessary. However, if parts are small and the capacity of the container is relatively large, then a smaller number of cards will be required.

$$\text{Number of Kanbans } (N) = \frac{d \times (t+s)}{c} \qquad (1)$$

Where: N = number of Kanbans

d = hourly demand

c = capacity of container

t = average time to obtain a replacement box (in hours)

s = safety stock (in hours)

For the system to operate well, the rules must be strictly observed. The box must contain only the exact number of parts shown on the Kanban card, no more, no less. Only the appropriate box for that part may be used to transport it. The box must contain only good, usable parts. A box must never be supplied without a Kanban card. The box must be emptied completely before being returned to the supplier.

Example

An assembly line makes 100 washing machines per day and the motors are supplied by Kanban in containers holding five units. The working day is eight hours. A safety stock of two hours is required.

It can be seen immediately that 20 (= 100/5) containers of motors will be required each day, but how many boxes should there be in the circuit? Empty containers are picked up every hour to be taken back to the goods receiving area, awaiting collection when the next delivery arrives from that supplier. This supplier delivers every two hours, and the supplier is about half an hour away from the washing-machine assembly company. The supplier usually refills the boxes within an hour of their arrival and then they go out on the next delivery run. Once at the washing-machine company, it may take up to an hour before the boxes are delivered to the assembly area. The total time in this refill circuit is summarized in Table 4.2.

Let us now substitute this data into formula 1:

d = hourly demand = 100/8 hours = 12.5 units per hour

c = capacity of container = 5 motors per box

t = average time to obtain a replacement box (in hours) = 7 hours

s = safety stock (in hours) = 2 hours

$$\text{Number of Kanbans } (N) = \frac{d \times (t+s)}{c} = \frac{12.5 \times (7+2)}{5} \approx 23$$

It is concluded that we need 23 containers and cards in the circuit. We can see that, at any one time, there could be five full boxes waiting for assembly (safety stock of 2 hours = [12.5 × 2]/5), two or three boxes waiting to be returned to goods inwards (12.5/5), plus a maximum of five boxes waiting

TABLE 4.2 Time in the Kanban circuit

Stage	Maximum time required (hours)
Removal to goods receiving	1
Collection by supplier	2
Travel to supplier	0.5
Refilling by supplier and wait for next delivery to customer	2
Travel to customer	0.5
Delivery to assembly area	1
Total hours =	7

to be returned to the supplier ([12.5 × 2]/5), plus five boxes coming back from the supplier plus two or three boxes waiting to be delivered to the assembly area, plus some in transit for a short time (5 boxes for half an hour ≈ 2 or 3 on average). In practice, we would see how this number of Kanbans worked and then adjust it accordingly.

Further information

See Bicheno, J and Holweg, M (2009) *The Lean Toolbox*, PICSIE Books, Buckingham.

Reference

Japanese Management Association (ed) (1986) *Kanban: Just in time at Toyota: Management begins at the workplace* (tr DJ Lu), Productivity Press, Portland, OR

4.6 Kraljic matrix

Introduction

The procurement function has changed dramatically over the last 20–30 years, from a 'purchasing' activity that was regarded as primarily administrative, looking for the 'best value' items to buy, to a strategic function (see tool 4.22) that is capable of generating profit and competitive advantage for the business by sourcing from high-performing suppliers. One of the milestones in this transformation was a paper by Peter Kraljic (1983) in which he described a way of analysing the portfolio of purchased items and services. The purpose was to adapt the method of procurement to the complexity of the supply market, and the relative importance of that purchasing decision to the business.

The overall complexity of the supply market depends on such factors as the number of potential suppliers available, the rate of technological change, barriers to entry for potential new suppliers and potential transport complexity, perhaps due to distance or special packaging requirements.

The relative importance of the purchasing decision to the business depends on such factors as the overall value of the decision, the strategic importance of the item to the business and impact of the price of this item on profitability.

These two factors form the axes of a 2 × 2 matrix and an approach to the procurement task is defined for each quadrant (see Figure 4.3).

FIGURE 4.3 Kraljic matrix

	Material management (Leverage items) Group items together and negotiate with several potential suppliers 12–24 month contracts Negotiate delivery frequency	**Supply management** (Strategic items) Evaluate potential suppliers very carefully Set up long-term agreements Explore mutual cost reduction Invite supplier's experience for new products and projects
	Purchasing management (Non-critical items) Annual contracts Look for local suppliers Vendor-managed inventory	**Sourcing management** (Bottleneck items) Keep searching for alternative suppliers/products Devise contract to minimize risk Relationship development

Importance of purchasing decision (High / Low)

Supply market complexity (Low / High)

When to use

This is not an everyday tool but is useful for periodic re-evaluation of procurement approaches in the business. The relative importance of items or families can change over time as new products are introduced and the product mix changes. It can also be useful before the introduction of a new product in order to review the relative importance of its different components, assemblies or raw materials.

The Kraljic matrix is a good communication tool for explaining procurement methods and strategies to different user functions. Communication between the procurement function and user departments is vital to making the best supplier and product selections.

How to use

It is advisable to carry out a Pareto or ABC analysis (see tool 3.2) first in order to understand which purchased items or families have the greatest financial importance. Then the items or families can be placed in the quadrants, either by the procurement function or by discussion between procurement and user functions. Finally, the appropriateness of current procurement methods for each family can be reviewed against the methods appropriate to that quadrant.

Example

A manufacturing company has determined that its outsourced logistics and supply chain services fall into six main categories:

1 full vehicle ambient transport;

2 market distribution transport to customer;

3 global sea freight services;

4 global air freight services;

5 a single national distribution centre providing co-packing and returns management services;

6 pallet supplies.

After some discussion, they position each family into the matrix as shown in Figure 4.4. One of the outcomes of the discussion was to try to find alternative suppliers for some of the specialist transport and market distribution services where there was currently only a single supplier identified, and that fell in the 'sourcing management' quadrant. It was recognized that the security and development of the single national distribution centre was key and that the current supplier might not be the right partner for the joint development of after-care services.

FIGURE 4.4 Application of Kraljic matrix to outsourced logistic and supply chain services

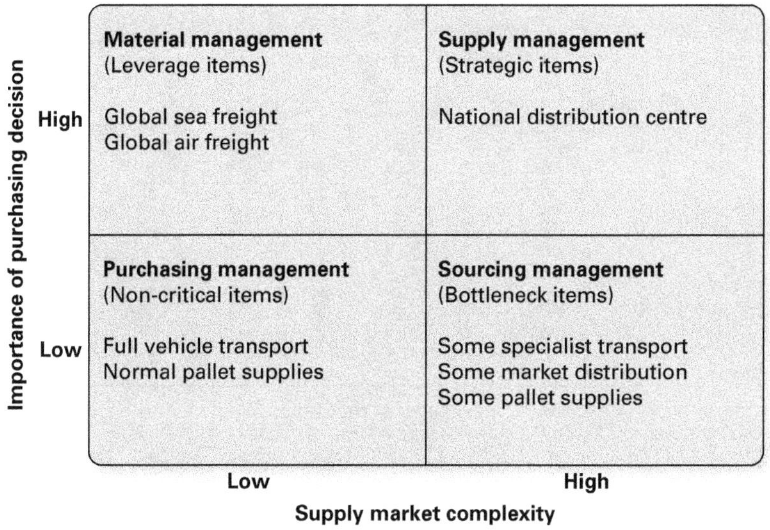

Global air and sea freight services had high spend and criticality in service for the company and needed to be tendered regularly.

(Example provided by Labyrinth Consulting, www.labyrinthsolutions.co.uk)

Reference

Kraljic, P (1983) Purchasing must become supply management, *Harvard Business Review*, September–October, pp 109–17 (or find out more by googling 'Kraljic matrix').

4.7 Maturity models

Introduction

The general purpose of a maturity model is to enable users to position themselves in terms of the level of advancement, or 'maturity', of the function or activity under consideration and thus to determine what to do next to seek improvement towards some kind of ideal or high-performing function or activity. Typically maturity is described at four or five levels, from low performing to high, but any number of levels can be included (see Figure 4.5).

FIGURE 4.5 Linking improving performance with maturity

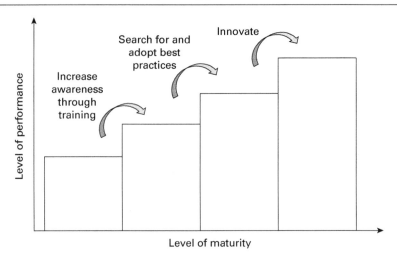

There is a good parallel between a maturity model for the logistics and supply chain function and the four 'stages in the evolution of manufacturing's strategic role' proposed by Hayes and Wheelwright (1984, 1985). At the lowest level of contribution to the business, they describe the manufacturing function as being 'internally neutral' where it is reactive and requires outside assistance to make strategic decisions. Looking outside the business, it can move to the next level of performance and become 'externally neutral' by adopting industry best practices. The next level, 'internally supportive', is achieved by ensuring that manufacturing strategy is developed from, and supports, the business strategy. The highest level, 'externally supportive', is achieved when manufacturing has a level of innovation in processes and technologies such that it is involved in major marketing and engineering decisions.

Maturity models have thus been created for many purposes and many different activities. They are particularly useful in logistics and supply chain management, as some companies still have a long way to evolve in terms of supply chain management while others have developed significantly in the last couple of decades. A maturity model enables a company to create a 'route map' for improvement to best performance.

A maturity model can be created for any 'pillar' of supply chain management, eg inventory management, warehouse management (see maturity scan for warehouse management in tool 1.18), information systems, transport or procurement, or an integrated model can be created to communicate overall direction.

When to use

A maturity model is a tool for determining strategy for the development of a function leading to improvement of the business. A functional workshop can be used to set up the first maturity model and thereafter it can be the basis of an annual review to discuss progress, how the model should be further developed to explain the long-term direction and agree on how the priorities for the next two to three years will be delivered.

How to use

Two approaches can be taken. The first is to task a manager with searching the literature for all existing models, selecting desired characteristics and then creating an initial model, perhaps with some alternatives at each stage. The second approach is to use the concept to develop a shared vision of how supply chain management should develop in your business, by means of a facilitated workshop involving all those concerned with the high performance of the supply chain. This might include, for example, representatives from marketing, the customer service function, accounting and operations. The outcome of the workshop should be an agreed, summarized diagram, rather like Figure 4.6, plus an action plan for moving to the next level of maturity.

FIGURE 4.6 Simplified supply chain management maturity model

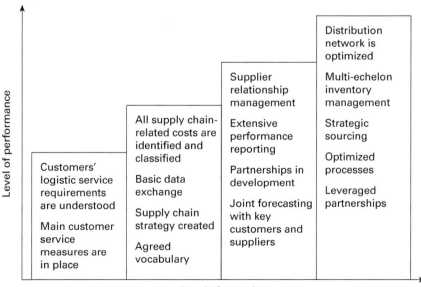

Example

Figure 4.6 shows a simplified example of a general maturity model for supply chain management.

Further information

See Lahti, M, Shamsuzzoha, A H M and Helo, P (2009) Developing a maturity model for supply chain management, *International Journal of Logistics Systems and Management*, 5 (6), 654–78.

A full supply chain maturity scan can be completed at: http://www.jvdbconsulting. com/english/supply-chain-maturity-scan.html

References

Hayes, R H and Wheelwright, S C (1984) *Restoring Our Competitive Edge: Competing through manufacturing*, Wiley, New York

Wheelwright, S C and Hayes, RH (1985) Competing through manufacturing, *Harvard Business Review*, January–February

4.8 Postponement

Introduction

'Postponement' is the term applied to the customization of a product at the latest possible time. One of the earliest well-documented examples was the Hewlett-Packard LaserJet printer. Instead of making all the different variants of the LaserJet printer at the factory, it was decided to produce a generic printer there, and ship the generic printers to the regional warehouses across the world. The final customization and packaging for a particular market was carried out at the warehouse. Although this finishing operation was slightly more expensive to carry out in the warehouse, the savings in transport costs and inventory massively outweighed this small disadvantage.

Another famous example is provided by Benetton, the Italian clothing group, which delays dyeing of knitted products until orders are received from the shops. Similar to HP, just one stock reference is held of each knitwear design and this stock may be transformed into a range of SKUs. In general, the advantages of postponement are:

- Having common product and associated processes until a very late stage encourages economies of scale, reduces the number of setups or changeovers required and reduces the amount of product to be managed.

- Adding variety as late as possible reduces the financial risk of holding inventory of less popular variants.

- Ability to meet rapidly increasing demand for those members of a product family that are selling well.

- Reduced number of SKUs to be managed.

- Early processes can be standardized, usually leading to advantages in processing time and cost.

Products subject to postponement are sometimes called 'T' products or 'mushroom' products, to indicate graphically that variety is introduced towards the end of the process.

When to use

When designing a product, or the production process, ask yourself if the components or processes that give rise to product variety can be delayed to the final stages of production, or even to the point of distribution.

How to use

First, consider the importance of product or service variety to your customers. For those products or services where variety is or could be important, consider how and when that variety is introduced.

It requires some imagination to review all the different ways in which variety can be introduced later in the sequence of processes rather than earlier, so that the product design and production processes are common for as long as possible. This may require a cross-functional team or process design review project.

Example

Flat laminated glass for architectural purposes is a 'sandwich' of glass and vinyl layers and is used in a number of security applications. For example, shop windows can be fitted with laminated glass to stop would-be thieves from entering the shop. Even though the glass will break under attack, the vinyl layer will usually prevent the aspiring robber from gaining access. Thicker and more complex 'sandwiches' enable the glass to become bullet-proof, such as is used on high-security delivery van windscreens and side windows.

Because of the number of layers involved, thick laminated glass can have very many different specifications and it was common at one time to make up the 'sandwich' for a specific order. In order to use the glass economically, the different glass layers were cut to size before laying up the 'sandwich'. However, the complexity of the production process meant that the customer would usually see a minimum lead time of at least 24–48 hours before the finished product was available.

It was recognized that one way of reducing the lead time to the customer would be to have stock sheets of thick laminate available, to a commonly accepted specification. Customers requesting thick laminate were offered a lead time of several days for their own specification or several hours if they accepted the standard specification laminate. On receiving an order for standard thick laminate, the stock sheet could be sawn to size and the edges finished. The total lead time for these operations was three to four hours. Customers were generally happy to pay a premium for speedy delivery.

In this example, two elements caused variety: the laminate specification and the size of the product. Both causes were addressed. The specification variety was eliminated by encouraging customers to choose a standard specification with the advantage of greatly reduced lead time, and the size variety was managed by introducing the variety at a much later stage in the process – final sawing.

The disadvantage was that stock of expensive product was held. This financial risk was minimized by holding a minimum amount of stock of a very small number of specifications, but which could nevertheless cover more than 50 per cent of applications if the customer was flexible enough to accept a slightly different specification.

Further information

Ronald Ballou (1988) gives a good summary of the principle of postponement and the types of firms that could be potentially interested: Ballou, R H (2004) *Business Logistics Management: Planning, organizing, and controlling the supply chain*, 5th edn, Prentice Hall, Upper Saddle River, NJ.

Early work in this area was carried out by Walter Zinn and Donald J Bowersox: Zinn, W and Bowersox, D J (1988) Planning physical distribution with the principle of postponement, *Journal of Business Logistics*, 9 (2), pp 117–36

An internet search for information about the HP Laser Jet printer supply chain will give rapid results.

4.9 Product Flow Path Design, by Fortna

Introduction

Product Flow Path Design, introduced by Fortna, defines the most cost-efficient and service-effective routes by which to move products from suppliers to customers. It provides a strategy, a business case and a prioritized road map for moving forward. It is seen as the critical link in the distribution network strategy cycle (see Figure 4.7).

To execute the Product Flow Path Design (PFPD), an important question often is: 'How many facilities do you need and where should they be?' Ideally, this is answered through a network optimization analysis. Network optimization takes an in-depth look into the estimated freight costs associated with alternative distribution facility locations.

Most often, a commercial software tool is used that has an optimization algorithm that essentially functions like a linear programming model to determine the minimum cost of alternative locations and product flows. (Examples of companies supplying this software are listed at the end of this tool.) It's a highly data-intensive and theoretical process requiring trained analysts. The most important input is identifying the alternative scenarios and flow paths to analyse. Rarely do these projects have sufficient time or budget to evaluate all the potential flow path scenarios or product segment permutations. So, a PFPD avoids sub-optimizing your study by providing a prioritized set of alternatives to evaluate.

The resulting network optimization analysis following PFPD is valuable input to the broader and more comprehensive requirements of a distribution network strategy. A distribution network strategy includes inventory deployment planning, service capability definition across channels, systems planning, and detailed financial budgeting. It is also based on practical constraints and considerations such as the availability of resources and logistics partners to execute and maintain the strategy.

Because all businesses change over time, the network strategy needs to be periodically re-evaluated. This need creates a loop back to PFPD.

A PFPD aims to answer three strategic questions:

1 What are the most effective and efficient methods (balancing cost and service) to flow unique product groupings from suppliers to customers or stores?

FIGURE 4.7 Outline of the distribution network strategy cycle

1) Define the future flow path design

Reassess over time

Product Flow Path Design

Emphasis:
- Physical attributes
- Supply chain characteristics
- Assessing alternative flow paths from supplier to customer
- High level business case and road map

Prioritize the areas in which to focus

3) Develop a detailed strategy and plan based upon practical constraints

Network Strategy

Emphasis:
- Actual location(s)
- Practical constraints and considerations
- Inventory deployment plan
- Service implications
- Detailed transition and human resource planning
- Detailed budgeting and cash flow requirements

Prioritize the alternatives to assess

2) Determine the number and general location of facilities

Network Optimization

Emphasis:
- No. and theoretical location of facility(ies)
- Service assumptions
- Freight cost analysis
- High-level warehouse and inventory costs
- Identifying minimum logistics costs of possible scenarios via optimization engine
- Financial justification

SOURCE: reproduced by kind permission of Fortna, www.fortna.com

2 What is the impact of the recommended product flow paths on existing operations (near and longer term)?

3 What is the supporting business case and migration plan to support the recommended changes?

Recommended tasks and deliverables from this effort are outlined in Figure 4.8.

The result can be a myriad of alternative flow paths depending on product attributes, source, lead times and destination. These can include direct shipments, global distribution centres, national distribution centres, regional centres, cross-docking and consolidation centres, local warehouses or a combination of the above. It is crucial, therefore, to produce a more manageable set of alternatives to evaluate. A sensible approach is to:

- apply deductive reasoning in developing a set of hypotheses for the potential future supply chain;

- allow business priorities to dictate where to focus your analysis;

- create a set of logical product segments by which to assess alternative flow paths;

- develop and use a financial model to compare the impact and sensitivity of each hypothesis versus your current operation, which becomes the baseline.

PFPD takes a holistic view of supply chain assets, service levels, cost to serve, profits and investments. The idea is to think outside the box, look beyond what you've done in the past, improve on benchmarked results, define the possibilities and evaluate what is practical.

Suppliers of supply chain network design software include the following:

Cast – http://www.llamasoft.com/cast-cast-flow/
Logic Net Plus – http://www.llamasoft.com/logictools/
Infor – www.infor.com/solutions/scm/
Supply Chain Optimizer – www.insight-mss.com
JDA – www.jda.com
Logility – www.logility.com/
Supply Chain Guru – http://www.llamasoft.com/supply-chain-guru.html
We Supply – www.wesupply.com

FIGURE 4.8 Tasks and deliverables in a Flow Path Design Project

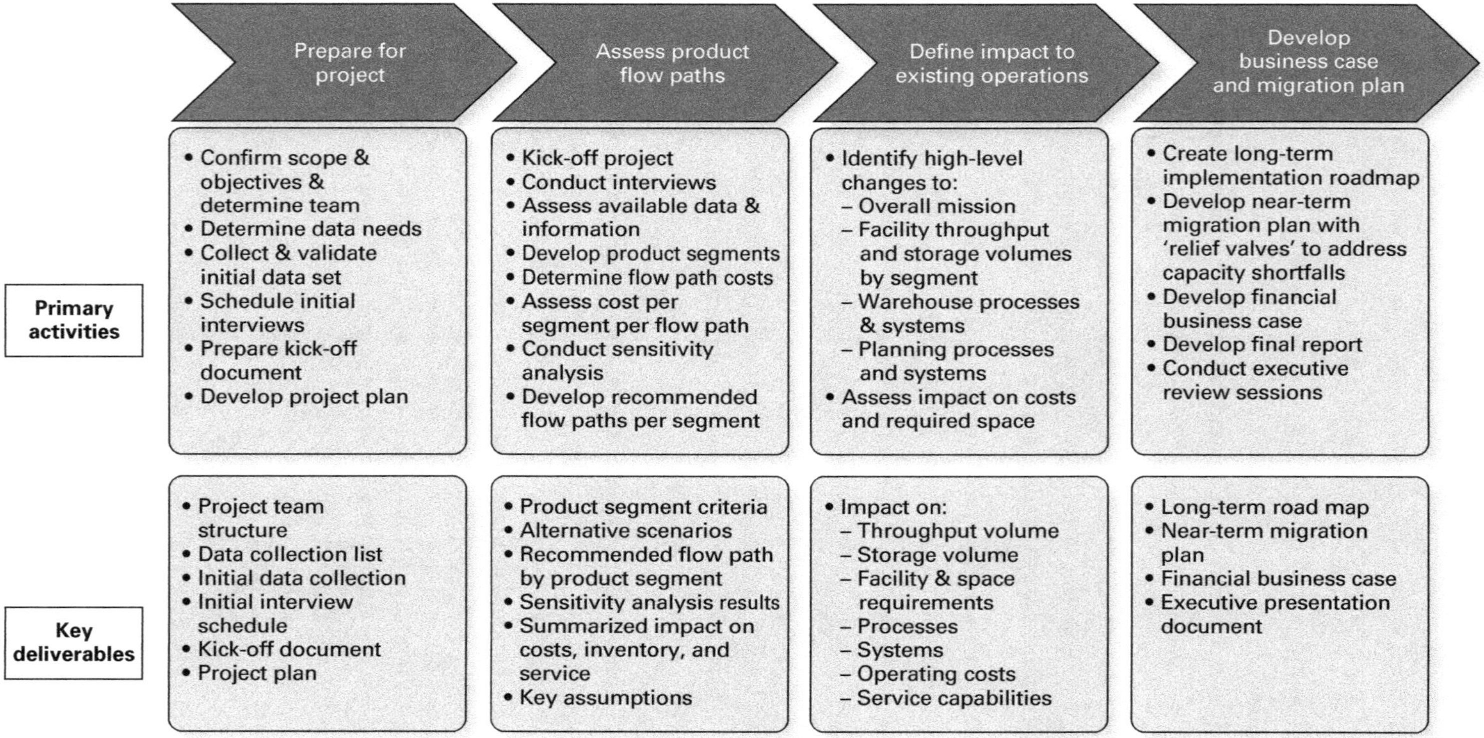

	Prepare for project	Assess product flow paths	Define impact to existing operations	Develop business case and migration plan

Primary activities	• Confirm scope & objectives & determine team
	• Determine data needs
	• Collect & validate initial data set
	• Schedule initial interviews
	• Prepare kick-off document
	• Develop project plan
		• Kick-off project
		• Conduct interviews
		• Assess available data & information
		• Develop product segments
		• Determine flow path costs
		• Assess cost per segment per flow path
		• Conduct sensitivity analysis
		• Develop recommended flow paths per segment
			• Identify high-level changes to:
			  – Overall mission
			  – Facility throughput and storage volumes by segment
			  – Warehouse processes & systems
			  – Planning processes and systems
			• Assess impact on costs and required space
				• Create long-term implementation roadmap
				• Develop near-term migration plan with 'relief valves' to address capacity shortfalls
				• Develop financial business case
				• Develop final report
				• Conduct executive review sessions

Key deliverables	• Project team structure
	• Data collection list
	• Initial data collection
	• Initial interview schedule
	• Kick-off document
	• Project plan
		• Product segment criteria
		• Alternative scenarios
		• Recommended flow path by product segment
		• Sensitivity analysis results
		• Summarized impact on costs, inventory, and service
		• Key assumptions
			• Impact on:
			  – Throughput volume
			  – Storage volume
			  – Facility & space requirements
			  – Processes
			  – Systems
			  – Operating costs
			  – Service capabilities
				• Long-term road map
				• Near-term migration plan
				• Financial business case
				• Executive presentation document

SOURCE: reproduced by kind permission of Fortna, www.fortna.com

4.10 SCOR®

Introduction

The Supply Chain Operations Reference (SCOR®) model is a product of the Supply Chain Council (SCC), which has merged with APICS. The model is a framework that links business process, metrics, best practices and technology features together into a unified structure to support communication between supply chain partners. It assists companies in improving the effectiveness of their supply chain management and related supply chain improvement activities.

SCOR® identifies five core supply chain performance attributes: reliability, responsiveness, agility, costs and asset management. Consideration of these attributes makes it possible to compare an organization that strategically chooses to be the low-cost provider against an organization that chooses to compete on reliability and performance.

Membership of the SCC is open to all companies and organizations interested in applying and advancing state-of-the-art supply chain management systems and practices. Member companies pay an annual fee to become involved and have access to:

- frameworks, benchmarking, templates and other resources developed from ongoing research efforts;

- professional development via training and certification programmes;

- networking via peer events and online portals.

Members include manufacturers, distributors, retailers and service providers as well as technology solution providers, business consultants, academic institutions and government organizations.

When to use

SCOR® is typically used to identify, measure, reorganize and improve supply chain processes.

How to use

SCOR® works through a cyclic process of:

- Capturing the configuration of a supply chain which is driven by:
    - plan: levels of aggregation and information sources

- source: locations and products
- make: production sites and methods
- deliver: channels, inventory deployment and products
- return: locations and methods
- enable: manage the supply chain.

- Measuring the performance of the supply chain and comparing against internal and external industry goals. Supply chain performance is focused on:

  - reliability: achievement of customer demand fulfilment on time, complete, without damage, etc
  - responsiveness: the time it takes to react to and fulfil customer demand
  - agility: the ability of the supply chain to increase/decrease demand within a given planned period
  - cost: objective assessment of all components of supply chain cost
  - assets: the assessment of all resources used to fulfil customer demand.

- Realigning supply chain processes and best practices to fulfil unachieved, or changing, business objectives. This realignment is achieved through a combination of:

  - classic process re-engineering from 'as-is' to 'to-be'
  - lean manufacturing analysis and process change
  - Six-Sigma analysis of defective processes
  - theory of constraints analysis of systems or processes to elucidate root-cause issues
  - ISO-9000-style process capture and control
  - Balanced SCOR® cards and benchmarking
  - a host of other combined industrial-engineering-based best-practice techniques in improvement.

The SCOR® process reference model contains:

- Performance metrics: standard metrics to measure process performance. There is a suite of key performance indicators but first-line metrics include:

  - the perfect order: on time, in full, damage free and complete document accuracy

- order fulfilment cycle time
- supply chain flexibility
- supply chain management cost
- cash to cash cycle time
- total cost to serve.

- Processes: standard descriptions of management processes and a framework of process relationships.

- Practices: management practices that produce best-in-class performance; they help companies:
  - Standardize processes: What is our standard way of operating this part/aspect of supply chains?
  - Identify alternative ways of operating the supply chain: How can we organize the process differently to address performance gaps?
  - Formulate a wish list of process configurations/automation.
  - Formulate a black list of undesired (move-away-from) process configurations.

- People: Training and skills requirements aligned with processes, best practices, and metrics.

Example

One of the success stories of SCOR® implementation is the use of this methodology by Siemens Medical Solutions for their 'computed topography' devices. These medical devices are made to order in Germany and China for customers all over the world. Several hundred employees were organized in teams for the project. Although the original aim of the project was to move supply chain processes to an e-business environment, there were stunning results in the supply chain itself. Delivery time was reduced from 22 to two weeks, costs were reduced by 30 per cent, and inventory reduced by 60 per cent.

Further information

SCOR® is copyright Supply Chain Council and APICS; see: http://www.apics.org/sites/apics-supply-chain-council/about-apics-scc and http://www.apics.org/sites/apics-supply-chain-council/frameworks/scor

4.11 Supplier relationships

Introduction

An important component of the inbound side of supply chain management – supply management – is the development of an appropriate relationship with each supplier. Kraljic's matrix (see tool 4.6) gives guidance on an overall approach to the procurement of different items according to the complexity of the supply market and the strategic importance of the item. In recent years, a lot more effort has been focused on identifying different kinds of relationships that may exist with suppliers and when each type of relationship is appropriate.

At one time the focus was on 'partnerships', a word that was much used – and abused. One useful classification is given by Lambert *et al* (1996), where they see a progression of relationships from 'arm's length' transactions, through three levels of partnership to joint ventures and finally, vertical integration. Rather than use the word 'partner', some companies identify 'preferred' or 'principal' suppliers, to indicate a relationship that is closer than 'arm's length'.

When to use

It is worth carrying out an annual review of the supplier base, looking at those suppliers that represent the top 80 per cent of spend. These are the key suppliers and a closer relationship with them can bring significant advantages. Stock and Lambert (2001) make the point that partnership is not a requirement for business success but not having a partnership where one is appropriate wastes the opportunity for competitive advantage. It is therefore useful to review the nature of the relationship with these key suppliers against the list of criteria below and consider whether there is any benefit in moving towards a closer relationship with any of them, and what this would entail.

How to use

Many companies recognize the advantages of closer links with their key suppliers. In purely economic terms, better understanding of how the other party works can save a lot of time and energy when placing and monitoring orders, or when sorting out problems. However, there can also be significant advantage in involving the supplier in new product development projects, or sharing plans regarding future demand and promotions (see CPFR® for example, tool 4.2).

FIGURE 4.9 Supplier relationships added to Kraljic matrix

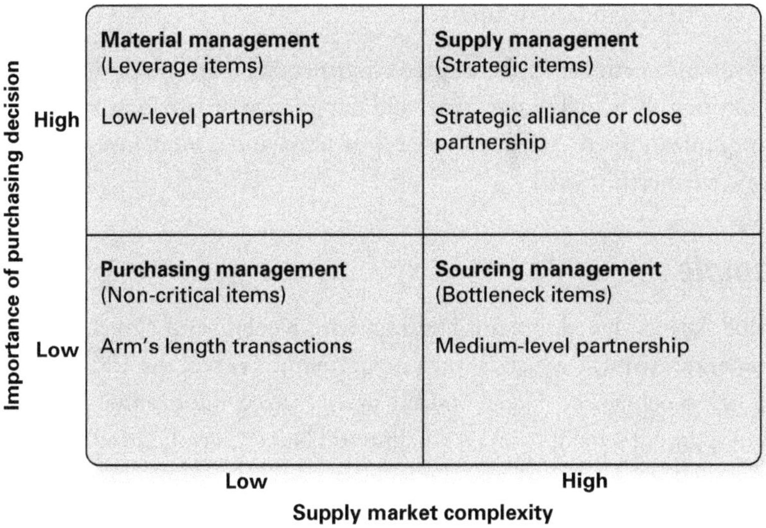

Looking at the Kraljic matrix again, one can allocate a type of supplier relationship according to the matrix quadrant (see Figure 4.9). To be more specific, the following points indicate some of the dimensions that can constitute the relationship:

- Giving information about production schedules to suppliers – the more they know about your exact requirements, the more likely they are to fulfil them on time and in full.

- Number of people in each business interacting with one another – the closer the relationship and the longer that it has been in existence, the more points of contact there are likely to be.

- How problems are resolved – fast resolution by joint discussion and investigation (looking after the final customer first) is preferable to reading the fine print of the contract to apportion blame.

- Date of termination of relationship – the closer the relationship, the less likely there is to be an envisaged termination date.

- Meetings to discuss how to work better together – members of both companies come together in a workshop to discuss how to streamline the ordering/delivery processes.

- Level of management effort required to maintain an expected level of supplier performance – close and healthy relationships are based on high levels of performance as well as trust.

- Involvement in new product design – suppliers in close relationships are consulted and involved in new projects, to engage their experience and innovations.

Finally, it is worth remembering that 'partnerships' are rarely built on the first meeting. It usually takes time and experience of working together for two organizations to achieve the level of trust and confidence required to make a partnership work.

Example

In 2008 Airbus signed a major contract with Kuehne and Nagel to manage and operate Airbus's logistics hubs in Germany, France, the UK and Spain. Although Kuehne and Nagel started by operating the existing warehouse facilities, the agreement foresaw Kuehne and Nagel consolidating the storage requirements and rationalizing the delivery network across Europe. Kuehne and Nagel had been working with Airbus since 2003, so both companies had had the opportunity to understand one another's needs and operations before Kuehne and Nagel were appointed 'lead logistics provider' for a significant contract period.

References

Lambert, D M, Emmelhainz, M and Gardner, J T (1996) Developing and implementing supply chain partnerships, *International Journal of Logistics Management*, 7 (2), pp 5–13

Stock, J R and Lambert, D M (2001) *Strategic Logistics Management*, McGraw-Hill, New York

4.12 Supply chain risk assessment

Introduction

Two other sections in this book discuss risk assessment and management: Warehouse risk assessment (tool 1.19) follows the recommended health and safety approach to managing risk in a warehouse, and supply chain risk mitigation and contingency planning (tool 4.13) describes the risks to monitor and what to do when things go wrong. This tool brings the other sections together to create a supply chain risk management framework, based on a simplified version of failure mode effect and criticality analysis

(FMECA), the methodology developed by NASA to eliminate the chance of a potential failure or mitigate its impact should it occur.

When to use

The first risk management plan can be set up at any time: the sooner the better! After this, it is highly recommended that an annual review takes place. An important event, such as a major contract or concern about a critical supplier or customer, could trigger a review of the plan before the anniversary review.

How to use

The overall approach is as follows:

1 Brainstorm the potential things that could go wrong at each stage of your supply chain, working systematically through the supply side, your operations, outbound side, customers and general business environment.

2 For each potential failure, use the SLD matrix in Figure 4.10 to award levels of severity of impact (S), likelihood of occurrence (L) and chance of detecting the failure before it occurs (D).

3 For each potential failure, calculate the criticality number (CN) from the product of S, L and D. Thus $CN = S \times L \times D$ (which will be a minimum of 1, maximum of 125).

4 Rank the potential failures in order of criticality, largest first.

5 Going down the list of potential failures in turn, starting with the highest CN, brainstorm ways of eliminating the risk. For each potential solution, estimate the cost of implementation and the practicality of the solution in eliminating the potential failure. For each potential solution, reassess the SLD values, find their product, and use this as an estimate of 'residual risk'.

6 If the risk cannot be eliminated, what mitigating actions can be taken to reduce the impact if failure occurs? For each potential solution, estimate the cost of implementation and the practicality of the solution in mitigating the potential failure. For each potential solution, reassess the SLD values, find their product, and use this as an estimate of 'residual risk'.

7 From all the solutions proposed for elimination or mitigation, choose the solution that gives an acceptable reduction in risk for an

acceptable cost to implement. Include this in an action plan, showing clear responsibilities for implementation and the target completion time.

8 Record the solution implemented and the residual risk.

9 Continue to monitor risks and review the plan periodically.

FIGURE 4.10 SLD risk assessment

	S	L	D
	Severity of effect	Likelihood of occurrence	Likelihood of detection
1	No direct effect on operating service levels	Probability of occurrence; once in many years	Detectability of the failure in the long term is very high
2	Minor deterioration in operating service levels	Probability of occurrence; once in many months	Considerable warning of failure before occurrence
3	Definite reduction in operating service levels	Probability of occurrence; once in some weeks	Some warning of failure before occurrence
4	Serious deterioration in operating service levels	Probability of weekly occurrence	Little warning of failure before occurrence
5	Operating service levels ceased	Probability of daily occurrence	Detectability is effectively zero

SOURCE: adapted from Slater (2005)

Example

A country in Africa was evaluating the idea of using container-based fuel stations for distributing fuel more widely across the country, in particular to rural areas. A specially designed 40-foot container would house two pumps, a supply of diesel and a supply of petrol. When the fuel supplies were exhausted, the whole container would be replaced by a full one.

Table 4.3 shows the beginning of the risk assessment, with the identification of potential problems and their CN ranking. Table 4.4 shows some of the potential solutions, and residual risk.

TABLE 4.3 Risk assessment part 1 – identifying and classifying the potential problems

Failure no	Potential failure or problem	L (1–5)	Effect of failure	S (1–5)	Cause of failure	D (1–5)	CN = L × S × D
1	Car/lorry crashes into the container	3	Explosion, death of driver	5	Poor driving skill	5	75
2	Attempts to steal fuel	4	Potential explosion	5	Container left in unsafe condition	3	60
3	Attempts to steal the whole container	1	Operation ceased, loss of asset	5	Criminal interference	5	25
4	Pump failure	2	Customer frustration	3	Poor maintenance	4	24
5	Leakage	1	Fire risk, environmental damage	5	Bad handling	3	15

TABLE 4.4 Risk assessment part 2 – action plan for elimination or mitigation of the risks

Failure no	Action	Target completion date	Whose responsibility?	Residual L (1–5)	Residual S (1–5)	Residual D (1–5)	Residual CN
1	Locate containers carefully, not near bends or other potentially hazardous places	03/2012	GM	2	5	5	50
1	Fencing around whole area to prevent accidental approach from road	Wait for budget		1	5	4	20
1	Protective posts or bars around edge of container zone, to take first shock of impact	Wait for decision on fence		2	5	5	50
2	Manned cabin – permanent guard	04/2012		2	4	3	24
3	Manned cabin – permanent guard	04/2012		1	5	3	15
4	Set up and follow maintenance plan	04/2012		1	3	2	6
5	Ensure drivers are trained to handle these containers carefully	04/2012		1	5	3	15
5	Appropriate equipment on site for handling leaks or fires	04/2012		1	4	3	12

It can be seen that location of the containers was thought to be critical in reducing their exposure to bad driving. Once located, however, only some kind of mechanical barrier would prevent a vehicle impacting the container, and a surrounding fence was believed to be the best solution. Unfortunately, this was expensive and needed a higher-level decision.

Meanwhile, it was decided to locate a manned cabin with a telephone to address the other potential problems. Placing equipment on site capable of handling leaks or fires is a mitigation measure in case the failure occurs.

The overall idea of using containers to deliver and dispense fuel in remote areas was believed to be feasible enough for further evaluation.

Further information

More rigorous approaches to FMECA can be found from any good textbook on total productive maintenance.

References

Gibson, R (2013) Know your risk, know your risk appetite for growth, *Focus*, **15** (5), pp 40–43
Slater, A G (2005) Vulnerability in the supply chain, Visiting Professor of Logistics, Huddersfield University, lecture notes.

4.13 Supply chain risk mitigation and contingency planning

Introduction

According to SCOR®:

> supply chain risk management is the systematic identification, assessment, and mitigation of potential disruptions in logistic networks with the objective of reducing their negative impact on the logistic network's performance. Potential disruptions can either occur within the supply chain (eg insufficient quality, unreliable suppliers, machine breakdown, uncertain demand, etc) or outside the supply chain (eg flooding, terrorism, labour strikes, natural disasters, etc).

Both are considered in an integral multi-phase approach for supply chain risk mitigation and contingency planning. SCOR® best practice suggests undertaking the following:

- Establish context: Define and document the objective and scope (internal and external) for managing risk.

- Identify risk: Collect and document all potential risk events that may impact the organization and prevent it from meeting its goals.

- Assess risk: Collect and document for each potential risk the causes, probability and consequences (understand the value at risk).

- Evaluate risk: Prioritize risks, determine for each risk whether mitigation actions are required or the risk is acceptable.

- Mitigate risk: Determine the actions required to eliminate, reduce, or accept and monitor the risks (risk mitigation plan).

- Monitor risk: Continuously monitor effectiveness of mitigation plans; identify emerging risks and changes in internal and external context.

A 10-step plan to avoid or minimize disruption in the supply chain has been put forward by JP Morgan Chase; this is an adaptation:

1 Undertake regular risk assessments – identify areas of concern:

- Political and labour issues.
- Physical and geographical risks such as weather.
- Market conditions.
- Oil prices.
- Currency fluctuation.
- Inflation.

2 Create a response team:

- Create an empowered group responsible for decision making during an emergency and communicate their actions throughout the supply chain.
- Ensure they have suitable competencies.
- Ensure access to communication lines.
- Both suppliers and customers have to be informed.
- Ensure you have trained staff to deal with the media.

3 Produce a contingency plan:

- Ensure that your suppliers also have a workable and realistic contingency plan.
- List details of emergency services.
- List details of providers of agency labour.

4 Give yourselves options:

- Establish and maintain relationships with alternative suppliers and logistics networks.
- Use multiple shippers, forwarders, ports and transport modes.
- Alternative power sources.

5 Test the contingency plan regularly:

- Review and update regularly.
- Run potential scenarios.

6 Keep documentation and information up to date:

- Ensure that telephone numbers and e-mail addresses are up to date.

7 Continue to track and be aware of current events likely to impact your supply chain:

- Weather patterns.
- Political unrest.
- Labour unrest.
- Labour shortages.
- Market conditions.
- Raw material shortages.
- Natural disasters, earthquakes, floods, volcanic eruptions.
- Terror attacks.
- Major fires.

8 Introduce cross-training:

- Develop a flexible workforce that can react quickly.
- Ensure staff have a cross-section of skills and abilities.

9 Save time and avoid congestion:

- Utilize quieter shipping routes.
- Move product away from ports quicker.

10 Back up and save all documentation:

- Ensure that this is done daily and stored off site electronically.

References

Supply Chain Operations Reference (SCOR®) model Overview – Version 10.0 supply chain http://www.apics.org/sites/apics-supply-chain-council/frameworks/scor SCOR® is copyright of APICS Supply Chain Council, http://www.apics.org/sites/apics-supply-chain-council/about-apics-scc

(Adapted from J P Morgan Chase Vastera cited in *The Unexpected Happens: Is your supply chain prepared?* by William Keenan, Jr, http://www.inboundlogistics.com/cms/article/the-unexpected-happens-is-your-supply-chain-prepared/)

4.14 Sustainable sourcing

Introduction

As natural resources become scarcer and as companies want to extend their level of corporate social responsibility (CSR) up the supply chain, sustainable sourcing is becoming more and more important in procurement.

Companies that are most closely involved are those that use natural materials directly in their product, for example palm oil, coffee beans and timber. Sustainable sourcing aims to ensure that the plantations and farms that produce these natural materials are managing their land and other natural resources in such a manner as to ensure that production can continue in the long term by putting as much back into the environment as is being taken out of it. For example, this includes replanting areas that have been harvested, managing water use and treating all waste products before releasing them back into the environment.

Nevertheless, all companies that buy goods and services can still implement sustainable sourcing, focusing on the carbon footprint (see tool 2.2) and overall environmental impact of the processes of their suppliers: use of energy, use of water, treatment of waste, packaging materials, etc. Note that sustainable sourcing will not be credible unless your company is also making clear progress to sustainability itself.

Another important impact of sustainability policies has been the CSR implications on the working conditions of the suppliers' employees. This has included ensuring that employees are paid correctly and have been trained for the work they do, so that they can work safely and efficiently.

When to use

Sustainable sourcing is a policy that must be agreed and supported by top-level management. Having decided how to approach this, the procurement function will review the existing supply base for sustainable practices and will be looking for commitment from all new suppliers.

How to use

Once top-level commitment has been obtained the procurement function will be asked to develop a company policy and then implement it. A good approach is to assemble an internal working party made up of interested members of different functions, including accounting and finance, marketing, operations and supply chain. Even though the focus will be on sustainable sourcing, information will be required from different functions. There will also be implications for different user functions and a learning process for the whole business.

The first task of the group will be to choose a focus area as a starting point. This could be one family of items or services and could be, for example:

- transport services;
- energy or water supplies;
- cleaning services;
- raw materials;
- components;
- equipment – taking a lifecycle viewpoint of the next purchase.

In general, it is a good idea to start with products where there is a clear environmental link, such as paper or food, or products where there could be high potential for cost savings over their lifetime, eg high-energy-consuming products. The first family will be used as a learning process, specifically to answer questions such as:

- What criteria will be used to assess sustainability in this case?
- How will sustainability be measured?
- What are the associated costs or risks?
- To what extent do suppliers meet the new requirements already?
- Will there be any kind of consultation process with key suppliers?
- How will suppliers be informed, eg next invitation to tender, quarterly communication?
- How will potential or new suppliers be informed about the new company policy?
- How can we help or support suppliers in their adoption of sustainable practices?

- How important are we to these suppliers? To what extent can we influence their sustainability programme?
- How will the success of our policy be measured?
- How will we react if a supplier is not interested or pays only lip service to our proposals?

It is always useful on a new project such as this to encourage the group members to carry out background research and provide summaries of their reading or visits to other members of the working party. This will suit some people more than others, but doing the underpinning research is essential education for the whole group. The main UK professional institutions are a good source of information, as well as a growing body of accessible books on the subject (eg Emmett and Sood, 2010).

Example

A high-profile sustainability programme was launched by Marks & Spencer in 2007. Known as 'Plan A' (there was no plan B), the project involved suppliers, customers and employees and covered the use of sustainable raw materials, environmental impact of the stores, eg energy and water use, waste, carbon footprint in distribution, healthy lifestyle and the final destination of its products. Its commitment has been unwavering and has brought many benefits for all concerned. More information is available on the website http://plana.marksandspencer.com

Further information

See Emmett, S and Sood, V (2010) *Green Supply Chains: An action manifesto*, Wiley, Chichester

These sites have a carbon footprint calculator to help companies in measuring their supply chain's impact on the environment: http://www.nef.org.uk/greencompany/co2calculator.htm and www.carbontrust.com/client-services/footprinting/footprint-measurement

4.15 Theory of constraints

Introduction

Eli Goldratt developed the 'theory of constraints' in the 1980s. Following on from his work on factory scheduling by starting scheduling from the bottleneck resource (Goldratt and Cox, 1984), the theory of constraints (Goldratt,

1990) was developed as a more general approach to improving business performance.

There have been many approaches to business performance improvement, but the theory of constraints is particularly relevant to supply chain management because one of its major pillars is reduction of inventory. A major outcome of applying the theory of constraints is improved flow through a resource or series of resources, which is also an objective of supply chain management.

Goldratt (1990) argues that there are only three ways to improve business performance:

1 Improve 'throughput', that is the rate at which saleable goods are output and can therefore generate revenue.

2 Reduce 'inventory' (for the same throughput), where inventory includes fixed assets as well as materials.

3 Reduce 'operating expense', which includes overheads and operating capital.

Crucially, this improvement process must be continuous (not just a quick fix), and also must involve everybody in the organization.

When to use

The theory of constraints can be used as the process for a business or supply chain improvement project. It is more suited to an ongoing improvement process than radical supply chain redesign.

How to use

The theory of constraints is an approach to business improvement that has captured the imagination of some managers. Through training, and often the involvement of an external change agent such as a consultant, these managers will lead business improvement projects. Advocates claim that it is a flexible method that can be used to attack almost any business problem effectively.

Goldratt (1990) outlines the main steps in the process of improvement using the theory of constraints:

Step 1: Identify the system's constraints. A constraint is anything that is preventing the organization from achieving its business development goals. Usually there are just three or four key constraints preventing the system from performing better. In general terms, these can be, for example, capacity, product quality or lead time.

Step 2: Having identified the system's constraints, there is no point in the non-constraining resources operating independently and at a higher performance level than the level at which the constraints will allow the whole system to operate. Thus the non-constraint resources should serve and supply the constraint resources. The second step is to identify how this can be done.

Step 3: Having identified how the non-constraint resources can serve and supply the constraint resources, the constraint resources take priority from now on, and all decisions regarding non-constraint resources are secondary to decisions and actions involving the constraints.

Step 4: Now is the time to consider how to 'break' the constraint by doing something about it, by making some improvement to the system. In the examples in step 1, solutions to a capacity problem might include working an extra shift or reducing downtime on a piece of equipment, whereas solutions to a product quality problem might include redesigning the product, refurbishing a piece of equipment or training operators in problem solving to identify and improve process quality themselves. Solutions to a lead-time problem might include reducing set-up times and batch sizes or increasing capacity.

Step 5: Clearly, if a constraint in one area or activity has been eased, then another area or activity becomes a constraint. Thus improvement is an ongoing process of identifying the next constraint and tackling it using the same steps. Thus we return to step 1.

Example

Case studies of successful implementations are available on the Goldratt Institute's website (see www.goldratt.com). Nike reports improving stock turns of socks from 2.3 to 7 within four months, and later to around 10, using the theory of constraints. Nike says that it did not change its IT systems or improve its forecasting but simply focused on the link between manufacturing and distribution. It was also able to reduce warehousing costs by $2 million per year and increase sales by 40 per cent during the peak season.

Reports from other companies are equally impressive and include improvements in on-time delivery, inventory reductions, increases in sales and reduced operating expense. *The Goal*, written by Goldratt, is certainly one of the most informative business books we have read and we recommend it as simple to understand and easy to read.

Further information

See http://www.goldratt.com/

References

Goldratt, E M (1990) *What Is This Thing Called Theory of Constraints and How Should It Be Implemented?* North River Press, New York

Goldratt, E M and Cox, J (1984) *The Goal*, North River Press, New York, now published by Gower Press

4.16 Time-based process mapping

Introduction

A number of methods exist for showing what happens over time: Gantt charts for example, but time-based process mapping aims to show movement of material or product through the supply chain over time. This forms the basis of an analysis to determine how and where time can be taken out of the supply chain to make it more responsive.

Removing time from the supply chain also removes inventory from the supply chain, thus reducing the amount of operating capital required to support the flow of materials and product from suppliers to final customers.

Time-based process mapping is one of a series of mapping techniques that can be used to analyse and improve supply chain operations. Others include value stream mapping, process mapping and relationship mapping.

When to use

This method can be used to demonstrate the movement of materials and product in the supply chain against time, with the purpose of identifying where time is wasted, thus resulting in excess inventory.

How to use

Time-based process mapping can be carried out at different levels. First, the main stages of the chain may be mapped against time, showing the flow of key raw materials through component production, to assembly and delivery or distribution to the final customer. Second, the time that each stage in the chain takes may be broken down into value-adding and non-value-adding time, or into its time-based components (moving, waiting, being processed, waiting for set-up, delayed by breakdown, etc).

Having plotted the time-based process map, questions must be asked about why each stage takes that time, what alternative methods or processes exist, or what problems must be solved for the time at that stage of the chain to be reduced.

Example

Let us consider the case of a product destined for a retail store that is assembled from a number of components. The assembler has sufficient knowledge of a key supplier's operations to include the timing of key stages there. Figure 4.11 shows these main stages on a time-based process map. Figure 4.12 shows some of the assembler's internal processes in more detail, breaking the key processes down into value-adding and non-value-adding time. We need to investigate the non-value-adding time.

FIGURE 4.11 Time-based process map

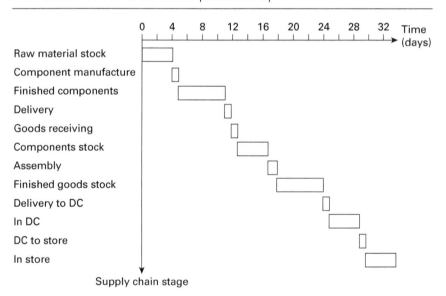

In this case, we might ask why component stock needs to be so high. Are some suppliers unreliable? Is customer demand completely unknown? We may also ask questions about the non-value-adding time in assembly. Can batch sizes be reduced? Would a better layout reduce movement time between operations?

FIGURE 4.12 Further detail of internal processes

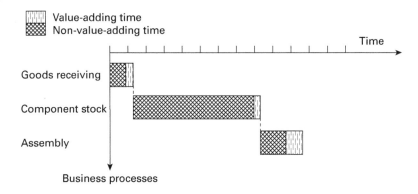

Other tools can now be used to investigate component stock and the high non-value-adding time in assembly, for example cause and effect analysis (tool 9.2), 5 Whys (tool 9.3) and flowcharts (tool 6.4).

Further information

Beesley, A (1997) Time compression in the supply chain, *Logistics Information Management*, **10** (6), pp 300–305

4.17 Time compression

Introduction

'Time is money!' is a phrase we hear so often, and it certainly applies in supply chain management. Every day that a product spends in the supply chain represents an amount of sunk operating capital, corresponding roughly to a day of sales. We talk easily of 'enough finished product stock to support sales for seven days'. If that finished stock could be reduced by just one day (and still be able to meet customer service targets), we could release the product cost component of a day's worth of sales, ie 'liberate' some operating capital.

Time compression methods aim to reduce lead time, be that production delivery or design lead time, by reviewing the tasks that are required and eliminating, changing or rescheduling those tasks. Liberation of operating capital is not the only benefit of reducing the time that product spends in the supply chain. Shorter lead times mean that production is closer to demand and can make more of what's selling well, or less of what is not selling, thus maximizing sales. Shorter lead times mean less storage is required, and fewer opportunities for obsolescence, damage and shrinkage of all kinds. Shorter design lead times mean that new technologies and materials can be incorporated into new products, and can reach the final customer before the competitors' products.

When to use

Whenever we see material queuing or waiting, we see operating capital tied up and time being wasted. This is true, for example, of work in progress queuing for a machine, or parcels waiting to be delivered and all product and material sitting in inventory. These are all candidates for time compression.

How to use

Time compression may be the objective of a major supply chain redesign or a small improvement project. For a major supply chain redesign, tools like SCOR® are used to plot flows or product from suppliers through all the stages of the supply chain to final customers. For a small improvement project, tools such as process mapping and layout diagrams may be created by a facilitated workshop to engage the people working in the area.

Ways of reducing the overall duration of a process or series of processes include:

- Reducing the process time, eg by improving the method such as using palm pilots to record stock quantities present, or using barcodes to identify a stock item being issued rather than keying in the item reference number.

- Carrying out two processes simultaneously – for example carrying out inspection and finishing operations on cars during the sea journey from one continent to another.

- Eliminating non-value-adding activities, eg eliminating correction of errors from a process by adding process control equipment to prevent the error occurring in the first place.

- Setting appropriate work priority rules so that the most important tasks are carried out first, especially where resources are shared.

Example

The stores area of a company carrying out servicing and maintenance of vehicles was also responsible for all goods receiving and dispatch. A disgruntled office employee observed that up to 48 hours could elapse between parcels being sent to the stores for dispatch and their actual removal off site by the carrier. Some of the parcels were parts being returned to the supplier and others were parts being sent to sister organizations. Complaints about delays in delivery were mounting up and came to a head.

An organization was brought in to run a time compression study, which included the stores operators taking part in a facilitated workshop focused on improving their way of working. A flowchart of the process used to receive and book in goods was created with the operators and analysed to minimize the effort and time required. A flowchart of the process used to dispatch goods was similarly streamlined. A 5S action plan (see tool 1.2) was carried out to reorganize the post room and set up clearly allocated areas for inbound goods, quarantine areas, holding areas, ready outbound goods and packing materials storage.

It was agreed that in future the carrier would collect parcels for dispatch three times a day. The lack of capacity of the stores operators to manage dispatch during busy periods resulted in training extra hands to help out with dispatch during these times, dispatch being less exacting than picking and issuing from stores. Priority rules were set up for the stores operators so that they knew when they should be working in dispatch or in the stores and when to call in the extra hands.

The overall result was that goods arriving were usually dealt with within an hour of arrival, and goods being dispatched usually left site within three hours of arriving in the post room. This had an impact on availability of product in the stores, cash flow in terms of credit from suppliers, and cash flow from customers of sister organizations that were able to complete their maintenance activities earlier than before.

Further information

Beesley, A (1997) Time compression in the supply chain, *Logistics Information Management*, **10** (6), pp 300–305

4.18 Calculating ordering cost

Introduction

Historically, ordering cost enabled some 'ideal' purchase quantity to be defined that minimized the total cost of stockholding and replenishment (see tool 3.11). Typically, 'ordering cost' was the total cost of replenishment, ie procurement, transport, goods receiving and inspection, and costs associated with returns or non-conformance. Today, we separate out from general overhead and other catch-all budgets all these supply chain costs so that better decisions can be made about movement of product through the supply chain. Here, we evaluate the cost of the procurement activity only, or average procurement cost per order because it is the most complex. The procurement function, like any other function, must look at the value it adds to the business against its own operating costs.

The costs of goods receiving and inspection may be taken as the time (eg, hours per week, month or year) spent on these activities multiplied by the hourly cost of employment of the person carrying out the task. Reducing the need for these activities, for example by making suppliers responsible for inspection before shipment, will result in a cost reduction. The costs associated with returns and non-conformance usually fall to the procurement function as they have to resolve the problems.

Procurement cost is also a base line against which to measure future reductions by means of 'soft orders' (electronic), blanket orders, longer contracts, VMI (see tool 3.17), grouping more items to fewer suppliers, etc.

When to use

It is not necessary to calculate procurement cost frequently but it is a useful exercise at the beginning of a supply chain management implementation project or supply chain cost reduction exercise. Thereafter, it can be reviewed every year or two.

Some small and medium-sized businesses outsource procurement to a specialist group in order to benefit from greater purchasing power. In this case, it is important to understand the internal procurement cost against the benefits and costs of external procurement.

How to use

As with any 'office-based' activity, the procurement function is embedded in the business and the costs of its activities are often divided between an operating budget for direct costs (salaries, expenses) and general overhead for indirect costs (telecommunications, IT systems, heating, lighting, etc).

The first stage is to complete Table 4.5 by obtaining as much data as possible from the accounting system and then making sensible estimates for the missing data. For example, heating cost can be estimated by taking the floor area occupied by the procurement function as a proportion of the total office floor area and using this as the proportion of total heating cost.

The second stage is to make use of this information by analysing the orders placed:

1 Calculate average cost per order placed (for use as a future comparator).

2 Carry out Pareto analysis to understand the spread of order cost and in particular the C orders – those 50 per cent of orders that likely account for 5 per cent of the total annual value of orders placed.

3 Carry out Pareto analysis based on number of order lines to find the C orders – those 50 per cent that have very few order lines.

4 Consider how these C orders can be reduced eg, by management credit cards, VMI, grouping items to fewer suppliers.

5 Consider the items on the B orders and look at where they are placed on the Kraljic matrix (see tool 4.6). Can they be moved to a more regular contract or agreement? Can the contract time be extended for some items?

6 Review the total procurement cost and cost per order.

(Table 4.5 can be downloaded as a template from http://howtologistics. com). In summary, a general expression of ordering cost against quantities delivered will not be obtained (as required for EOQ calculations) but total

TABLE 4.5 Cost data required to estimate total procurement cost

Category	Description	Estimated annual cost
Office space	Rental or depreciation	
	Taxes	
	General maintenance	
	Fire detection and extinction system	
	Office equipment – desks, chairs, etc	
	Insurance	
	Utilities – electricity, water, etc	
Office systems	Telecommunications	
	Computer hardware, software, support	
	Mobile phones	

(*Continued*)

TABLE 4.5 Cost data required to estimate total procurement cost (*Continued*)

Category	Description	Estimated annual cost
Direct employment costs	Salaries	
	Overtime	
	Agency costs	
Expenses	Staff cars	
	Transport, subsistence, accommodation costs	
	Training	
	Office consumables	
	Postal	
Cost of services consumed	Access control	
	Security	
	Fire system testing	
	Cleaning	
	Waste disposal	
Proportion of cost of shared functions	Legal	
	Personnel	
	Accounting	
	Inventory management	
	Production management	
	Transport	
	Logistics	
	Other	

procurement cost and average cost per order can be useful markers against which to measure progress in reducing operational costs during a project to improve supply chain or procurement efficiency.

Further information

Ordering cost is part of acquisition cost. See Burt *et al* (2003) or any comprehensive textbook on procurement or supply management for a further discussion: Burt, D N, Dobler, D W and Starling, S L (2003) *World Class Supply Management,* McGraw-Hill, New York.

4.19 How to calculate stockholding cost

Introduction

Calculating the costs associated with material flow, that is ordering, transport and stockholding costs, is one of the first stages in implementing supply chain management. It is essential to know these costs in order to make the best choice from among the many alternative options for procurement, transport, storage and warehousing.

For specialist transport or warehousing operations, it can be easy to access these costs. In other cases, they must be carefully separated out from overheads or shared facilities' costs. As a simple example, what is the cost of providing hardware, software and support for the computer system in the finished goods store of a factory? In this case, perhaps the number of terminals as a proportion of all terminals across the site might yield a proportion of system cost that could be allocated to the warehouse. This is just one element of a multitude of costs that must be added together to understand the real cost of holding stock.

When to use

Stockholding cost is part of the first stage of a supply chain management project. Recalculation every two to three years should suffice unless there are major changes to some of the factors.

How to use

Select a person to do this who is tenacious, capable of searching through cost data and making sensible estimates. Complete the template in Table 4.6 as far as possible and arrive at a total annual cost.

To this must be added the financial investment in the stock and, particularly, the loss to the business of having capital tied up in the stock. Some companies use lost opportunity cost for this; others use the bank interest rate.

Since the loss to the business of the financial value of the stock is usually expressed as a percentage of its value, it is common to express total stockholding cost as a percentage of the value of the stock rather than as a dollar/pound cost. Both figures are useful. The most important point is that a year-on-year reduction is sought, either as a reduction in the stock value or the cost of holding stock or both.

TABLE 4.6 Template for estimating annual stockholding cost

Category	Description	Estimated annual cost
Building	Rental or depreciation Taxes Maintenance Fire detection and extinction system Office equipment	

Storage	Depreciation of:
	    Racking
	    Shelving
	    Pallets, totes, boxes, etc	

Packaging consumables	Stretch wrap, bubble wrap, boxes, tape, etc	
Mechanical handling equipment (MHE)	Depreciation Fuel, tyres, lubricants,etc Maintenance	
Services	Utilities: water, gas, electricity, steam MHE maintenance and repair Pallet maintenance and repair Environmental control Pest control Access control Security Fire system testing Cleaning Waste disposal	
Systems and communications	Hardware Software System support Telephone/internet Staff mobile phones	

(*Continued*)

TABLE 4.6 Template for estimating annual stockholding cost
(*Continued*)

Category	Description	Estimated annual cost
Personnel	Full employment costs (salary plus overheads) Overtime Staff vehicles Training Personal protective equipment	
Safety/security	Insurance Special licences	
Stock losses	Spoilage/breakage Obsolescence Shrinkage: theft; errors in location, counting, issues from stock	
Costs of shared or relocated inventory	Transport to other sites Returns to supplier	
Proportion of cost of shared functions	Personnel Site maintenance Accounting Legal Project engineering Other	
	TOTAL:	

Some people say that if you have a warehouse, you might as well fill it! In supply chain thinking, we are always trying to reduce the amount of inventory (thus increasing stock turns). If this frees up part of the warehouse, then rent out that space to another business and receive some income for it. If you are renting the warehouse anyway, move to a smaller one.

Further categories of costs are shown in tool 8.1, activity-based costing. A comprehensive table can be downloaded as a template from http://howtologistics.com

Further information

A good description of the elements of stockholding cost can be found in any good textbook on supply chain management, logistics or warehousing, for example: *Strategic Logistics Management* by J R Stock and D M Lambert, published by McGraw-Hill, 2001.

4.20 Sales and Operations Planning (S&OP)

Introduction

For many people, S&OP is just a module in the Enterprise Resource Planning (ERP) system or process to balance future demand and supply but research into top-performing companies has shown that a good S&OP process is an important element of supply chain and business success. On a rolling basis, S&OP provides a continuously renewed coherent plan that is created jointly and followed by the supply functions (procurement and production) and demand (sales and distribution) functions. The plan states how much will be produced and sold over the coming months. Involving Finance supplies the confidence that the plan is feasible, and that the cash and profit implications are understood. The critical success factor is that all functions involved take ownership of the plan and contribute to its maintenance and execution. In large companies with multiple sites, product families and markets, S&OP may be carried out at site level as well as at regional and corporate levels. Achieving a good balance between sales and production ensures that customer demands are met with minimum inventory and greatest production efficiency.

Using S&OP for demand and supply balancing is beneficial at the operational level. However, the S&OP can provide an effective cross-functional forum for discussion of future business shape and performance. Conducted at the most senior levels, this form of S&OP provides an important tactical and strategic vehicle for business management. Sometimes the higher level planning is called Integrated Business Planning, to distinguish it.

Quantities are usually expressed per product family in broad brush terms, in whatever units have common meaning in the business, eg tonnes, dollars, square metres, millions of units and so on. Depending on the sector, the horizon can be one to five years (ideally 18 months or longer).

Having agreed the plan, it then becomes the basis for more detailed capacity planning, materials forecasting, the procurement budget, recruitment (if necessary), and other plans that ensure that the overall plan is executed.

When to use

S&OP is necessary when the company's products are sufficiently complex or numerous to warrant a higher level process than a master production schedule (MPS). However, S&OP can still be valuable in smaller organizations in developing a shared business plan and a forward-looking view of the company.

How to use

The following steps are carried out in each monthly cycle:

1 Supply side progress against the current plan is monitored using a group of key performance indicators (KPIs) including supplier performance, procurement expenditure, production volumes, stocks, percentage achievement of plan, production costs, etc.

2 Sales progress against the current plan is monitored using a group of KPIs including sales volumes, revenue, percentage achievement of plan, delivery achievement to customers, service levels achieved, etc.

3 The Sales function updates the demand forecast and makes this available to the Production and Supply Chain functions. Note that good forecast accuracy is critical for realistic S&OP (see tools 4.2 and 4.3). Product launches, promotions, new market entries or other non-routine events are flagged up.

4 Taking into account projected available inventory in future and safety stock requirements, the Production function updates the production forecast. Major changes in capacity (shutdowns, new/ closing facilities, etc) are flagged up.

5 The Supply Chain function reviews the sourcing requirement and flags up any potential problems.

6 The demand (sales) and supply (procurement and production) forecasts are then used as the basis for a number of sub-calculations, carried out either by the S&OP module in the ERP system or in Excel, including:

- revenue forecast

- production cost forecast

- feasibility of obtaining all parts and materials in time by using macro-bills of material, ie the most critical items due to long lead times or other market difficulties

- estimation of the labour workload and the capacity required on the most heavily loaded machines by using macro-routings, ie operations on bottleneck and near-bottleneck workstations

- proposing alternative scenarios if production and supply cannot be balanced, for example products may need to be allocated to customers or markets if capacity is constrained

- procurement budget forecast and cash flow projections.

7 Supply chain analytics may be used to spot trends, identify cause and effect links and hence enhance the information available during S&OP decision making.

8 An S&OP information pack is created and circulated to the managers of the key functions involved. Each manager prepares for the monthly S&OP meeting, which may require some extra preparation on potential solutions if problems are anticipated. A cover sheet using traffic light indicators allows focus on areas that need attention.

9 The team discusses the results of the sub-calculations and adjustments are made until final agreement is reached between all parties on a feasible and coherent S&OP. The S&OP is then used as the basis for MPS. Once a management team becomes familiar with the S&OP process, it has been found that it is more efficient to focus on exceptions and key issues rather than going through every detail of the plan each month.

10 The team executes the plan and monitors its progress. Any serious deviations are investigated and logged for future learning. Thus the cycle recommences.

Example

Wacker Polymers (see URL below) has made available a slide set that explains its S&OP process. The plan covers the next 18 months and is updated monthly on a rolling basis. It enables the business strategy to be realized and resources to be planned. The plan is expressed in dollar terms and also units.

Using 18 month forecasts, first the demand plan is reviewed, then the supply plan. The supply plan is then agreed and used as the basis for the revenue forecast, procurement planning, production and distribution plans, and financial and sales planning.

In consequence of better S&OP, improvements have been seen in four key measures: improved forecast accuracy, improved adherence to production schedules, reduction in inventory days of supply (stock cover) and improved financial forecast accuracy. The process seems to be working so well that S&OP meetings have become boring – a sign of success!

Further information

Propokets (2012) and Iyengar and Gupta (2013) give good introductions to S&OP. Wallace and Stahl present a comprehensive guide to sales and operations planning. Ling *et al* provide a good overview of S&OP deployment to drive business performance and its use in more complex business environments. They also provide a means of assessing the maturity of S&OP use in a company.

Wacker Polymers presentation can be found at: http://fr.slideshare.net/guestdd5f19/ executive-sop-case-study-gpseg-1915590

References

Iyengar, C and Gupta, S (2013) Building blocks for successful S&OP, *Supply Chain Management Review*, November, pp 10–17

Ling, D, Coldrick, A, Bissell, B and Whitewood, D (2010) *Breakthrough Sales & Operations Planning*, Touchmark Publishing, Tukwila, WA

Propokets, L (2012) *S&OP: What you can learn from the top performers*, *Supply Chain Management Review*, May/June, pp 28–35

Wallace, T F and Stahl, R A (2008) *Sales and Operations Planning: The how-to handbook*,T. F. Wallace and Company, Montgomery, OH

4.21 Omni-channel distribution

Introduction

Armed with mobile technology, today's consumers want to be able to make purchases quickly and simply, no matter where they are. That's why retailers must offer customers all manner of ways to place orders and be able to subsequently process them intelligently and efficiently. Furthermore, the returns process has to be as slick if not better, to ensure consumers receive their money back promptly and, from an operational perspective, the goods are back on sale as quickly as possible.

Retailers are looking to move away from multi-channel retailing where each buying stream is separated, to omni-channel retailing where they are utilizing all the available channels to provide a consistent brand experience that in turn can lead to a more efficient operation. According to Streatfield

(2014) sales growth in an omni-environment comes through ease of consumer access, better informed choices and enhanced customer services. Stock visibility across all the channels and the ability to choose the most cost-effective dispatch location – DC, fulfilment centre, store, supplier – will improve efficiency and safeguard margins. To enable companies to see at a glance how well organized their omni-channel fulfilment is, Supply Chain Movement and Manhattan Associates has developed a self-assessment model.

When to use

This tool enables companies to see, at a glance, where they are in terms of their capability for omni-channel fulfilment.

How to use

Retailers need to answer two groups of questions on 'Customer friendliness and convenience' and 'Fulfilment competence'. The answers to the questions will place the company within the grid in Figure 4.13. Example questions include the following:

Customer friendliness and convenience

- Can consumers choose between several delivery options (locations, time windows, transport)?
- Can consumers select an express option (collect from a store within a couple of hours)?

Fulfilment competence

- Does the company have various stock-holding points for deliveries (DC, supplier, stores, in transit, etc)?
- Does the company have real-time insight into all types of stock (available stock, allocated stock, etc)?

Scores are allocated for each 'yes' answer and the total for each question group determines the position of your company on the grid (for example the position indicated in segment 3).

Segment 1

Your customers have little or no choice about where and when they order; it is decided for them. The product range is limited and takes hardly any account of customer preferences. The method of supply is still very traditional. In fact, you are still operating much as a traditional market trader (bottom left).

FIGURE 4.13 Omni-channel fulfilment capability

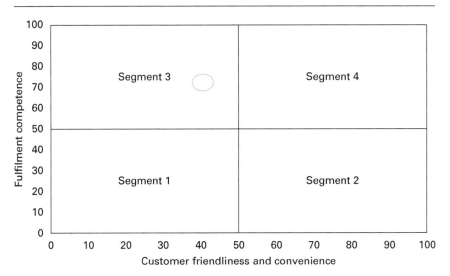

Segment 2

You are very customer focused and listen carefully to their specific needs. You are very flexible in responding to consumer demands. Your product range can be adapted easily, but is not unlimited. The delivery possibilities are limited to just a couple of traditional methods. You can be compared with a classic tailor (bottom right).

Segment 3

You offer considerable choice with a large product range. Customers have a reasonable amount of flexibility regarding the time of day that they can place orders. How you process their orders is still fairly traditional; the various sales channels are not aligned. Your company can be compared with a traditional department store (top left).

Segment 4

Your company is definitely moving with the times by offering an extensive product range tailored to customer needs at all manner of locations, from which customers can order at any time they wish. You also make full and innovative use of the internet and social media. You offer very diverse and flexible delivery and return options including click and collect and timed deliveries. Your company really is an omni-channel store (top right).

The full questionnaire can be found at www.supplychainmovement.com/self-assessment-model-for-omni-channel-fulfilment/. The self-assessment model for omni-channel fulfilment by Supply Chain Movement and Manhattan Associates is at http://www.supplychainmovement.com/

References

Hewitt, M (2014) Are omni-channel returns your weakest link?, *Logistics and Transport Focus,* **16** (9), pp 46–7
Streatfield, P (2014) Omni-channel retailing: a journey driven by disruptive change, *Logistics and Transport Focus,* **16** (9), pp 38–43

4.22 Strategic procurement

Introduction

Strategic procurement is the result of a major evolution of the purchasing function over the last 30 or so years. The name acknowledges the strategic importance of good procurement practices. Depending on the sector, the function is involved in 70–90 per cent of company expenditure (ie, just about anything that is not salaries or depreciation) and a business of any size would do well to make sure that its expenditure is funnelled through the procurement function as far as possible.

A good proportion of this expenditure is supply chain-related and effective procurement is an important element of supply chain management. It is critical that supply chain management, and hence procurement, has board level representation.

When to use

Many companies can improve their procurement practices and this tool is intended to give you some insight into how strategic procurement can help your business.

How to use

Use this tool to review the procurement activity in your business. If you would like know more about these ideas, shown in Table 4.7, see the further information section.

TABLE 4.7 Some of the best practices which form strategic procurement

What	What is involved
Analysis of purchased items	Set up families of similar items Use ABC Pareto analysis to identify items and families in each class Set up appropriate procurement strategy for each item/family according to its importance ie, aim to spend more time on the most important or valuable items (see tool 4.6)
Category management	Divide up the purchased equipment, services and materials into logical 'categories' which are then allocated to individual procurement professionals. These category managers then develop specialist knowledge of the supply market. This is particularly useful for centralized procurement of A and B items (see below). It also prevents duplication, inefficiency or vendor proliferation in large organizations with multiple sites/countries
Supplier selection	Set up clear procedures for selecting suppliers depending on importance and value of item, involving users where appropriate, including technical and quality assessments, financial stability, transport options, delivery reliability, ability to contribute to new product development Look at the local, national, regional and worldwide supply markets as appropriate
Minimum number of suppliers	Choose suppliers that the business wants to work with rather than the 'best' supplier for each individual item. The business works to ensure good performance from those suppliers is achieved across a wider range of items. A number of different functions could be involved as well as procurement eg, quality, production planning, transport
Supplier status range	Suppliers may be approved, preferred, lead, sole supplier etc. Set up appropriate supplier relationships (tool 4.11)
Supplier management	Provide close or real-time links with suppliers through access to Extranet, a platform or portal, to share forecast demand, order history, recorded delivery performance and in some cases actual sales information (eg, EPOS)

(*Continued*)

TABLE 4.7 Some of the best practices which form strategic procurement (*Continued*)

What	What is involved
Communication with suppliers	Visit suppliers periodically (depending on location and importance of supplier), and give them regular feedback on performance eg, through platform or portal as above Communication could also include participation in joint workshops regarding problem solving, new product development, closer cooperation on planning and forecasting, etc
Total cost of acquisition	In addition to the invoiced amount, take into account the cost of transport, cost of rejects, administrative effort required to work with this supplier, training, commissioning, consumables, etc
Lifetime cost of equipment	In addition to the invoiced amount for equipment, take into account the installation, commissioning, operating and maintenance costs, shipping and packaging, spare parts requirements, consumables, training, etc
Cooperation with key user functions	Remember that procurement 'serves' internal users and can only do this effectively by being involved as early as possible in development projects such as new products, new facilities, etc. This may require engaging with user departments to explain the role of procurement and the value they add to the business
Supply market monitoring	Keep up to date with the main players and new developments in the supply markets for key items and families
Supply chain risk analysis	Carry out periodic risk assessments on key suppliers, major items, new projects, etc
Information management	Use an appropriate module or package eg, SAP Ariba
Centralization vs decentralization	Use ABC analysis to set policy for centralized or decentralized procurement of different items or categories eg, centralized procurement for A and B items/families and C items where aggregated demand across all branches or sites or countries makes it worthwhile

Example

A procurement professional was appointed to a small business to take over all the procurement activity that had previously been handled by the Managing Director (MD) and his assistant. The MD made the decisions and the assistant executed them. While the MD could claim that company expenditure was being carefully controlled, this did not mean that procurement was being handled analytically or in the best long-term interests of the company.

The procurement professional immediately started analysing the item catalogue, set up families, identified different purchasing approaches for the different families, formalized a supplier database and reviewed all purchase orders (POs) placed over the previous 12 months. The majority of POs were individual transactions, many to the same companies. Supply agreements were set up with key suppliers with forecasts of aggregated demand.

After a couple of years of reviewing and renewing the supplier base, the purchasing budget had reduced by nearly 15 per cent, supplier performance had increased and production shortages severely reduced (thus reducing the amount of time spent on expediting).

As a rule of thumb, we can say that a procurement professional can reduce the cost of purchases by about 10 per cent over two years if the expenditure has not yet been analysed methodically. Thereafter, year on year reductions of 3–5 per cent can be expected depending on the sector. This is not about 'squeezing' suppliers nor is it about 'switching and baiting'. It is about choosing good and reliable suppliers, especially for key items, setting appropriate working relationships with them, securing supplies where the supply market is difficult, working closely and cooperatively with internal user functions and involving suppliers in future projects.

Further info

See www.cips.org for all matters regarding procurement, training, industry news, events, etc; www.purchasingchessboard.com identifies 64 methods from ATKearney's experience that reduce cost and increase value with suppliers.

The following standard textbooks are highly recommended (for UK and the United States):

Baily, P, Farmer, D, Jessop, D and Jones, D (2005) *Purchasing Principles and Management,* FT Prentice Hall, Harlow (UK)

Lysons, K and Farrington, B (2006) *Purchasing and Supply Management,* FT Prentice Hall, Harlow (UK)

Burt, D, Dobler, D and Starling, S (2004) *World Class Supply Management,*
    McGraw-Hill, New York (USA)
Monczka, R, Handfield, R, Giunipero, L, Patterson, J and Waters, D (2009)
    Purchasing and Supply Chain Management, South-Western, Mason, OH (USA)

4.23 Supply Chain Strategy, by Julian Amey

Introduction

Twenty years ago companies developed manufacturing strategies or, in some cases, operations strategies. It is now recognized that while manufacturing can be an important capability, the company really needs an effective supply chain strategy. This recognizes the shift that many companies have made from being pure 'manufacturers' to ones with more complex sourcing arrangements and that customers, products and markets are what drive company performance. Indeed, certain experts would say that companies now compete on their supply chains, necessitating a clear well formulated and executed supply chain strategy.

The supply chain strategy must be created to support the company's (or business unit's) strategy and commercial ambition. Developing the supply chain strategy requires a clear understanding of customer and market requirements, the products and services that need to be delivered and how the company competes and delivers value to its customers.

The strategy must be forward looking. Although it may seek to address current performance issues, it must consider the future needs of the company and the supply chain (eg, what product launches are required, what the cost and cash pressures are, in what markets expansion or contraction will occur, how the company's operating or selling model may need to change). This is necessary because of the likely time that it will take for some facets of the strategy to be implemented. An effective strategy will install the necessary capabilities ahead of their requirement in order to create a leading organization.

A supply chain strategy can have many dimensions and areas to address. These could include:

- Supply chain performance in areas such as customer service and inventory.
- Sourcing arrangements and supply chain configuration/re-configuration: asset strategy, make vs buy, supply base.
- Geographical reach: customer base, supply base, logistics services.

- Product portfolio: new product introduction, product divestments, product lifecycle-driven changes.

- Cost and cash pressures.

- People: skills and talent development, recruitment, organization development.

- Operating model changes: global vs regional vs local, value adding service offerings.

- Technology: manufacturing capabilities, technology transfer.

- Processes and systems: streamlining or harmonizing processes, information management capabilities.

- Infrastructure.

There is the temptation to put too much into the strategy. This should be avoided. It is important to be realistic and focus on the crucial elements that will deliver the most benefit or the changes most critical to future success. Typically a good strategy should be simple and clear with a number of key principles or messages. A simple focused strategy is easier to communicate and to gain buy-in than a complex one. It is also more likely to be implementable.

The strategy should not be seen as a document. To add value, the strategy needs to be implemented. This will require good project management and communication.

When to use

A company should always have a valid and up-to-date supply chain strategy. Because of the pace of change of business conditions and competitive environments, the strategy should be reviewed at least annually and will probably require revision every three years, the likely time horizon for implementation of the previous edition.

How to use

The supply chain strategy must be developed in consultation and collaboration with other functions in the company. Key amongst these will be:

- Research and Development – to understand the future product/service portfolio and plans for new product introduction.

- Sales and Marketing – to understand the commercial plans, long-term forecasts and geographical ambitions.

- Finance – to understand the financial imperatives and constraints (eg, cash flow, profitability, tax).

As part of the strategy's development, a business case should be created since the strategy is likely to involve change. Resources will be needed to effect the change. Hence the business case should justify the effort and resources required. A strong financial case will also generate commitment within the business towards implementation.

Implementation of the strategy will not happen by accident. Effective project management with a clear plan is essential.

Example: AstraZeneca

Following the merger of the pharmaceutical companies Astra and Zeneca in 1999, an Operations strategy was generated that focused on the immediate issues of company integration and the imperative of launching major new products. In 2001, the strategy was radically revised to become a supply chain strategy that addressed issues of poor customer service and high inventories through:

- implementation of lean and demand-driven supply to reduce lead time and improve efficiencies to provide capacity headroom for new products without major capital investments;
- lifecycle management of products;
- greater emphasis on outsourcing;
- shifting the focus of the Operations from being a manufacturing organization to one focused on customer service and supply.

Implementation of the strategy debottlenecked supply of certain products leading to increased sales, reduced inventory by circa $500 million and raised customer service levels to >99 per cent. In consequence, Operations' reputation was enhanced and it was seen as a great place to work.

Following attrition in the company's new product portfolio leading to absence of the expected product launches and confronted by impending patent expiries of a number of major brands, in 2006 the strategy was revised to:

- place more aggressive focus on the continued implementation of lean supporting a continued drive to reduce cost of goods;
- full end-to-end supply chain management by organization realignment and implementation of advanced planning systems to provide full supply chain visibility;

- inventory optimization to free up cash for investment in licensing opportunities;
- stronger regional focus to align with the sales organization;
- shifting the geographical footprint to align with future growth in emerging markets; and
- much greater focus on outsourcing to avoid significant capital investments and manage risk.

Further information

More information can be found in:

Chopra, S (2015) *Supply Chain Management: Global edition: strategy, planning, and operation,* Pearson, Harlow

Christopher, M (2005) *Logistics and Supply Chain Management,* FT Prentice Hall, Harlow

Hill, T (1993) *Manufacturing Strategy,* Macmillan, London

Slack, N, Brandon-Jones, A and Johnston, R (2013) *Operations Management,* Pearson, Harlow

Outsourcing tools

5.1 Outsourcing

Introduction

Outsourcing is about recognizing a task or process that isn't your organization's core competence and getting a third party to operate it more efficiently and hopefully more cost-effectively. There are many models to guide companies through the process of determining whether to outsource, how to go about outsourcing and how to ensure that the implementation is successful.

We have looked at a number of different models and combined the best elements of each to ensure a complete end-to-end process. We have also simplified the model and taken into account the likely benefits and barriers to outsourcing.

When to use

There are many situations when a company needs to evaluate whether outsourcing logistics can be a fundamental part of an ongoing strategy. This model enables the company to assess its current situation and decide whether to outsource or not. Part two of the model (Figure 5.3) provides a methodology for outsourcing and implementation.

How to use

Before tackling the main model, there is a simplified version produced by Kate Vitasek *et al* (2010) which can be seen in Figure 5.1.

FIGURE 5.1 Simple outsourcing decision model

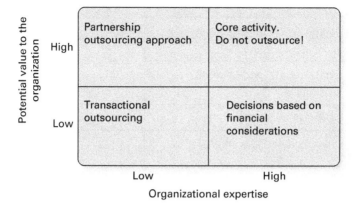

Main model

At each stage in the model there are a number of questions that need to be discussed, the answers to which will, in part, determine the next steps (Table 5.1). We aren't always going to get absolute yes and no answers; however, there is likely to be a preference one way or the other. If it is a genuine 'don't know', you will need to undertake further work. The term 'logistics' can be replaced by any other function in the company, such as facilities management, IT, procurement, customer service, etc. (A printed version of the questionnaire can be downloaded for free from http://howtologistics.com)

TABLE 5.1 The outsourcing decision matrix

	Don't know	Yes	No
Current situation			
Is logistics a core activity within our business (define what is 'core')?		R	O
Is logistics critical to our business?		R	O
Do we have the expertise (core competence) internally?		R	O
Do we compare favourably against our competitors in logistics terms?	BM	R	O
Does our logistics operation give us differentiation?		R	O
Are we able to leverage economies of scale within the operation?		R	O

(Continued)

TABLE 5.1 The outsourcing decision matrix (*Continued*)

	Don't know	Yes	No
Are there internal political reasons for retaining an in-house operation?		R	O
Do we have sufficient capital to fund a logistics operation?		R	O
Are we a risk-averse company?		R	O
Do we worry about losing control of a key activity?		R	O
Does operating our logistics give us greater flexibility?		R	O
Is there a likelihood of a loss of crucial expertise if we outsource?		R	O
Do we have sufficient wider market knowledge?		R	O
Can outsourcing threaten our corporate image?		R	O
Are we able to manage industrial relations issues internally?		R	O
Feasibility of outsourcing			
Is the availability of suitable suppliers a problem?		R	O
Is comprehensive market and product knowledge essential for our business?		R	O
Do we have greater capability than the potential suppliers?		R	O
Are there constraints to outsourcing (list constraints), eg • Legal, eg TUPE (EU law, Transfer of Undertakings, Protection of Employment) • Existing leases on buildings and equipment • Unionized environment?		R	O

TABLE 5.1 The outsourcing decision matrix *(Continued)*

	Don't know	Yes	No
Is our logistics operation very complicated?		R	O
Are there likely to be technological issues with outsourcing?		R	O
Are there confidentiality and security issues with outsourcing logistics?		R	O
Do we have problems finding suppliers with the right cultural fit?		R	O
Do we have the capability and expertise to undertake value-adding services?		R	O
Cost and service			
Are service levels likely to decline if we outsource?	BM	R	O
Are costs likely to increase if we outsource?	BM	R	O

O = Consider Outsourcing strongly

R = Retain in-house and optimize performance

BM = Benchmark (see tool 7.6)

Follow the suggestion indicated by the majority of yes and no answers. There may be a requirement to undertake a benchmarking exercise to fully assess the current logistics operation and examine the feasibility of outsourcing. If the majority of the answers point towards outsourcing, we need to follow a process to ensure that it runs smoothly (see Figure 5.2).

Further information

There are numerous books to choose from on logistics outsourcing. Kate Vitasek *et al*'s book on vested outsourcing takes us away from traditional outsourcing to more collaborative relationships: Vitasek, K, Ledyard, M and Manrodt, K (2010) *Vested Outsourcing: Five rules that will transform outsourcing*, Palgrave Macmillan, New York.

FIGURE 5.2 Stages of an outsourcing process

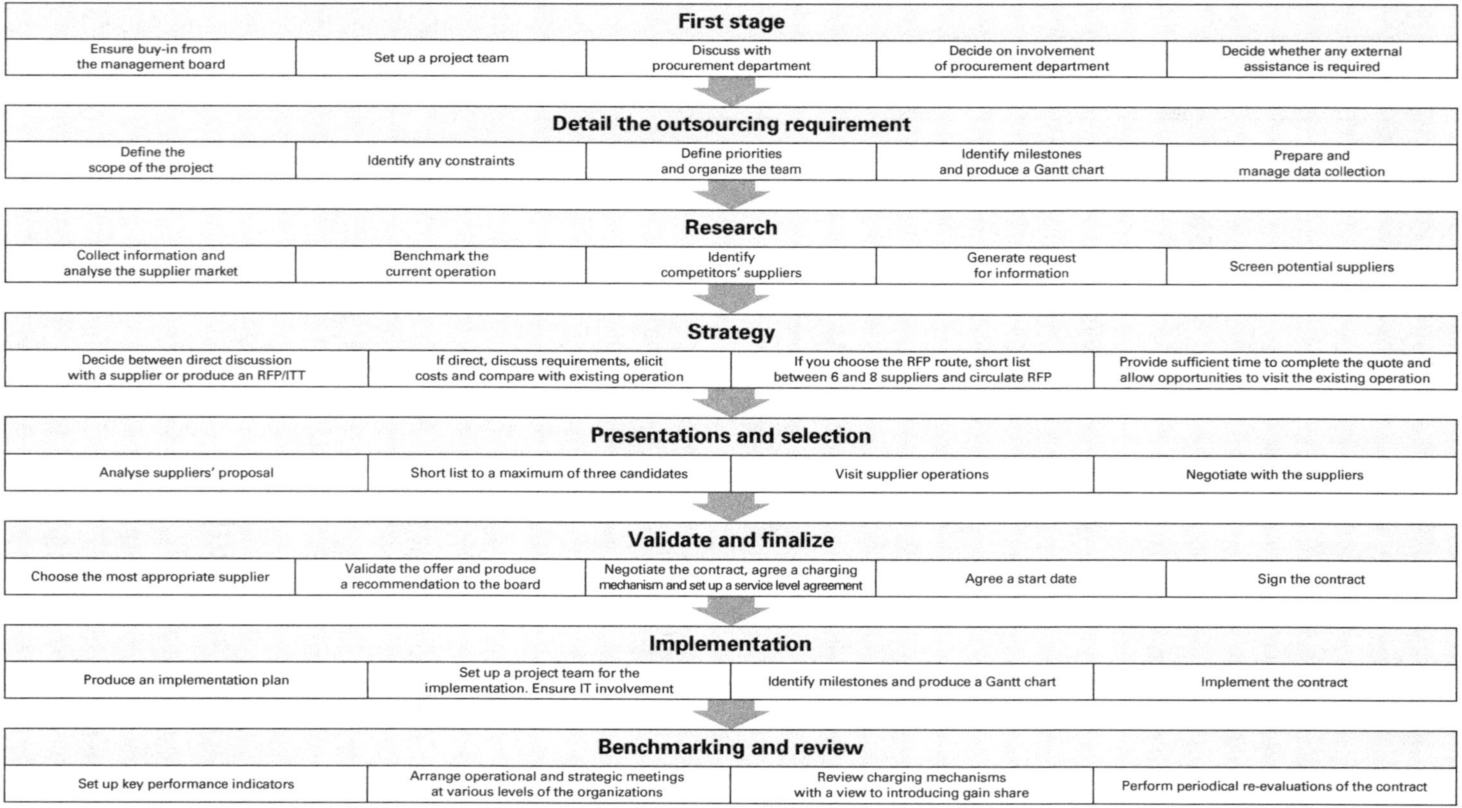

First stage
- Ensure buy-in from the management board
- Set up a project team
- Discuss with procurement department
- Decide on involvement of procurement department
- Decide whether any external assistance is required

Detail the outsourcing requirement
- Define the scope of the project
- Identify any constraints
- Define priorities and organize the team
- Identify milestones and produce a Gantt chart
- Prepare and manage data collection

Research
- Collect information and analyse the supplier market
- Benchmark the current operation
- Identify competitors' suppliers
- Generate request for information
- Screen potential suppliers

Strategy
- Decide between direct discussion with a supplier or produce an RFP/ITT
- If direct, discuss requirements, elicit costs and compare with existing operation
- If you choose the RFP route, short list between 6 and 8 suppliers and circulate RFP
- Provide sufficient time to complete the quote and allow opportunities to visit the existing operation

Presentations and selection
- Analyse suppliers' proposal
- Short list to a maximum of three candidates
- Visit supplier operations
- Negotiate with the suppliers

Validate and finalize
- Choose the most appropriate supplier
- Validate the offer and produce a recommendation to the board
- Negotiate the contract, agree a charging mechanism and set up a service level agreement
- Agree a start date
- Sign the contract

Implementation
- Produce an implementation plan
- Set up a project team for the implementation. Ensure IT involvement
- Identify milestones and produce a Gantt chart
- Implement the contract

Benchmarking and review
- Set up key performance indicators
- Arrange operational and strategic meetings at various levels of the organizations
- Review charging mechanisms with a view to introducing gain share
- Perform periodical re-evaluations of the contract

References

McIvor, R (2000) A practical framework for understanding the outsourcing process, *Supply Chain Management*, 5 (1), pp 22–36

Richards, G (2014) *Warehouse Management*, 2nd edn, Kogan Page, London

5.2 To 4PL or not to 4PL

Introduction

The decision to outsource your logistics operations is difficult enough, but then you have to decide what type of organization to place the contract with – third-party logistics providers (3PL), lead logistics providers (LLP) or fourth-party logistics providers (4PL©)?

In terms of definitions, 3PLs will utilize solely their own resources on the contract. Lead logistics providers will utilize their own assets and those of others to operate the contract, whereas, according to Accenture, which came up with the name, 'A 4PL© is an integrator that assembles the resources, capabilities, and technology of its own organization and other organizations to design, build and run comprehensive supply chain solutions.' A true 4PL© has the following attributes:

- non-asset owning company – in terms of warehouses and trucks;
- sophisticated IT systems;
- a strategist that manages all logistics operations on behalf of companies;
- is expected to provide the most cost-effective logistics systems to its clients;
- an intermediary between the shipper and the transport companies;
- develops contracts on behalf of the shipper with an optimum number of transport and warehousing providers.

Working with 4PLs© offers the following advantages:

- the ability to step back from the day-to-day operations to see the big picture;
- a neutral party looking to optimize your supply chain rather than their own assets;
- an ability to select the best 3PLs for the task required;
- an unbiased service;

- ability to instigate shared user transportation for clients;
- greater access to resources and greater flexibility;
- greater information flow through sophisticated supply chain systems;
- single point of contact;
- seamless key performance indicators;
- shared interest with customer, better view of whole market;
- payment by results options such as profit share schemes;
- a global reach in many circumstances.

The disadvantages are:

- reliant on partners to provide the service;
- profit on profit;
- reluctance on the part of 3PLs to work for 4PLs©;
- a confusing marketplace as to who are the true 4PLs©.

When to use

When reviewing your supply chain operation and your current outsourcing arrangements.

How to use

Table 5.2 is a straightforward yes or no questionnaire that will give you the opportunity to decide whether working with a 4PL© is right for your company.

TABLE 5.2   4PL© decision-making process

Question	Yes	No
Section 1		
1. Does your organization struggle to manage increasing levels of supply chain complexity?		
2. Do your customers' supply chain demands exceed your organization's capacity to deliver?		
3. Do you wish you had full visibility throughout your supply chain?		

(Continued)

TABLE 5.2 4PL© decision-making process (Continued)

Question	Yes	No
4. Would you like to have access to the technology capabilities to integrate processes and logistics providers across your supply chain?		
5. Can you make better use of your capital currently dedicated to supply chain assets such as staff and IT?		
6. Do you wish you had experienced supply chain managers within the company?		
7. Are you operating warehouses and manufacturing plants globally with little coordination between them?		
8. Are you looking to expand your business globally?		
9. Is neutrality and objectivity fundamental to your choice of logistics provider?		
10. Is your relationship with your suppliers and logistics providers adversarial?		
11. Is dealing with a multitude of logistics providers taking up too much management time?		
12. Are you under pressure from your customers to become more environmentally friendly, with an expected target of carbon neutrality?		
13. Are you happy to enter into a longer-term partnership?		
14. Are you happy to share resources with your competitors?		
15. Are you comfortable having 'all your eggs in one basket'?		
16. Do you want your logistics contracts to be based on a gain share/cost reduction basis?		
17. Are you looking for more than a task- or functionally-oriented logistics provider?		
Section 2		
A. Do you consider the supply chain critical to your organization's success?		

(Continued)

TABLE 5.2 4PL© decision-making process *(Continued)*

Question	Yes	No
B. Is supply chain management a core competency within your company?		
C. Is full control of your supply chain very important to you?		
D. Do you undertake regular supply chain reviews so as to improve efficiency and reduce costs?		
E. Do you have full visibility throughout your supply chain?		
F. Is the relationship with your current logistic providers important to you?		
G. Is neutrality and objectivity fundamental to your choice of logistics provider?		
H. Does your company have a policy against single supplier sourcing?		
I. Is having internal supply chain and logistics expertise important to you?		
J. Are you risk averse?		

If you have answered yes to the majority of the questions in Section 1, it is definitely worth considering 4PL© companies. If you answered yes to the majority of questions in Section 2, a 4PL© may not be a preferred option. (A printed version of the questionnaire can be downloaded for free from http://howtologistics.com).

Further information

This can be obtained from the book written by Paul Van den Brande: https://www.shopmybooks.com/BE/en/book/paul-van-den-brande/4pl-book-never-should-have-been-written (Van den Brande, P (2010) *4PL: The book that should never have been written,* Noble House Group)

Reference

Bade, D J and Mueller, J K (1999) New for the millennium: 4PL, *Transportation and Distribution,* 40 (2), pp 78–80

5.3 A risk-based approach to logistics outsourcing

Introduction

There are several iterations and stratifications of logistics and supply chain outsourcing solutions and the nature of the industry allows for bespoke service offerings, with an eagerness among service providers to avoid a one-size-fits-all solution, although a number of proposals are presented on that basis. A large number of customers of logistics service providers (LSPs) remain very pre-scriptive in their control of their LSPs and have an ongoing role in managing the outsourced relationship. It is also not always clear what degree of risk each service offering entails for the customer and the service provider.

A risk-based approach

This approach is illustrated in Figure 5.3, which describes a pyramid of out-sourcing solutions, balancing them with the degree of control and risk inherent to the parties involved.

FIGURE 5.3 Control vs risk of outsourced solutions

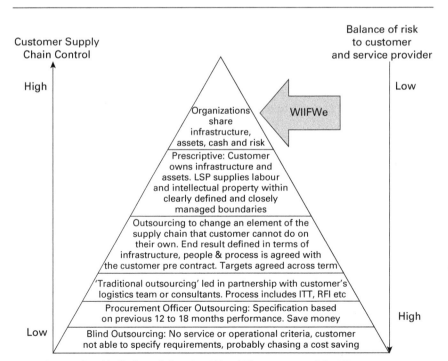

SOURCE: reproduced by kind permission of Dr Richard Gibson, Yusen Logistics UK

At the base of the pyramid lies 'buying' the *blind outsourcing* decision, where customers aspire to a better state of affairs and see outsourcing as a route to a better way of working. There are few or no criteria and the solution is left to the incoming service provider; the balance of risk is high for both parties in the absence of agreed success criteria. In this environment the LSP may encounter a dynamic environment with a high degree of scope drift and this poses a significant risk to any long-term commercial arrangement.

The next step on the pyramid is *procurement officer outsourcing*, which is focused on saving money using performance over the previous 12 to 18 months as a benchmark from which to make logistics procurement decisions. This commoditization of logistics procurement does not rely on a high degree of ongoing control from the customer supply chain team, if indeed there is one in situ. There is a high risk that this purchase will move to another provider at the end of the contract term, and this is not a basis for the long-term success of such an agreement.

Traditional outsourcing is the tried and tested formula developed in the post-World War II era. The familiarity with the process and pitfalls ranks this element a medium risk to the customer and service provider and requires a medium level of supply chain control on behalf of the customer. Concepts such as 3PL, LLP, 4PL© and 5PL sit in this element.

The next step on the pyramid is using *outsourcing to change an element of the supply chain;* this is when the activity moves from functional to transformational and warrants a higher degree of control from the customer. Because this is transformational outsourcing, it may be assumed that it will be part of the customer's overall supply chain management strategy, with clearly defined objectives. The service provider becomes a means to an end with a specific remit and timescale to follow as it executes part of the customer-driven project.

The *prescriptive* step sees the balance of power in the longer-term relationship moving from the service provider to the customer. Requiring a greater degree of control, the customer typically owns the infrastructure and assets, while the service provider supplies labour and intellectual property within clearly defined and closely managed boundaries. The customer benefits from having a service provider for short-term flexibility in other parts of its supply chain and for speedy supply chain access to new markets as well as territories. This step is very much a master–servant relationship and because it is prescriptive, the balance of risk to both the customer and service provider is low.

The top segment of the pyramid moves the relationship into an equity-sharing arrangement, where both organizations *share* assets, cash and risk in delivering the supply chain solution. Customer and supplier are locked in a mutual arrangement with a common suite of brand delivery objectives. The behaviour set exhibited by both may be described as 'what's in it for we' (WIIFWe) (Vitasek *et al*, 2010).

The model links some iterations of outsourced logistics service provision with the degree of control expected from the customer and a risk of engagement profile for the logistics service provider.

Summary

The pyramid in Figure 5.3 may be used to define and assess the risk profile of a logistics outsourcing strategy. The risk is defined in terms of 'low to high' for the parties involved; it looks at the process as a whole and is thus not blinkered to one point of view. The optimal relationship is balanced between both parties and demonstrates a WIIFWe set of behaviours.

Reference

Vitasek, K, Ledyard, M and Manrodt, K (2010) *Vested Outsourcing: Five rules that will transform outsourcing*, Palgrave Macmillan, New York

5.4 Supply chain and logistics outsourcing

Introduction

The Supply Chain Satellite is a strategy assessment tool developed by a group of logistics professionals and academics (see www.supplychainsatellite. com). They have combined their specialist experience to develop a framework for logistics outsourcing. The tool consists of a detailed questionnaire, a sophisticated scoring model and an in-depth analysis covering all possible logistics outsourcing strategies. Based on your answers you will be provided with an analysis of your current situation and the best-in-class strategy towards outsourcing logistics activities.

When to use

When reviewing your supply chain strategy and when contemplating outsourcing all or part of your logistics and supply chain operation.

How to use

The online questionnaire can be found at www.supplychainsatellite.com. Once completed your answers will be scored, weighted and subsequently plotted into the Outsourcing Strategy Assessment model. The model consists of two axes, x and y, that form the basis of your position.

X. Added value of your supply chain

This axis measures the extent to which your supply chain and specifically your logistics process adds value to your product. It determines whether, and to what extent, differentiation of your logistics processes can impact your competitive position. Indirectly this axis also measures the impact of logistics on your bottom line since a differentiated logistics model will justify higher margins.

Y. Complexity of your supply chain

This axis forms the unit of measure for the complexity of your logistics operation. It measures how easy it is to standardize your logistics processes. It is a fundamental factor that highly influences the type of relationship you will have with a logistics service provider. The four segments shown in Figure 5.4 are discussed below.

FIGURE 5.4 Supply Chain Satellite matrix

1. Price buyer

Cost containment in the logistics chain is your main objective. You have limited or no need for the highly specialized logistics competences of the 3PL. This makes it easy for you to select a provider. You make sure you know the cost leaders among the LSPs and develop relations with them in each geographical market.

Minimizing the logistics cost as part of the final selling price of your product represents an important source of competitive advantage. It can lower the price for which you can offer your product to the end user, or improve your margin. The logistics operation should contribute to these objectives but does not, in itself, impact the perceived value of your products.

2. Do it yourself

You do not outsource or hardly outsource any logistics activities and have no need to develop relations with LSPs. Because of your highly customized handling and shipping requirements you have custom-built these capabilities yourself. Other reasons for your situation could be that you are locked into an insourced logistics operation. Reorganization costs would outweigh the potential benefits of outsourcing. Alternatively, you could have had previous negative experiences with LSPs or you are sceptical about the true cost of outsourcing.

3. Expertise buyer

Your logistic activities are complex and you have a wide portfolio of products, suppliers and customers. Product lifecycles are short and you face critical time-to-market requirements in a volatile market. Logistics outsourcing in principle should be a long-term commitment to the LSP as this allows you to capitalize on continuous improvement and cost reduction. LSPs are selected on specialist expertise, technologies and assets and will be deployed in those parts of the supply chain where they bring substantial benefit.

4. Strategic partner

Your logistic activities are complex and of high strategic importance. You have a wide portfolio of products, suppliers and customers. Product lifecycles are short and you face critical time-to-market requirements in a volatile market. Your contracts with LSPs aim to facilitate long-term commitment. Together with your LSPs you work on a programme of continuous improvements in service levels, flexible delivery options, lead times, warehouse efficiency and eventually cost reduction.

Undecided

There is no or almost no conscious strategic approach. You either take conflicting approaches to the management of your logistics operations or you lack a clear approach. There can be many possible reasons for this lack of strategic direction. In a positive scenario you find yourself in a transitional period where a strategy is defined but far from implemented. Conflicting views within the supply chain function or in your company's strategic management can also cause logistics processes and improvement projects to even each other out and result in a status quo.

General management tools

6.1 Critical path analysis

Introduction

PERT (Programme Evaluation and Review Technique) and CPM (Critical Path Method) were developed in the 1950s and were responsible for saving many months in the duration of major projects by managing the timing and the order of implementation of tasks more efficiently. An important part of these techniques is identifying the critical path. This is the group of tasks that determines the overall duration of the project. If one of these activities runs over the planned time, the whole project will be completed late, unless further resources can be used to claw back the time lost. In practice, the 'near critical' tasks are also monitored closely, ie those tasks that have very little 'slack' time and that could become critical if a problem occurs and they overrun by more than the amount of slack.

When to use

Everybody has projects in their life! Getting married, buying a flat, moving house are all projects and there are certainly many more in our logistic careers, eg re-planning the distribution network, looking for 30 per cent inventory reduction over the next two years, buying a major piece of new equipment, setting up a supplier conference. All of these can be well managed using project management methods.

How to use

There are five stages:

1 Identify all the activities that must be carried out in order to complete the project and determine what must be completed before each task can start, ie identify the 'sequential dependency' of each task.

2 Estimate the most likely time required to carry out each task.

3 Using these times, calculate the overall duration of the project, assuming that each activity starts at the earliest possible moment and that each activity is completed on time.

4 From the overall duration of the project, calculate the latest time at which each activity can start, assuming that all activities finish on time.

5 After the calculations in steps 3 and 4, the critical path can now be identified.

Example

We are going to set up a project network for the preparation phase of a project to improve inventory accuracy. During a team meeting, we decide that there are seven top-level activities. A brief description of each activity is given in Table 6.1, and each activity is given a code from A to G, for simplicity. The 'predecessors' of an activity are those activities which must be completed before the activity in question can start, eg we need to obtain the results of last year's stock-take before we can classify the sources of deviation (differences between physical stock level and recorded stock level) found.

TABLE 6.1 List of activities with predecessors and expected duration

Activity description	Activity code	Predecessors	Duration (elapsed time in days)
Obtain last year's count results	A	–	2
Obtain all process charts	B	–	6
Get system access for all team	C	–	3
Classify main sources of deviation	D	A	4

(Continued)

TABLE 6.1 List of activities with predecessors and expected duration (*Continued*)

Activity description	Activity code	Predecessors	Duration (elapsed time in days)
Team carries out self-evaluation of ability to use main processes	E	C	5
Set targets for accuracy improvement	F	A	1
Create overall plan for improvement	G	B, D, E	8

A precedence diagram can be drawn from this information (see Figure 6.1). Activities A, B and C can all start as soon as we have clearance to start the project. As soon as activity A has finished, D and F can start, and so on. Note that nothing comes after F or G (no other activity has either of these activities as a predecessor), so we know that they both go into the end point.

FIGURE 6.1 Precedence diagram

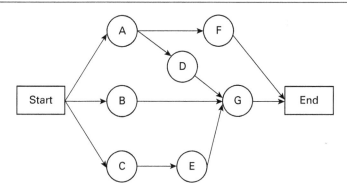

We now work forwards through the network (ie from start to end), calculating the earliest time at which each activity can start, assuming that all activities finish exactly on time. Remember that all predecessor activities must be completed before the successor activity can start, eg B, D and E must *all* be finished before G can start (see Table 6.2).

TABLE 6.2   Results after forwards analysis

Activity	Predecessors	Duration (days)	Earliest start	Earliest finish
A	–	2	0	0 + 2 = 2
B	–	6	0	0 + 6 = 6
C	–	3	0	0 + 3 = 3
D	A	4	2	2 + 4 = 6
E	C	5	3	3 + 5 = 8
F	A	1	2	2 + 1 = 3
G	B, D, E	8	8	8 + 8 = 16

The earliest start time of an activity is when all predecessor activities have finished. The earliest finish time of an activity = earliest start time + duration. Note that by convention we start at time 0.

It can be seen that we need 16 days to complete this preparation phase of the project. This is considerably less than the total of all the elapsed days required for each activity. If we carried out only one activity at a time, we would require 29 days (the sum of all durations). This method allows us to calculate the duration of a project when some activities are being carried out simultaneously.

Now comes the tricky part! We want to find the *latest* time at which each activity can start, and to do this we will work backwards through the network. Remember that we must now allow enough time for all the following ('succeeding') activities to take place.

Table 6.3 shows the backwards calculation. We start at the end of the project and know that activities F and G must finish by time = 16, for a 16-day project. The latest start time of G (time = 8) becomes the latest finish time of its predecessors, B, D and E. The latest finish time of A will be governed by the latest start times of D and F. We must allow enough time for D and F to finish so that G can start on time, so we take the smaller latest start time, which is the latest start time of D, which is time = 4.

TABLE 6.3 Results after backwards analysis

Activity	Predecessors	Duration (days)	Latest start time	Latest finish time	Slack (days)
A	–	2	4 – 2 = 2	4	4 – 0 – 2 = 2
B	–	6	8 – 6 = 2	8	8 – 0 – 6 = 2
C	–	3	3 – 3 = 0	3	3 – 0 – 3 = 0
D	A	4	8 – 4 = 4	8	8 – 2 – 4 = 2
E	C	5	8 – 5 = 3	8	8 – 3 – 5 = 0
F	A	1	16 – 1 = 15	16	16 – 2 – 1 = 13
G	B, D, E	8	16 – 8 = 8	16	16 – 8 – 8 = 0

Finally, we can calculate the amount of slack time for each activity as shown in the final column of Table 6.3:

Slack = latest finish – earliest start – duration

'Critical' activities have no flexibility in their start and finish times, so they have zero slack. It can be seen that activities C, E and G have zero slack and it can also be seen that these activities lie end-to-end through the network. These activities form the 'critical path' and must be managed particularly carefully if the project is to finish on time.

Critical path analysis is just one element of project management. Good project management also requires people management skills, good time- and cost-estimating skills, and it is well worth attending a training course to learn more and then take part in a major project to gain experience of using these skills. Project management is an extremely powerful tool to have in your toolbox!

(This example can be downloaded for free from http://howtologistics.com).

Further information

An excellent reference book is Meredith, J R and Mantel, S J (2009) *Project Management: A managerial approach*, 7th edn, Wiley, Hoboken, NJ. The standard for project management certification in the UK is Prince2. Many software packages of greatly varying cost and sophistication are available.

6.2 Decision matrix analysis (DMA)

Introduction

Decision matrix analysis is a quasi-scientific method to aid decision making when there are many different factors to take into account and a number of alternative options or courses of action. It is particularly useful when a group of people must make a joint decision since it allows the discussion to be more objective, giving some distance from individual 'pet' projects.

This can be an effective tool when there are a significant number of competing alternatives and a myriad of factors that need to be taken into account. This tool can assist managers in making a choice where there isn't a clear and obvious outright candidate, supplier or product. Being able to use DMA means that you can take decisions confidently and rationally, at a time when a team is finding it difficult to come to a consensus.

In all cases, a method of this nature improves the quality of discussion, moving the arguments away from the subjective and closer to the objective.

When to use

This is a useful technique when you have a difficult choice to make where you have a number of alternatives and many different factors to take into account. This could be, for example, the choice of some major piece of equipment, location of a new plant or warehouse, or for comparing tenders. Note that the method does not make the decision for you – it is not that sensitive – but it does enable a more objective and analytical discussion to take place among a group of decision makers, or the range of options to be narrowed down to the last two or three.

How to use

Identify the key criteria that will be used to compare the different options and give them a relative weighting from 1 to 5 (where 5 is most important). Each factor is allocated to a row in the decision matrix. Each option is allocated to a column in the decision matrix.

Working across each row, score each option on a scale of 1 to 5 (where 5 is best) on how well it meets the criterion. Multiply the score awarded by the weighting to arrive at a sub-total for that criterion for that option. Add up all the sub-totals for that option to arrive at a total score. The option with the highest score is the most logical choice based on the scores and weightings allocated.

When using this tool, don't assume that it is totally objective. If the scores are very close, further analysis should take place. Utilize a spreadsheet to compile the figures as this will enable you to change weights and scores very quickly and produce overall totals in a much faster time.

Example

The following is taken from an outsourcing exercise where a company was looking to change supplier for its warehousing and pallet load distribution operation. It is a comparison based on the tender responses and presentations made by the 3PLs.

All of the criteria were discussed internally and given weights based on the consensus of opinion. Each member of the management team involved in the decision-making process scored the contractors based on the criteria. The weighting and scoring criteria were:

Weighting	*Score*
1. Nice to have	1. Very poor
2. Fairly important	2. Poor
3. Important	3. Average
4. Very important	4. Good
5. Most important	5. Excellent

Table 6.4 is an amalgamation of the scores from each of the management team involved. As can be seen from the table, the contract is likely to be placed with either Company C or Company D after further discussion and negotiation. (A spreadsheet version of the matrix can be downloaded for free from http://howtologistics.com)

References

Turner, S (2002) *Tools for Success: A manager's guide*, McGraw-Hill, London
http://www.mindtools.com/pages/article/newTED_03.htm

TABLE 6.4 3PL decision matrix

Decision matrix Service/Benefit	Weight	Company A Score	Total	Company B Score	Total	Company C Score	Total	Company D Score	Total	Company E Score	Total
Total cost	5	3	15	2.8	14	1.8	9	4.5	22.5	5	25
Purchasing power for outbound deliveries	5	3	15	2.3	11.5	4.8	24	4.8	24	1.5	7.5
On-site pick and pack experience	4	2.5	10	1.8	7.2	4.8	19.2	4.8	19.2	2.8	11.2
Staff flexibility	4	4	16	3.8	15.2	4.5	18	4.3	17.2	2.3	9.2
System ability to deal with multiple clients	4	2.8	11.2	4.5	18	4	16	3.5	14	1.5	6
Management team we are comfortable working with	4	2.8	11.2	3.5	14	4	16	3.8	15.2	3.3	13.2
Dedicated senior contract management	3	3.5	10.5	2.8	8.4	2.5	7.5	3.5	10.5	5	15
End-to-end supply chain management capability	3	2.8	8.4	3.8	11.4	4	12	3.3	9.9	2.3	6.9
Proven WMS capability	3	4	12	3.8	11.4	4.3	12.9	4.3	12.9	1.3	3.9
Current use of scan technology within the warehouse	3	3.3	9.9	2.8	8.4	4.3	12.9	3.5	10.5	1	3

Decision matrix Service/Benefit	Weight	Company A		Company B		Company C		Company D		Company E	
		Score	Total	Score	Total	Score	Total	Score	Total	Score	Total
Pool of capable management talent	3	3.5	10.5	3	9	4	12	3.8	11.4	1.3	3.9
Capacity to expand	3	3.8	11.4	4.3	12.9	2.5	7.5	4	12	3	9
Proposed service levels	3	2.8	8.4	3.8	11.4	4	12	3.5	10.5	3.5	10.5
Suitability of space	3	2.8	8.4	4.5	13.5	3.5	10.5	3.8	11.4	3	9
Implementation costs	3	1	3	4	12	3	9	3.8	11.4	5	15
Payment terms	3	3	9	3	9	4.8	14.4	3	9	3	9
Southern European owned sites	2	3.5	7	2.3	4.6	4.8	9.6	2.8	5.6	1.3	2.6
Existing supplier/ understanding of culture	2	2.3	4.6	4	8	3	6	2.8	5.6	4.8	9.6
Implementation timescale	2	3.8	7.6	3.5	7	3.8	7.6	4.3	8.6	1.5	3
Other customer synergy	2	3	6	3.3	6.6	4.8	9.6	3.8	7.6	2	4
Total score			**195.1**		**213.5**		**245.7**		**249**		**176.5**

NOTE: Scores are rounded up or down based on decimal places.

6.3 DMAIC: a process improvement tool

Introduction

The DMAIC tool tends to be synonymous with Six Sigma. The tool is used to identify problems, develop ideas on how to improve the process, produce a solution and finally ensure that the fix is sustainable. DMAIC is not exclusive to Six Sigma and can be used as a framework for other improvement applications.

DMAIC stands for Define, Measure, Analyse, Improve and Control. All of these steps are necessary and are undertaken in that order (see Figure 6.2):

1 Define. Document what is known about the problem, assess and clarify the facts, set objectives and put together a project team to work on the problem.

2 Measure. Decide what is to be measured and how to measure it. Ensure that the measures are specific, the data easy to collect and monitor. At this stage the process needs to be tested to ensure feasibility.

3 Analyse. The data collected are analysed to determine the root cause of the problem. A gap analysis can be undertaken to identify differences between current performance and the target performance.

4 Improve. At this stage, ideas for improvement can be discussed. The most feasible ideas can be tested and the most effective idea introduced.

5 Control. Finally, once introduced, the improvements need to be monitored to ensure continued success.

Process documents need to be produced together with a system of continuous improvement. At this stage, the new ideas can be shared and, as in the 8D model (see tool 9.4), the project team should be recognized for their efforts.

When to use

This tool is used to identify problems and form ideas on how to solve them and ensure that there is no recurrence.

FIGURE 6.2 DMAIC

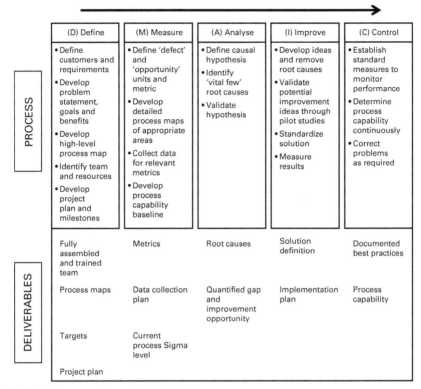

(D) Define	(M) Measure	(A) Analyse	(I) Improve	(C) Control
• Define customers and requirements • Develop problem statement, goals and benefits • Develop high-level process map • Identify team and resources • Develop project plan and milestones	• Define 'defect' and 'opportunity' units and metric • Develop detailed process maps of appropriate areas • Collect data for relevant metrics • Develop process capability baseline	• Define causal hypothesis • Identify 'vital few' root causes • Validate hypothesis	• Develop ideas and remove root causes • Validate potential improvement ideas through pilot studies • Standardize solution • Measure results	• Establish standard measures to monitor performance • Determine process capability continuously • Correct problems as required

PROCESS

Fully assembled and trained team	Metrics	Root causes	Solution definition	Documented best practices
Process maps	Data collection plan	Quantified gap and improvement opportunity	Implementation plan	Process capability
Targets	Current process Sigma level			
Project plan				

DELIVERABLES

SOURCE: diagram courtesy of Precision CEM

How to use

Let's take achieving 'Daily cycle counting for 98–100 per cent inventory records accuracy' as the project at hand:

- Define what our goal is: 98–100 per cent daily inventory records accuracy.

- Measure where we are now: take a sample cycle count of a mixture of A, B, C and D items.

- Divide the total count into the amount correct: let's say 10 items were counted and six were correct = 60 per cent inventory records accuracy for this trial count. This is far from good enough.

- Analyse: why were four counts incorrect? Analyse the transaction detail in the warehouse management system (WMS) to find the root causes for the four variances: warehouse counts to computer counts.

- Improve: improve through daily cycle counting of A, B, C and D items throughout the warehouse. As you find root-cause errors, do a root-cause error frequency distribution and eliminate these root causes by writing standard operating procedures (SOPs).

You should be holding steady at 98–100 per cent daily inventory records accuracy if you follow this proven system.

The key now is C = Control. You must maintain and control this 98–100 per cent inventory records accuracy level through daily cycle counting and root-cause analysis. This control step is the most critical step. You can reach this point, but it has to be maintained and controlled. When you do control this level of inventory records accuracy, you can consider eliminating the annual wall-to-wall physical inventory count if this is also agreed with your auditors.

(Using DMAIC Aside From Six Sigma, by Chuck Intrieri for The Good Word, experienced Third Party Logistics (3PL), Logistics, and Warehouse Operations Consultant. Article used with permission.)

6.4 Flow charts

Introduction

Flow charting is a method of recording work or business processes, or for explaining how to navigate through a series of decisions. There are many other methods for doing this, including techniques from method study, information systems analysis, and business process re-engineering, to name a few. However, standard flow charting can be powerful and useful for improving work or business processes.

The basic flow charting method uses symbols for operation or activity, decisions, the start and end points, and links to the next stage, either following immediately or elsewhere on the chart (see Table 6.5).

TABLE 6.5 Flow chart symbols

Symbol	Meaning	Rule for use
(oval)	Start or end	Make sure that there is only one start point and one end point in the diagram
(rectangle)	Operation (rectangle)	Multiple inputs are possible, but only one output
(diamond)	Decision (diamond)	One input, multiple outputs (which must cover all eventualities, and with no overlapping between options)
(arrow)	Arrow to next stage	Check that the arrow shows direction of flow
(circle with A)	Link to another part of the chart	Ensure that the link continues elsewhere, ie if there is an 'A' end point, there is also one 'A' start point somewhere else

When to use

Flow charts are a good means of recording a current business process or 'as-is' situation that you want to analyse and streamline. When the new process is designed, the 'to-be' process, it can also be communicated as a flow chart. A flow chart can therefore be used as a communication tool for discussion leading to redesign, or for presenting or formalizing a work procedure.

How to use

The most common method of creating a flow chart of a business process is for the person creating the chart to interview the person carrying out the business process. The interviewer makes notes or may sketch the activities as they are described. Later, the interviewer constructs the flow chart. Actually drawing out the flow chart can give rise to questions about the logic of the procedure or the sequence of activities, and it is often necessary to go back to the person carrying out the process to check the details. The process of constructing the final flow chart often offers ideas for improvement. The process chart can be shown to all involved and used as the basis for a discussion about potential improvements. Eventually, a 'to-be' process can be developed, tested and implemented. The flow chart thus becomes the reference document of 'what should happen' and for future checking of 'conformance to process'.

Example

Figure 6.3 shows a flow chart for goods receiving. Note how the links ensure that there is only one start point and one end point, and a clear way through the chart ('P.O.' is purchase order).

FIGURE 6.3 Flow chart for goods receiving

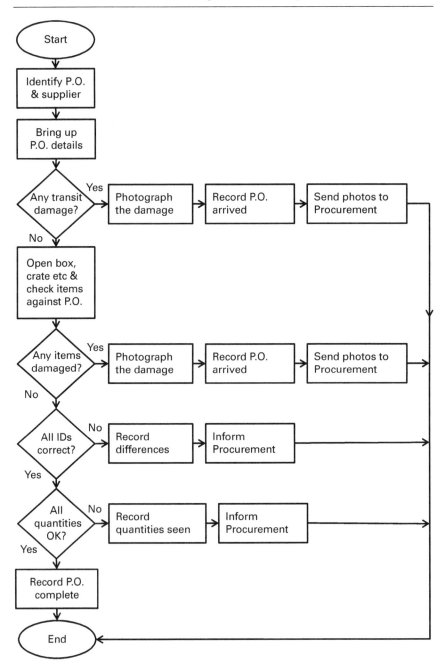

Further information

Obolensky, N (1996) *Practical Business Re-engineering*, Kogan Page, London

6.5 Gantt charts

Introduction

Gantt charts were developed by Henry Gantt, an American engineer and consultant who lived and worked in the late 19th and early 20th centuries. A Gantt chart shows what happens to a job or a resource over time. It is a good way of drawing out a schedule.

Time is always shown on the horizontal axis and resources or jobs on the vertical axis. A resource can be an operator, a piece of equipment, a functional team or group, or even a department. Jobs or tasks are allocated to the resources, with a start and finish time, in order to create a schedule. Gantt charts are also used in project management to show which activities will be taking place at any time and can also be used to show the allocation of resources to tasks.

The primary applications of Gantt charts, be it for project management or production scheduling, include:

- finding the overall lead time to complete a job, a series of tasks or a project, after being processed through several resources;
- finding the overall planned level of utilization of these resources as a result of this schedule;
- checking that resources are not double-booked and that jobs or people are not expected to be in more than one place at a time;
- improving use of the resources, or overall completion time, by scheduling jobs or tasks in a different way;
- measuring progress against the schedule.

When to use

Gantt charts are used in project management for planning and visualizing the schedule of tasks that must be carried out and for reviewing the use of resources throughout the project. In production planning, Gantt charts are used to allocate jobs to production resources, to create a production schedule for a series of jobs and a group of resources.

How to use

It is important to understand the sequential dependency between tasks so that the tasks can be carried out in the correct order. For example, the steel framework structure of a new warehouse will not be erected until the foundations have been laid.

Example

A Gantt chart will be created for the small project network illustrated in tool 6.1. The project has seven activities and the critical path was found to be C–E–G (see Tables 6.6 and 6.7).

TABLE 6.6 List of activities

Activity description	Activity code
Obtain last year's count results	A
Obtain all process charts	B
Get system access for all team	C
Classify main sources of deviation	D
Team carries out self-evaluation of ability to use main processes	E
Set targets for accuracy improvement	F
Create overall plan for improvement	G

TABLE 6.7 List of activities after full time analysis has been carried out

Activity	Predecessors	Duration (days)	Earliest start	Earliest finish	Latest start	Latest finish	Slack
A	–	2	0	2	2	4	2
B	–	6	0	6	2	8	2
C	–	3	0	3	0	3	0
D	A	4	2	6	4	8	2
E	C	5	3	8	3	8	0
F	A	1	2	3	15	16	13
G	B, D, E	8	8	16	8	16	0

To build the Gantt chart (Figure 6.4), we start by placing time on the horizontal axis, then laying out the critical activities, C, E and G, end-to-end across the chart. Now the non-critical activities can be added to the chart. By default, they are shown to start at the earliest possible start time. The latest finish time of the non-critical activities is also shown so that the amount of slack can be distinguished. It can be seen that activities A and D share two days of slack. This slack could be used before A starts, between activities A and D, or, as shown, after D.

Activities B and F also have slack. By convention, this is shown as occurring after the activity, but the activity could start at any time, so long as it is completed by the latest finish time. The latest finish time is shown by a dotted line: end of day 8 for activities B and D, end of day 16 for activity F.

FIGURE 6.4 Gantt chart

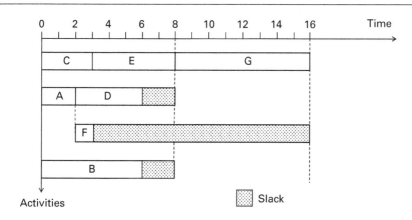

The Gantt chart can now be used to look at the resources required for each activity and for all the activities scheduled for each day. For example, we may be considering how many person days are required and these can be shown on the chart.

Further information

See Meredith and Mantel (2009) for how Gantt charts are used in project management and Slack *et al* (2010) for how Gantt charts are used in production scheduling. An example Gantt chart for an implementation project can be downloaded from http://howtologistics.com

References

Meredith, J R and Mantel, S J (2009) *Project Management: A managerial approach*, 7th edn, Wiley, Hoboken, NJ

Slack, N, Chambers, S and Johnston, R (2010) *Operations Management*, FT Prentice Hall, Harlow

6.6 Mind maps

Introduction

The 'brain' of a computer operates in a purely linear fashion; our brains do not. Brains work by comparing, processing and integrating information; in essence, they work associatively. Every single thought that we produce is linked to other thoughts, sights, sounds and concepts.

Mind maps were developed by British psychology author Tony Buzan. Tony also hosted a BBC TV series called 'Use Your Head'. During this show, Tony frequently and enthusiastically used a 'tree-like' diagram to visualize his thoughts while also using colours to highlight key words and phrases.

The reason we often 'sketch' things in this format is down to the fact that this 'map' takes on the same structure as our memory, ie it is associative. It is an easier way to see and recognize things and thus recall them. Mind mapping is therefore a way of 'brainstorming' (see tool 9.1) or making notes but in a more visual way.

When to use

When you want to brainstorm a particular problem and then provide a visual representation to both yourself and your colleagues.

How to use

The brainstorming potential of a mind map is immense. You start with a basic problem and put it at the centre of the 'map' and then generate ideas from it. As you generate these ideas, other thoughts come to mind that are then added to the major spurs. By presenting your thoughts in this visual way a better overview is frequently gained. Colours and pictures can be used to accentuate the data.

The mind map shown in Figure 6.5 has been produced in response to an enquiry to outsource a logistics operation. The diagram shows the thought processes that the person went through when thinking about the task in hand. Figure 6.5 is a simplified version; Figure 6.6 shows how complex a mind map can be. We can see that the central theme is inventory management but with a number of sub-themes such as finance and logistics.

FIGURE 6.5 Mind map for outsourcing a logistics operation

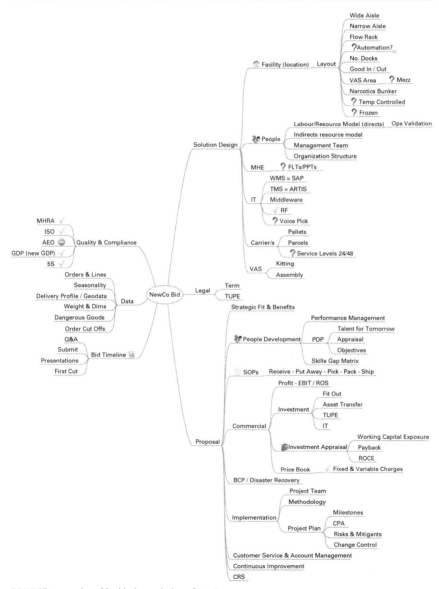

SOURCE: reproduced by kind permission of Joe Fogg

FIGURE 6.6 Mind map for inventory management

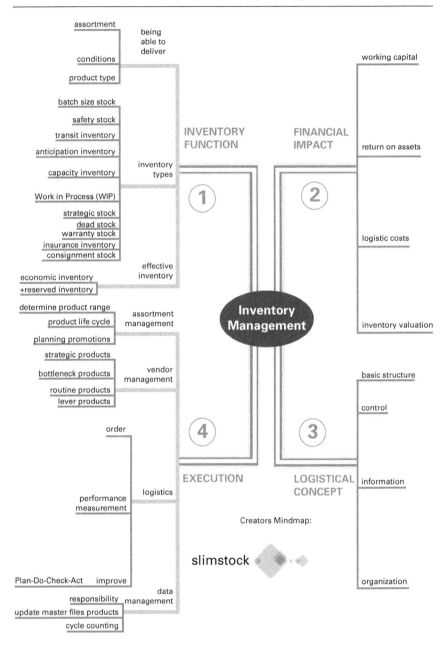

The inventory management mind map replaces pages of text that the reader would find difficult to take in all at once. The map not only provides information but also helps in decision making. (The full version of this mind map can be downloaded from http://howtologistics.com).

Utilizing a mind map enables you to quickly understand, identify and absorb the structure of a subject. However, more important and due to the fact that a mind map is the 'same shape' as your memory, it enables you to recall the information.

Further information

Free mind map software can be found at: http://freemind.sourceforge.net/wiki/
   index.php/Main_Page
(With thanks to Joe Fogg of Arvato and Richard Evans from Slimstock.)

6.7 The PDCA tool

Introduction

The PDCA tool (Plan, Do, Check, Act) or Deming Cycle, named after W Edwards Deming, a business improvement and quality guru, is an approach to change and problem solving. The four phases in the cycle involve:

Plan: identifying and analysing the problem.

Do: producing and trying a potential solution.

Check: measuring how successful the test solution is and analysing whether it can be improved in any way.

Act: implementing the improved solution fully.

When to use

The Deming Cycle or PDCA is an excellent, well-ordered, precise method for problem solving. It can be utilized in a number of areas such as:

- assisting in the implementation of Kaizen or continuous improvement practices, enabling the cycle to be repeated over and over as new areas for improvement are discovered and resolved;

- pinpointing new resolutions and improvements to processes and practices that are repetitive;

- investigating a range of possible new solutions to problems, evaluating and improving them before selecting the most appropriate for full implementation;

- avoiding the waste of resources that accompanies full-scale implementation of an average or deficient solution.

PDCA is a proven method for removing waste or inefficient cost in an operation, resulting in increased value. In our example below, Nissan Motor Parts (NMPC) uses PDCA as part of its continuous improvement process. It is in a competitive environment and needs to have high performance levels.

Nissan uses PDCA when examining larger change events that require more time and perhaps investment but are critical for the business performance. These are not in the gift of any one team, so require senior managers' support through active participation. They rely on data for objective root-cause analysis and for testing possible solutions before implementation. Projects tend to be more data intensive.

According to Nissan, the use of PDCA supports the development of leaders and team members by providing a place for people to work together and grow their skills for continuous improvement. It not only increases confidence in individuals but also develops a good spirit in the workplace. It becomes a place to apply individual expertise and a place to learn about the expertise of others by working cross-functionally in the supply chain.

Nissan uses it as a training opportunity and it becomes a place of ownership, ie when a group of people make a change for the better in their part of the business they will implement the change and follow the standard operating procedure, which is the written record of the changed procedure.

A mutual respect grows among colleagues: 'If your colleague made the change you support that change when you are deployed in that task because you need your colleague to reciprocate.'

How to use it

The following is a case study example from Nissan Motor Parts UK. Figure 6.7 shows the model that Nissan uses.

Project title: Physical Picking Claims Improvement Project

Problem: NMPC receives dealer orders and then processes them in a manual picking process. When carrying out this task there is the risk of a team member in the supply process making a physical error resulting in a dealer claim and loss of value for the part. This is at a cost of £563,869 per year.

Target: A reduction of physical errors by 10 per cent equating to a reduction in claims value of £56,386 in total. This is equal to 1,007 physical error claims.

Approach: Use of PDCA and DMAIC (see tool 6.3).

FIGURE 6.7 PDCA/DMAIC model produced by Nissan

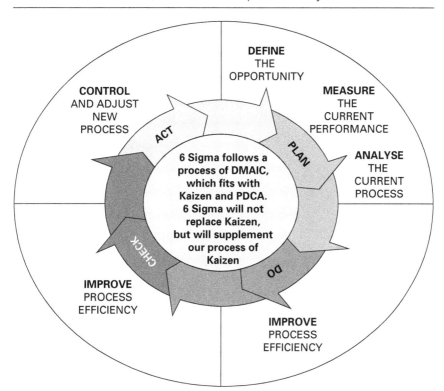

SOURCE: reproduced by kind permission of Bruce Taylor, Nissan

Step 1. Plan (Define, Measure, Analyse)

Define the opportunity and set up a project team.
Undertake a stakeholder analysis (see Table 6.8).
Produce a communication plan (see Table 6.9).

The stakeholder analysis and the communication plan together form the engagement plan.

The group discussed the best methods to engage the stakeholders effectively and maintained this approach throughout the project. It was decided that the critical group of 'Pickers' would be communicated to via a 'Roadshow' type of presentation. The use of the same presenting team and the opportunity to ask questions provide consistency and transparency.

This technique was employed from start to finish for both this project and the sub-projects that came from it:

- Produce process maps to assess the current situation.

- Measure and validate the data for the current situation.

- Determine the influencing factors of below-par performance and chart them (see Figure 6.8).

TABLE 6.8 Stakeholder analysis

Stakeholders' name and group	Project Impact on Stakeholder (SH) H/M/L	SH level of influence on success H/M/L	SH current attitude +/0/-	Explanation of current SH attitude	SH score H=3, M=2, l=1, + =1, 0=2, -=3	Action plan for SH
Pickers	H	H	+	Monetary reward and self worth	7	Consult and involve at each step using skills
TL	H	H	+	Time back, morale of team, monetary reward, self worth	7	Consult and involve at each step using skills
Management	H	H	+	KPI uplift, morale of team, monetary reward, self worth	7	Consult and involve at each step for approval at gateway review
Gatekeeper	H	H	+	Time to focus elsewhere	7	Consult and involve at each step using skills
Dealers	H	L	+	Service improvement	5	Dealer Conference

SH   Stakeholder
TL   Team leader
H/M/L High/Medium/Low

TABLE 6.9 Communication plan

Audience/to who	Media	Purpose	Topic of discussion/ key message	Owner	Frequency	Notes/ Status
Pickers	Visit teams in person to brief progress	Engage and prepare audience for coming changes gaining input	Intentions and plan to utilize skills of pickers	Team	25/03 then as required	Detail to be discussed to ensure ownership and involvement
TL	Face to Face	Inform and encourage feedback	Intention and current status	Team	Launch and post Gateway review	
Management	Face to Face	Inform and encourage feedback	Intention and current status	Team	Launch and post Gateway review	
Gatekeeper	Face to Face	Recognize role	As per picker	Team	As all above	
Dealers	Conference/ intranet	Inform	Relay result of better service	Team	At finish	

FIGURE 6.8 Performance chart

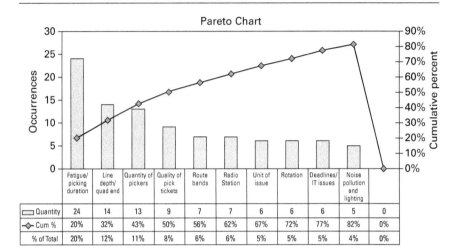

At the next stage, which is the Analysis stage in DMAIC, the team looked to identify the root cause or causes of the problem or opportunity. Using the data produced, the problem is analysed and 'drilled down' to gain a better understanding of what and where the root causes are.

Step 2. Do (Improve)

A 'quick win' was identified that saw Nissan provide its pickers with the opportunity of a free eye test. Out of 77 who took the test, 33 required glasses. A number of people were not aware they needed them. Everyone was given the option to have free glasses up to a cost of £50 and everyone was able to choose from a variety of styles.

Other solutions were identified, scored and ranked by effectiveness, feasibility, cost and duration. The top five ideas were evaluated and a risk analysis carried out. The ideas were later either implemented or a separate project team was set up to look at return on investment and feasibility.

Step 3. Check

The group identified a loophole in the way that the existing claims tracker calculated overall claims scores for operatives. The existing tracker allowed operatives to score points towards merit-based pay reviews even when they were performing poorly in key areas. This was due to the way that the tracker took a percentage of the overall score for each area and enabled one good performance to guarantee a minimum score.

A new tracker with a new calculation was developed to remove this loophole and enable like-for-like comparison between operatives. This ensures that the operatives who need the most assistance get the most coaching and in good time.

Step 4. Act (Control)

Many of the new processes have been introduced and others are currently being fully evaluated in terms of feasibility and cost, with the project teams due to report back on the results.

Result

The 10 per cent reduction was equivalent to a drop of 1,007 claims over the year. Nissan achieved a reduction of 582 claims in four months. If this is maintained it is forecasting an annual saving of 1,746 physical error claims. This equates to a 23 per cent reduction in physical errors.

At an average of £55.97 a claim, it has so far saved £32,574 in four months. If this continues, the projected saving over a 12-month period will be £97,723. Implementation resource costs were approximately circa 300 hours @ £15.15 per hour = £4,650 = net saving in first year of £93,073.

The introduction of tools such as PDCA and DMAIC has resulted in staff working together in teams to ensure continuous improvement and in many instances exceed the targets initially set.

Further information

Further information can be found at: http://www.mindtools.com/pages/article/newPPM_89.htm

(With thanks to Bruce Taylor from Nissan UK for his input.)

6.8 Radar chart

Introduction

This tool can be used to show the gap between actual and targeted performance and present it visually. Normally you would include 6–10 organizational factors. Radar charts can also be used to compare alternative methods or equipment and their efficiency against expected results.

When to use

When you wish to present to a customer or show internal colleagues where there are gaps in performance. The chart clearly shows which factors require the most attention.

How to use

Decide on the performance categories to be measured and compared (KPIs can be taken from the lists shown in tools 7.2, 7.3 and 7.4). Ensure that each category has consistent measures both for the target and actual performance. These can be shown as percentages or scales from 0–10 or 0–5, for example. Then, produce the chart:

1 Draw a diagram with as many sides as there are performance categories. In Figure 6.9 we have drawn a heptagon.

2 Label each of the outside points with the performance category.

3 Draw lines from the outside points to the centre of the shape.

4 Beginning from the outside, draw parallel lines from the outside to the inside at increments denoting the performance figures. This can be from 5 (excellent performance) to 0 (poor performance) or you can use percentages as shown in Figure 6.9. Ensure that the number of lines drawn equates to the number of increments.

5 Plot the target scores and connect each of the target scores.

6 Plot the actual results figures and link them.

7 Once complete, evaluate the figures and look for areas for improvement.

Figure 6.9 looks at seven specific KPIs related to warehouse operations and plots the difference between target and actual performance. As can be seen in the figure, there are issues in terms of paperwork accuracy as well as damaged items, which both impact perfect order attainment. On-time delivery is ahead of target:

FIGURE 6.9 Radar chart

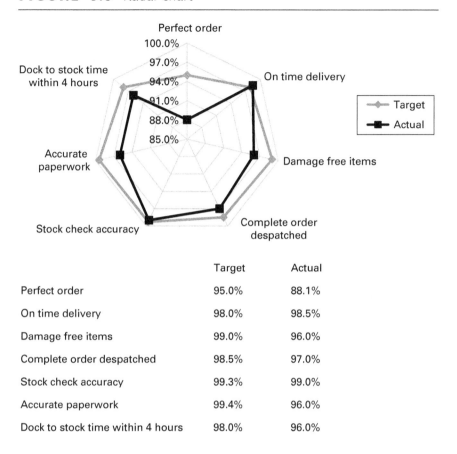

	Target	Actual
Perfect order	95.0%	88.1%
On time delivery	98.0%	98.5%
Damage free items	99.0%	96.0%
Complete order despatched	98.5%	97.0%
Stock check accuracy	99.3%	99.0%
Accurate paperwork	99.4%	96.0%
Dock to stock time within 4 hours	98.0%	96.0%

With regard to performance improvement, it is important to focus on the biggest gap in the most important category.

Further information

Radar charts are found in Excel and PowerPoint and are easy to construct.

6.9 SWOT analysis

Introduction

Undertaking a SWOT analysis enables companies to identify their Strengths, Weaknesses, Opportunities and Threats. Strengths and weaknesses tend to concentrate on the internal situation, whereas opportunities and threats look outside the organization. It is a strategic tool to identify the company's current situation and how it needs to adapt to future challenges.

When to use

When the company is looking to change strategy or make certain strategic decisions as a result of a performance issue, an acquisition, governmental intervention or in response to a change in the market.

How to use

The first step is to assemble a group of people to identify the strengths and weaknesses of the company and potential and existing opportunities and threats. The group should be cross-functional and all points should be considered and evaluated. This can be done through brainstorming (see tool 9.1).

The next step is to draw out a four-box grid as shown in Table 6.10. This grid can be used to record the points discussed. Continue the discussion until the list is exhausted for all four areas. As for a number of the other tools, honesty and openness are vital for the success of this exercise.

Example

Let us take for example both the US and UK postal services. They are under threat from the growth of the internet in terms of a reduction in letters posted, but have an opportunity to expand with an increase in e-commerce, both business to consumer and consumer to consumer. Table 6.10 shows an example of a SWOT analysis for these corporations. As can be seen in the table, a threat could potentially be an opportunity, such as the possibility of being privatized.

Once the table is completed, produce a plan to maximize the strengths, compensate for the weaknesses, understand and look to combat the threats and take advantage of the opportunities.

TABLE 6.10 SWOT analysis for postal service

	Strengths	Weaknesses
Internal	Nationwide coverage	Strength of labour unions
	Worldwide/European network through partnerships	Industrial unrest among long-term workers
	Advanced technology – readable post codes, digital signature capture, online mailshots	Uniform charge for 1st class mail (UK)
	Door-to-door service	Loss making in the main
	Recognizable and strong brand	Lower revenue generated per employee compared to competition
	Cost advantage	High employee costs
	Property portfolio	
	Large database of individuals and companies	
	Retail and financial business	
	Opportunities	**Threats**
External	Growth of online shopping globally	Electronic communication such as e-mail and text messaging
	Growth of C-to-C business (consumer to consumer)	Online greetings cards
	Last-mile deliveries for other organizations	Increasing number of competitors
	Large number of collection points and drop-off points	Fuel price increases
	Privatization	Economic slowdown
		Reduction in government support
		Increased postal deregulation
		Being privatized and broken up
		Industry consolidation
		Internet banking

Further information

Further information can be found in Ansoff, H I (1987) *Corporate Strategy*, Penguin, Harmondsworth.

6.10 Team selection – building a successful team, by Belbin

Introduction

Whether we are putting together a team for a specific project or for a new company, we want to ensure that we have a good mix of talent and capability in the team. Some of the tools we have discussed have required putting a team together to brainstorm strategy or tackle problems. We need to ensure that our team make-up is capable and able to work together to achieve the specific goal.

An ideal team size is between 7 and 15 people. According to Belbin (1981):

> A team is not a bunch of people with job titles, but a congregation of individuals, each of whom has a role which is understood by other members. Members of a team seek out certain roles and they perform most effectively in the ones that are most natural to them.

Belbin's Team Role Questionnaires are used to identify people's behavioural strengths and weaknesses in the workplace. This information can be used to:

- build productive working relationships;
- select and develop high-performing teams;
- raise self-awareness and personal effectiveness;
- build mutual trust and understanding;
- aid recruitment processes.

The Belbin Team Role Self-Perception Inventory (BTRSPI) was designed to measure behavioural characteristics that individuals display when working in teams.

When to use

When putting a team together to undertake a particular task, solve a problem or start a new company.

How to use

Identify the skills required for the particular task, then identify the types of people required. There are a number of different behavioural analysis tools on the market, but for this exercise we will concentrate on one of the most famous – Belbin. Belbin suggests that each person has a number of different traits and behaves differently depending on what they are involved with and whom they are with. To understand each potential individual, each person completes a questionnaire that is analysed by the Belbin team and a report is produced.

The team roles that Belbin identifies are used widely in thousands of organizations all over the world today. By identifying our team roles, we can ensure that we use our strengths to advantage and that we manage our weaknesses as best we can. Sometimes this means being aware of the pitfalls and making an effort to avoid them.

As with many areas that require people to work together, it isn't only down to skill but also to attitude and culture. When building a team, you need to know how the team members are going to work together. Do they complement each other and will they get on for the duration of the project?

An individual does not have one team role, but a combination of preferred, manageable and least preferred roles. The distribution and interrelation of these roles across an individual's profile have a great influence on the way the roles will be played out in practice and experienced by others.

While individuals may claim to prefer or enjoy a particular role, it does not necessarily mean that they can or should play only this role. The theory of team roles is concerned with acknowledging strengths and weaknesses.

Belbin can also be used as a recruitment and selection tool. Team roles provide an insight into working and team relationships, but the profiles should not be used as the sole basis for making recruitment decisions. Each team role is outlined in Figure 6.10.

Team roles are clusters of behaviour, rather than individual traits or characteristics. It is envisaged that a candidate will have more than one preferred team role.

An individual's team roles can be analysed into three categories:

1 *Preferred roles* – those roles the individual is comfortable playing and which come naturally.

2 *Manageable roles* – those roles which an individual can play if required for the benefit of the team. These may be cultivated to broaden the individual's team-working experience.

3 *Least preferred roles* – those roles the individual does not naturally or comfortably assume. It is generally recommended that the individual avoids contributing in these areas, lest the pitfalls of the behaviour outweigh the strengths.

FIGURE 6.10 Team role descriptions

	Team Role	Contribution	Allowable weakness
	Plant	Creative, imaginative, free-thinking. Generates ideas and solves difficult problems.	Ignores incidentals. Too pre-occupied to communicate effectively.
	Resource Investigator	Enthusiastic, communicative and outgoing. Explores opportunities and develops contacts.	Over-optimistic. Loses interest once initial enthusiasm has passed.
	Co-ordinator	Mature, confident, identifies talent. Clarifies goals. Delegates effectively.	Can be seen as manipulative. Offloads own share of the work.
	Shaper	Challenging, dynamic, thrives on pressure. Has the drive and courage to overcome obstacles.	Prone to provocation. Offends people's feelings.
	Monitor Evaluator	Sober, strategic and discerning. Sees all options and judges accurately.	Lacks drive and ability to inspire others. Can be overly critical.
	Teamworker	Co-operative, perceptive and diplomatic. Listens and averts friction.	Indecisive in crunch situations. Avoids confrontation.
	Implementer	Practical, reliable, efficient. Turns ideas into practical actions and organizes work that needs to be done.	Somewhat inflexible. Slow to respond to new possibilities.
	Completer Finisher	Painstaking, conscientious, anxious. Searches out errors. Polishes and perfects.	Inclined to worry unduly. Reluctant to delegate.
	Specialist	Single-minded, self-starting, dedicated. Provides knowledge and skills in rare supply.	Contributes on only a narrow front. Dwells on technicalities.

SOURCE: reproduced by kind permission of Belbin

There is much debate on what 'makes a team'. But what are the key factors? Size and selection are critical. If there are too many people in a team, roles and behaviours start to overlap, causing problems. Too large a team can also lead to conformism and focus on a single leader. A smaller team ensures that each voice and contribution is heard and valued.

A team should be put together for a specific purpose. Each team member should be chosen to ensure that the correct balance of skill and behaviour is achieved. Each team member will be seen as being important to the task in hand and vital to the success of the project.

Once the team has been assembled, you need to explain the task in full and ensure full commitment. Finally, ensure that roles, responsibilities, values and objectives are made clear and understood by all the participants.

Further information

Belbin, R M (1981) *Management Teams: Why they succeed or fail*, Butterworth-Heinemann, Oxford
The BTRSPI is available from Belbin Associates at http://www.belbin.com

Performance management tools

7.1 SMART

Introduction

Many companies operate with far too many key performance indicators (KPIs), which leads to problems not only in terms of the time taken to capture and analyse the data but also the relevance to the staff of some of the measures. This tool focuses management on a number of aspects in relation to KPIs.

When to use

When a company is looking to introduce performance measures, there are a number of stages that need to be followed. A company needs to choose the KPIs that are right for it and its customers and will lead to improved performance.

How to use

The first known uses of the mnemonic SMART appeared in the November 1981 issue of *Management Review* by George T Doran. It gives guidance to managers to ensure that the correct measures are chosen. When deciding on a KPI, that measure needs to pass five tests:

> S – *Specific*. The measure has to explain exactly what the company is measuring and why. This includes the specific area to be measured, how it is measured and who is involved in the measurement. It needs to be clear and unambiguous to all involved. For example, 'On time

delivery' relates to the number of orders that were delivered to the client at the time requested. This can be expressed as a percentage based on the number of on-time deliveries divided by the total number of deliveries made within a particular time frame. A less specific measure would be customer satisfaction, which is, as we will see next, more difficult to measure.

M – *Measurable*. The performance indicator has to be measurable. You need to be able to compare the current figures with past data, or data from other sources such as budgets, competitors, peers. The measure needs to be objective rather than subjective, with little room for ambiguity.

A – *Achievable*. There is no point in setting targets that cannot be achieved under any circumstances. This leads to demotivation. The performance measure also needs to challenge staff and therefore should not be set too low either. An on-time delivery target of 100 per cent every time is probably not achievable, yet a delivery target of 50 per cent on time should be easily achievable and therefore not a realistic target.

R – *Relevant*. The indicator also needs to be relevant to the business. It should dovetail with other parts of the business and assist in achieving the company's overall goal and vision. The specific goal needs to take you somewhere. This can be seen clearly in the Balanced Scorecard tool (see tool 7.5) where different departments share the same goals but have their own specific targets in order to achieve these goals.

T – *Time based*. This covers a number of areas. We need a time frame over which to measure so that we can compare year-on-year data, for example, and we also need a target date to ensure that everyone knows we are working towards a deadline.

Finally, according to Matthews (2013), KPIs need to be future focused:

- A clear vision will drive KPIs.
- Effective KPIs will drive effective behaviours.
- Effective behaviours will drive effective performance.
- Effective performance drives sustainable profit.

References

Doran, G T (1981) There's a SMART way to write management's goals and objectives, *Management Review*, 70 (11) (AMA Forum), pp 35–6

Matthews, E (2013) www.performetrix.co.uk

7.2 Performance measurement and quality improvement

Introduction

'If you do not measure, you cannot manage', or so the theory goes. According to a survey by Aberdeen Group (2010), best-in-class companies are 1.9 times more likely to utilize established standards against which employees can be measured. They are also 2.7 times as likely to undertake employee-specific data collection. The companies will use both individual and group performance metrics to monitor, motivate and encourage the workforce.

KPIs are introduced into companies to both measure and control performance:

- To measure in order to: extend vision and strategy to performance, create a discipline and communicate the non-negotiables, ie those targets that are essential.

- To control so as to: expose gaps between aspirations and actual performance and to close those gaps.

- To change behaviours and future performance: let people know what a good job looks like and create understanding, change attitudes and align energies.

KPIs should not primarily be thought of as measures but as drivers and enablers of vision – they should help take you where you want to go by translating your vision into effective performance.

When to use

When looking to improve performance within the company.

How to use

You have to translate the board's vision into 'bite-sized chunks' to let every employee know 'what a good job looks like'. To achieve this you need to:

- *Structure* the plan, ie determine the scope of the activities to be measured and identify the organization and department-level objectives.

- *Communicate* the plan.

- *Drive* the plan by determining the operating processes and methods required and set the goals.
- *Measure* against the plan.
- *Support* employee behaviours through training and mentoring.
- *Report* progress.
- *Initiate* remedial action where required.
- *Benchmark* excellence to create best practice (see tool 7.6).

You need to monitor performance against the criteria that are important to your customers (service). You also need to monitor performance against the criteria that are important to you (costs).

Do not introduce too many measures, as you will end up spending too much time measuring and not enough time managing and controlling. To ensure success you need to:

- produce accurate data;
- validate and ensure completeness of data;
- target the correct audience;
- put emphasis on user ownership;
- react to changes in business activity;
- measure against historical data but also benchmark current best practice;
- simplify processes and measurements to ensure ease of maintenance;
- spend less than the savings gained from improved productivity.

Finally, these KPIs need to be focused on the future, lead to behaviour change and help you realize your vision.

Table 7.1 provides examples of eight measurements for four key business drivers that are introduced in the Balanced Scorecard tool (tool 7.5). Taking customer service as an example, Table 7.2 provides details of each of the KPIs for customer service together with standards and targets. As discussed in tool 7.1, these need to be SMART.

In Table 7.2, 'critical' is a situation in which, unless improvement is introduced quickly, the business will fail. A failing score denotes a requirement for immediate action to be taken to prevent the operation reaching a critical stage where loss of business is inevitable. A standard is that which must be achieved for the warehouse/team/individual to be seen as being satisfactory

TABLE 7.1 Eight measurements for each of the four perspectives of the Balanced Scorecard

	Customer service and satisfaction	Financial performance
1	On-time delivery	Operational cash flow
2	Orders in full first time	Budget v actual
3	Correct documentation	Days' sales outstanding
4	Damage claims	Overtime costs
5	Perfect order	Inventory days of supply
6	Total order cycle time	Logistics cost as a % of sales
7	Customer complaints	Logistics cost per unit shipped
8	POD returns	Stock loss/stock obsolescence
	Business process improvement	**People and environment**
1	Forecast accuracy	Employee turnover
2	Stock accuracy	% turnover spent on training
3	Dock to stock time	Training days per employee
4	Picking accuracy	Accident levels
5	Returns percentage	Sickness and absence
6	Space efficiency percentage	Carbon emissions/carbon footprint
7	Order to completion time	Level of waste
8	Audit results	Energy usage

– this is the minimum level of acceptable performance. Finally, a target is a level of performance above standard that is desirable to achieve in order to impress and stretch the warehouse/team/individual. It is likely to be best in class in the industry.

Performance results need to be communicated both internally and externally. This can be achieved through regular operational meetings – weekly, monthly and/or quarterly. Results can be posted on notice boards for all staff to see.

TABLE 7.2 Performance indicators for customer service with standards and targets

1. Customer service and satisfaction

Key indicator	Precise definition	Critical	Failing	Standard	Above standard	Target	How verified?
On-time delivery	Number of orders delivered on or before the agreed-upon time, against total number of orders received, expressed as a %	<90	<95	97.5	98.5	99.5	System check/ manual records
Orders in full first time	Number of orders which shipped completely, as per the initial order, against total number of orders received, expressed as a %	<90	<95.5	98	99	99.5	System check/ manual records
Correct documentation	Number of orders for which the customers received an accurate invoice and other required documents etc, against total number of orders dispatched expressed as a %	<96	<98	99.3	99.7	100	System check/ manual records
Damage claims	This measures the number of customer orders received in good and usable condition expressed as a % of total orders dispatched	97.5	98.5	99.5	99.8	99.9	System check/ manual records
Perfect order	The result of multiplying the above four metrics together	75.8	876	94.4	97	98.9	System check/ manual records
Total order cycle time	The time taken in hours from placement of order to receipt of order by the customer	>72	48–72	40	33	30	System check/ manual records
Customer complaints	Time taken in hours to fully answer a customer query/complaint	48	24	6	4	2	System check/ manual records
Back orders	Back orders as a % of total orders received	>8	>4.5	2	0.6	0.2	System check/ manual records

SOURCE: Table adapted from Performetrix

As for incentives, these can be individual or team based. In the case of outsourcing, a gain share arrangement can be introduced where logistics service providers share in the savings and productivity increases they have instigated.

To complete the process, ensure that the KPIs are aligned within the company – a customer's perception could be totally different from that of individual departments. For example:

- 100 per cent dispatch of what's available from the warehouse doesn't mean it's what the customer ordered – the order may have been stock adjusted before being sent to the warehouse for picking.

- Dispatch within 24 hours of the warehouse receiving the order from sales may not have been 24-hour dispatch from receipt of the customer order – it could have sat on someone's desk for a day!

Further information

See Rushton, A, Croucher, P and Baker, P (2010) *The Handbook of Logistics and Distribution Management*, Kogan Page, London

Further information on automating your performance management system can be found at http://www.performetrix.co.uk/

Further information on performance management within warehousing can be found at www.WERC.org

References

Heaney, B (2010) [accessed 3 June 2016] Labor management: instill accuracy, efficiency, and productivity in the warehouse and retail store, http://www.kronos.com/showAbstract.aspx?id=13036&rr=1&sp=y&LangType=1033&ecid=701610000005jmCAAQ

WERC (2015) [accessed 30 December 2015] DC measures 2015, WERC Watch, Spring, http://www.werc.org/DCMeasures2015/

7.3 Performance measures for freight transport

As discussed in the previous tool, it is not a good idea to have too many KPIs. Here we have provided a comprehensive list from which you can choose those most relevant to you as a company and for your customers. Table 7.3 shows examples of freight transport KPIs. It is not suggested that all of these measures are introduced.

TABLE 7.3 Examples of performance indicators for freight transport

Key performance indicator	Description
Cost indicators	
Average cost per unit delivered (£)	Average cost of delivering a specified unit (eg a pallet or tonne of goods)
Total whole vehicle cost (pence per mile/kilometre)	Total cost of your fleet per mile/kilometre. Made up of running, standing and driver costs
Average running cost (pence per mile/kilometre)	Average cost of running your fleet per mile/kilometre. These are the costs incurred for running the vehicles (fuel, tyres, lubricants and maintenance)
Average standing cost (cost per day based on number of days worked per annum)	Average standing costs for your fleet. Standing costs are those incurred whether or not the vehicle is running – depreciation of the vehicle, road fund licence (vehicle excise duty), operator licence fees and insurance
Operational indicators	
Asset efficiency	Average utilization of fleet in cubic capacity or tonnes carried (outbound and inbound)
Vehicle fill efficiency	This calculates the percentage of actual load carried against the potential capacity of the vehicle fleet (tonnes or cube)
Average miles per gallon/km per litre	Average fuel consumption rate for your fleet or by individual truck and driver
Total empty miles/km run ('000s)	Total number of miles/km run by your fleet without a payload
Total miles/km run ('000s)	Total number of miles/km run by your fleet
Percentage empty running total	Total distance run by your fleet without a payload as a % of total miles/km run
Average time utilization	This calculates the percentage of time that the vehicle fleet was actually in use against the potential time available
Demurrage time	Excess time spent at premises waiting to load or be unloaded

(Continued)

TABLE 7.3 Examples of performance indicators for freight transport (*Continued*)

Key performance indicator	Description
Service indicators	
Percentage of late deliveries/on-time deliveries	Late/on-time deliveries made by your fleet as a % of total deliveries
Percentage of damaged items	Damaged items as a % of total items delivered
Number of claims	Number of claims received as a % of total deliveries
Correct paperwork	Number of delivery notes/invoices etc completed correctly/total number of deliveries
Compliance	
Overloading	Total number of overloads in the fleet as a % of loads moved
Traffic infringements	Total number of traffic infringements in the fleet as a % of vehicle movements
Drivers' hours infringements	Total number of drivers' hours infringements in the fleet as a % of trips
Maintenance	
Failed safety inspections	Percentage of failed or overdue safety inspections for your fleet as a % of total safety inspections
Vehicle maintenance downtime (VOR)	% time vehicles off road (VOR) due to maintenance/accidents
Total maintenance cost (pence per mile/kilometre)	Total cost of maintaining the fleet per mile/kilometre
Vehicle downtime	Percentage of defects rectified in 24 hours total
Environment	
CO_2 produced per km	Average CO_2 produced (kg) per mile/km travelled by your fleet
Total CO_2	Total CO_2 emissions produced by the fleet over a period
Safety indicators	
Accident record	Time lost through incidents as a % of total working days
Accident record	Number of days/miles/km since last reportable incident

Further information

http://www.transport-research.info/sites/default/files/project/documents/20060728_
160031_57628_Key%20Performance%20Indicators_Final_Report.pdf

7.4 Warehouse KPIs

Table 7.4 shows some examples of KPIs that can be applied in a warehouse. It is not suggested that all of these measures are introduced; choose the ones that are important to you as a company and to your customers.

TABLE 7.4 Examples of performance indicators for a warehouse

Key performance indicator	Description
Cost indicators	
Average cost per unit shipped (£)	Total cost of warehouse operations/total units shipped
Warehouse costs as a percentage of cost of goods sold	Total cost of warehouse operations/Cost of goods sold (as per the P & L statement)
Warehouse costs as a percentage of sales	Total cost of warehouse operations/Total sales (as per P & L Statement)
Cost per order shipped	Total cost of warehouse operation/Total orders shipped from warehouse
Actual cost per activity	Actual cost by activity/Expected (budget) cost
Productivity indicators	
Orders picked per hour	Orders picked and packed/Total warehouse labour hours
Product Lines picked per hour	Lines picked and packed/Total warehouse labour hours
Items picked per hour	Items picked and packed/Total warehouse labour hours
Pallets picked per hour	Pallets picked/Total warehouse hours worked
Cases picked per hour	Cases picked/Total warehouse hours worked
Service indicators	
On-time despatch	Total orders shipped on time/Total orders shipped
Order fill rate	Orders filled completely/Total orders shipped
On time in full first time	Orders filled completely first time and delivered on time/Total orders

(Continued)

TABLE 7.4 Examples of performance indicators for a warehouse (*Continued*)

Key performance indicator	Description
Damage free shipments	Damage free items shipped/Total items shipped
Paperwork accuracy	Orders shipped with correct paperwork/Total orders shipped
Order accuracy	Orders shipped without errors/Total orders shipped
Line accuracy	Lines shipped without errors/Total lines shipped
Order cycle time	Actual ship date – customer order date
Internal order cycle time	Actual order ready time – customer order receipt time (hours)
Perfect order completion	Orders shipped on time, in full, damage free, with correct paperwork/Total orders shipped
Dock to stock time	Time taken from vehicle arrival to input onto sales system
Utilization Percentage	
Operator hours	100 × Labour hour used/Labour hours available
MHE utilization	100 × MHE hours used/MHE hours available
Picker utilization	100 × Actual case pick rate achieved/Expected cases to be picked
Pallet locations	100 × Pallet locations occupied/Pallet locations available
Environment	
Total CO_2	Total CO_2 emissions produced by the warehouse over a period
Safety indicators	
Accident record	Time lost through incidents as a % of total working days
Accident record	Number of days since last reportable incident
Near miss reports	Number of near misses reported each month

(*Continued*)

TABLE 7.4 Examples of performance indicators for a warehouse (*Continued*)

Key performance indicator	Description
Other measures	
Workforce turnover	Number of operatives leaving/average number of operatives employed over the year
Inventory days on hand	Average inventory value/Average cost of goods sold daily
Inventory count accuracy	Items in correct locations in correct quantity/Total number of locations counted
Inventory days of supply	Current total inventory value/(Total annual cost of goods sold/365)
Inventory shrinkage	Items lost and damaged/Total items in stock (in quantity or value)

Further information

WERC (2015) [accessed 30 December 2015] DC measures 2015, WERC Watch, Spring, http://www.werc.org/DCMeasures2015/

7.5 Balanced Scorecard

Introduction

Much has been written on the Balanced Scorecard and we cannot do full justice to the subject in a few pages; however, we will outline the premise and suggest how you can begin the process and decide whether this is a performance tool you can use in your own company.

Kaplan and Norton (1992), who developed the Balanced Scorecard, believe that you cannot judge the performance of a company solely through financial measures. They suggested three other areas that required a company's attention. The model is now made up of four areas, namely: financial; customer satisfaction; internal practices and procedures; and training and development. The first two perspectives are relevant to the here and now (customers and shareholders) and the last two are relevant to the future (people and processes), thus forming a balanced approach. Many writers have looked to enhance the model by including other aspects within the business that require the attention of staff at all levels throughout the organization.

Figure 7.1 shows an adaptation of the Balanced Scorecard model produced by Performetrix, a producer of software to enhance the Balanced Scorecard. As can be seen, environmental issues have been added to the people quadrant. The Balanced Scorecard is no longer just a simple performance measurement framework, but has evolved into a strategic planning tool and management system.

FIGURE 7.1 Adaptation of the Balanced Scorecard

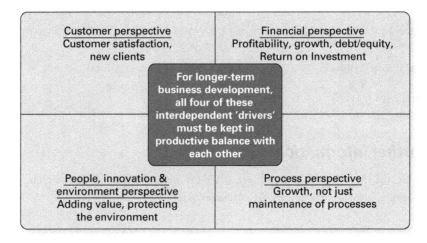

SOURCE: reproduced by kind permission of Performetrix

When to use

When the company is looking to establish and formalize a performance measurement system and instil a culture of continuous improvement. Note that a Balanced Scorecard will take some time to set up.

How to use

The premise is to begin with a vision, determine a strategy or strategies to achieve it and then break these down into activities that have their own measurements. The ideal scenario sees departments within the company all working towards the same vision, with relevant and related KPIs.

First, you need to set out the company's vision and the strategies to achieve this. A SWOT analysis (see tool 6.9) is a good tool in this respect. The perspectives mentioned above need to be clear and understandable to all, both within and outside the business. The top-level scorecard needs to be translated into more detailed plans and tasks and each department given measures and goals that will play a part in achieving the overall vision of the company.

The following steps need to be taken (this can take up to two months to complete):

1 As with the majority of new initiatives, you need to gain board commitment.

2 Find a suitable project owner.

3 Confirm/review/revise your company vision.

4 Define your four business perspectives and ensure clarity and understanding.

5 Formulate the overall strategic aims.

6 Identify the critical success factors and create your initial KPIs with unambiguous definitions. Ensure they are SMART (see tool 7.1).

7 Create the metrics for your KPIs (see tools 7.2, 7.3 and 7.4). Each measure has objectives and targets that are measured against actual performance.

8 Analyse the measures and ensure that they provide 'balance'.

9 Establish a comprehensive top-level scorecard and filter through the organization.

10 Translate the vision into a strategy and the strategy into day-to-day tasks.

11 Produce both long- and short-term goals.

12 Develop an action plan to achieve these goals.

13 Continuously review and be prepared to change.

Figure 7.2 is an example of how a warehouse operation can assist in the success of the company's vision by providing a performance that leads to the achievement of the goals set.

The use of a Balanced Scorecard in this example should result in:

- greater staff safety;
- better practices and procedures;
- fully trained and inspired employees;
- improved communication and information systems;
- a significant increase in customer satisfaction;

FIGURE 7.2 Warehouse operation Balanced Scorecard

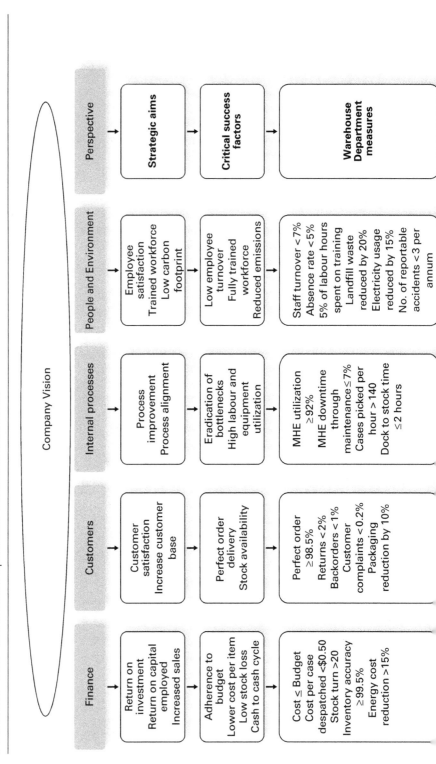

- improved environmental credentials;
- increased profit.

A software program that can help companies in setting and reviewing their performance can be found at http://www.performetrix.co.uk/

Further information

See the original papers by Kaplan and Norton (1992, 1993, 1996) and their book (1996), listed below.

References

http://www.businessballs.com/balanced_scorecard.htm [accessed 5 March 2013]

Kaplan, R S and Norton, D P (1992) The Balanced Scorecard – measures that drive performance, *Harvard Business Review*, Jan–Feb, pp 71–9

Kaplan, R S and Norton, D P (1993) Putting the Balanced Scorecard to work, *Harvard Business Review*, Sep–Oct, pp 134–42

Kaplan, R S and Norton, D P (1996) Using the Balanced Scorecard as a strategic management system, *Harvard Business Review*, Jan–Feb, pp 75–85

Kaplan, R S and Norton, D P (1996) *The Balanced Scorecard*, Harvard Business School Press, Boston, MA

Turner, S (2002) *Tools for Success: A manager's guide*, McGraw-Hill, Maidenhead

7.6 Benchmarking

Introduction

According to Natarjan (2005), benchmarking is:

> the practice of being humble enough to admit that someone else is better at something and being wise enough to try to learn how to match and even surpass them at it. It is a systematic approach to business improvement where best practice is sought and implemented to improve a process beyond the benchmark performance.

Best practice as it is today is not the best possible practice. 'As good as' is not 'better than'. It is not a substitute for creativity and innovation.

Benchmarking is a way of comparing your own performance with that of your peers, be they internal or external, to find out how efficient and effective your business or department is compared to others. By identifying high-performance or best-in-class operations, you can learn what it is they do that allows them to achieve competitive advantage. It also provides you with targets based on other operations currently achieving these levels of performance. Note that, according to Sweeney (2007):

> Benchmarking is not about copying other companies' approaches; rather it is about learning and *adapting* appropriate practices so that they can be usefully *adopted* in an effort to improve efficiency and/or effectiveness (*adapt* before *adopting!*). Companies do not need to be the world's best at everything. All companies have finite resources and benchmarking can help to identify where these resources should be targeted.

When to use

- When you need to understand your own business performance.
- When you want to identify areas for improvement.
- When the competition is stealing a march on you and you need to discover what they are doing better.
- When you need to manage and accelerate change within the business.
- When you are looking to set performance targets that can be proven to be achievable.

How to use

Step 1

Decide the critical success factors or areas of improvement that you want to measure. Don't choose processes that do not have a significant effect on the business or sufficient potential for improvement.

Step 2

Have a detailed knowledge of your own operations and processes. Gather sufficient data to be able to compare accurately with other operations.

Step 3

Decide whether to benchmark internally or externally. Mondelez (previously Cadbury) compares the internal performance of its warehouse with that of its third-party logistics providers. If you are looking to compare performance with your competitors, you need to choose carefully. At the bottom of this section there is a list of specific supply chain and logistics benchmarking clubs you can join to share data and best practice.

A point to note here is that accurate benchmarking relies on companies being open, honest, willing to collaborate and respect confidentiality. According to Turner (2002), there is a benchmarking code of conduct that states: 'Never ask for something you would not be prepared to share in return.'

TABLE 7.5 Stages of benchmarking (Sweeney, 2007)

Stage	Explanation
DEFINE	
Select the area to be studied	Think about what your customers want from the business. What are the issues likely to attract and retain business today and in the future?
Define the process to be benchmarked	Think about those processes that can really make an impact on the business. Think about the parts of the business that add value for the customer and can produce a competitive edge.
Identify potential benchmarking partners	Who do you consider the best in the industry? Who is regarded as being world class in this area? Are there companies in other industries with a reputation for excellence?
Identify the data required, sources and appropriate methods of collection	Brainstorm ideas for the type of data that you can collect to measure the performance of your own and the benchmark company. Alternatives to contacting external companies include trade fairs, company accounts, journals, magazines, customer surveys etc – these can all provide useful information.
ANALYSE	
Collect your data and select benchmarking partners	From all the ideas created from the Define stage you need to evaluate the various options. Take into account factors such as the quality of the data, the cost and time involved in collecting it and whether you are prepared to share the data with other companies. An independent consultant or educational establishment can provide anonymity and independence in this.
Determine the performance gap	Make honest comparisons between your performance and that of the companies you are benchmarking. You need to identify areas where there is significant room for improvement and which will contribute to business success.

(Continued)

TABLE 7.5 Stages of benchmarking (Sweeney, 2007) (*continued*)

Stage	Explanation
Establish the difference in the process	Examine the benchmarked company in more detail. Dig beneath the data to understand what they are actually doing better than you and, more importantly, how they are doing it.
Target future performance	Once you have understood the potential for improvement, you need to develop realistic targets for internal improvement projects.
IMPLEMENT	
Communicate and gain commitment	The data collected during the Analysis stage can be used to convey the scale of the problem and potential for improvement. This can help to create acceptance and commitment to the improvement process.
Adjust targets and develop improvement plan	Individual improvement projects should be established to address the areas for improvement. Plans and targets for these projects should be developed by the people who will be running them, not necessarily the benchmarking team.
Implement and monitor	There is no point in benchmarking if you are not going to make improvements. You need to implement any changes and monitor them to ensure they are achieving what you expected.
REVIEW	
Review progress and recalibrate	Note that the best in the business is always improving on current performance, so you need to continue the process. If you are fully satisfied with a particular area, look for others to improve.

Example

Table 7.6 shows a benchmark exercise for a leisure clothing producer. As can be seen, most companies provided comprehensive information, with a few exceptions. The companies were all able to measure their own performance against their peers and concentrate on their areas of weakness, be it stock turn, items picked per hour or cost as a percentage of sales.

TABLE 7.6 Example benchmark exercise – clothing producer

Measure	Company A	Company B	Company C	Company D	Company E	Company F	Company G
Stock turn	7	8	20	5.2	11	7	7
Logistics costs as a % of sales	6.04%	NK	8–10%	NK	Reluctant to share	Reluctant to share	4.7%
Warehouse costs as a % of sales	3.16%	2.90%	3.2%	2–5%	2.75%	3%	4.25%
Lines per hour picked	Not measured	Not measured	50	9.3	Not measured	8	8
Units per hour picked	79.4	48	Not measured	Not measured	89	Not measured	Not measured
Shipping accuracy	99.89%	99.9%	98%	99.2%	99%	98.2%	98.6%
Stock accuracy	99.89%	99.995%	99.6%	98.66	99%	97.5%	98.1%

A word of warning: not every competitor or peer for that matter will have exactly the same product and order profile, for example, and therefore an exact comparison is rarely achievable.

Some benchmarking clubs and reports

UK

Logmark – http://www.ciltuk.org.uk/Membership/Organisation/Benchmarking Logmark.aspx

Palmark – http://www.ciltuk.org.uk/Membership/Organisation/Palmark.aspx

United States

APQC – https://www.apqc.org/

CSCR – http://www.smeal.psu.edu/cscr/bench/trans/transportation-benchmarking-consortium-1

DLMB Consortium – http://dlmbc.com/benchmarking-clients

WERC – http://www.werc.org/

Australasia

Benchmarking Success – http://www.benchmarkingsuccess.com/default.asp

Other benchmarking sites

www.benchmarking.com
www.benchnet.com

References

Natarjan, R (2005) *Technical Education, Current status and future direction*, vol III, ICFAI University Press, India

Richards, G (2014) *Warehouse Management*, 2nd edn, Kogan Page, London

Sweeney, E (2007) Supply chain benchmarking and performance measurement: towards the learning supply chain, in *Perspectives on Supply Chain Management and Logistics – Creating competitive organizations in the 21st century*, Blackhall Publishers, Dublin, ch 15, pp 283–94

Turner, S (2002) *Tools for Success: A manager's guide*, McGraw-Hill, Maidenhead

Financial management tools and ratios

8.1 Activity-based costing (ABC) and time-driven activity-based costing (TDABC)

Introduction

ABC is a financial cost accounting model. It differs from traditional finance models as it attempts to allocate all costs, including overheads, directly to each product, activity or customer.

Traditional cost accountancy models allocate indirect costs or overheads on the basis of volume or as a percentage of total direct cost. In a traditional costing model, all products and customers are allocated the same percentage overhead irrespective of activity, such as management time spent on them. As a result, low-volume products and smaller customers are not always allocated the true cost of producing or servicing them. This can result in under-priced products and customers being either under- or overcharged. This became very apparent to the author when he became customer services manager for a leading 3PL. With over 25 clients, it always seemed to be the smallest client that took up a large percentage of time, rather than the large corporate clients – yet costs were spread across the clients, based on their volume of business.

This becomes more difficult when we look to allocate costs such as the human resources, finance, sales and marketing, IT and health and safety departments. ABC assigns the cost of each activity in an organization to all products, services and customers according to the actual consumption of the resource.

The main drawback to ABC is the time it takes to gather all of the information and to accurately allocate the indirect and overhead costs. A further drawback is the fact that not all costs can be allocated precisely. With this in mind, Kaplan and Anderson (2004) came up with time-driven activity-based costing, which will be discussed in the last section of this tool.

When to use

This tool is for companies that want to be more accurate in terms of allocating costs. It can also be used to identify non-value-adding processes such as relabelling or double checking. Time-driven ABC also highlights available capacity and areas for productivity improvements.

How to use

To illustrate the tool we have used the example of a shared user third-party warehouse. First, we need to gather the overall cost of the business by category:

1 Identify the major elements of cost within the company:

   a Employee costs:

   Warehouse

   Administration

   Direct management and supervision.

   b Building costs:

   Rent

   Rates

   Insurance

   Security

   Utilities

   Maintenance

   Cleaning and waste

   Rack depreciation.

   c Equipment costs:

   Forklift trucks

   Stretch-wrap machines

   Conveyors

   Automated Storage and Retrieval System (AS/RS)

   Scanners, voice, pick to light systems.

d Material costs:

Pallets

Stretch-wrap

Packaging

Labels

Paper.

e IT and telecoms:

Hardware

Software

Maintenance

Monthly rental.

f Inventory holding costs:

Obsolescence

Damage

Interest

Insurance

Stock counting.

g Support department costs:

Finance

Sales and Marketing

Customer Services

HR

Health and Safety

Legal.

2 Identify and define the relevant activities carried out in the company:

a In-handling

b Put-away

c Storage

d Order picking

e Replenishment

f Value-adding services

g Dispatch.

3 Determine the relationships between activities and costs.

4 Identify cost drivers to assign costs to activities. These can include number of pallets stored, orders processed, pallets received, etc.

5 Any costs that cannot be attributed to specific activities should be pooled together with other one-off costs, such as donations to charity, and termed residual costs.

Points to note here are that the cost of collecting, analysing and allocating the data should not outweigh the benefits, and that allocation within 5–10 per cent is acceptable in the initial stages.

Finally, when asked how much time staff spend on activities, they neglect to mention the idle time, including breaks, waiting for instructions, delays, etc. This needs to be addressed by examining the warehouse management or labour management systems or undertaking time-and-motion studies.

Example

In the standard ABC model the information shown in Table 8.1 applies for a warehouse with a total cost of £3,500,000.

In terms of the traditional costing model, it is likely that the IT and telecoms cost will have been combined with the support costs and allocated equally across all of the activities. As we can see in Table 8.1, the support costs are allocated based on the time involved on each activity by the support staff.

Having calculated the total cost by activity, we can now identify the cost drivers. For example, in terms of in-handling we can choose the number of pallets and/or cases received, and for order pick we can use the number of orders processed or the number of cases picked. In the case of in-handling, if both pallets and loose cartons are received the cost will need to be broken down further, as shown in Table 8.2.

Time-driven ABC

In time-driven ABC (TDABC), Kaplan and Anderson (2004) have come up with a simpler version of ABC. They suggest that managers need to work out the resource required to service a transaction, product or customer. We therefore need to know the cost in time units (and space if we are discussing warehouses) and the time taken per activity.

First, we need to estimate the actual productive time of the staff. This can be done by interrogating WMS and LMS systems or initially producing a

TABLE 8.1 ABC model

Cost Centres	Total cost (£)	Warehouse activities						
		In-handling	Put-away	Storage	Order pick	Replenishment	Value adding services	Despatch
Direct employees	862,000	10%	5%		55%	10%	10%	10%
Supervision and management	200,000	10%	5%		55%	5%	15%	10%
Building	1,400,000	10%		75%			5%	10%
Equipment	386,000	15%	5%	5%	45%	10%	5%	15%
Material	38,000	15%		40%	15%		25%	5%
IT and telecoms	200,000	10%	5%	20%	45%	10%	5%	5%
Support costs	414,000	10%	5%	20%	35%	5%	15%	10%
Total	3,500,000	371,200	103,100	1,207,300	998,400	175,500	287,100	357,400
Potential cost drivers		No of pallets	No of pallets	No of pallets/ locations	No of orders	No of pallets	No of units	No of pallets
		No of loads	No of cases	Square metres	No of items	No of cases	Time taken	No of loads
		No of cases	No of units	Cubic metres	No of lines	No of lines	No of staff	No of cases
		No of units	Cube/weight	No of units	No of units	No of locations		No of orders

TABLE 8.2 Cost allocation

Activity	% time spent	Allocated cost	Volume	Rate per item
In-handle pallets	13.9%	51,556	52,000	0.99
In-handle cases	86.1%	319,644	1,395,000	0.23
Total		£371,200		

guesstimate. For example, where staff are working a 45-hour week we can guesstimate their productive time at 80 per cent of the total available hours. This equates to 36 hours per week.

When reporting the time it takes to undertake a task, it is unlikely that staff will include such things as delays, preparation time and breaks, either scheduled or non-scheduled. We therefore need to check the WMS system again or undertake a time-and-motion study for the various tasks. In terms of the in-handling example, we end up with Table 8.3, based on the time taken to undertake each of the tasks.

TABLE 8.3 Time-driven ABC

Activity	Unit time (minutes)	Volume	Total minutes	Total cost (£)	Cost per unit
In-handle pallets	1.154	52,000	60,000	39,600	0.762
In-handle cases	0.3	1,395,000	418,500	276,210	0.198
Total capacity used			478,500	315,810	
Total supplied			561,600	371,200	
Unused capacity			83,100	55,390	

If we base our calculations on five staff members, we have a productive time of 36 hours × 5 staff × 52 weeks × 60 minutes, which gives us a cost per minute of £371,200/561,600 = £0.66. In Table 8.3 we see that the cost per unit is lower than in the traditional ABC method and we end up with £55,390 of unallocated costs and 1,385 spare hours. Based on the above figures, we know that we have additional capacity for increased volumes and additional clients. We can also determine whether, by further increasing productivity, we can reduce the headcount by at least one person.

Figure 8.1 shows that a percentage of support costs/overheads and some of the unallocated activity costs end up as residual cost, and therefore they are not allocated to specific products or customers unfairly, as they would be in a traditional overhead allocation system. These costs become indirect until they are reduced, removed or allocated to new customers.

FIGURE 8.1 Cost allocation based on consumption

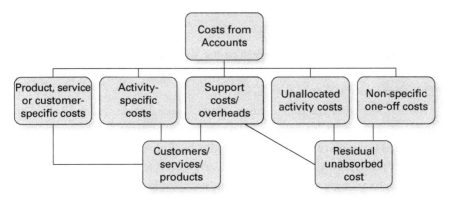

SOURCE: adapted from FSN © 2013 FSN Publishing Limited

Further information

Further information and articles can be found at: http://www.brighthub.com/office/finance/articles/78752.aspx [accessed 25 October 2012]

References

Anon (2007) [accessed 25 October 2012] Introducing activity based costing (ABC) and activity based management (ABM), http://www.fsn.co.uk/channel_bi_bpm_cpm/introducing_activity_based_costing_and_activity_based_management.htm

Kaplan, R S and Anderson, S R (2004) Time driven activity based costing, *Harvard Business Review*, **82** (11), November, pp 131–8, p 150

8.2 Value tree financial model, by Enrico Camerinelli

Introduction

To ensure the existence of the causal relationships between financial performance and operational decisions, the mapping of financial metrics to operational metrics has to be proven. Operational metrics abound: on-time delivery, logistics costs, warehouse management costs, manufacturing productivity and forecast accuracy. Financial metrics are best represented by the following elements from the balance sheet and income statement.

From the income statement

- Revenue – the top-line figure par excellence of the income statement. It is clearly directly related to how supply chain operations are performed.

- Cost of goods sold (COGS) – quantifies the cost of producing a product or service to be sold to the market. It represents the total costs of acquiring raw materials and turning them into finished goods.

- Selling, general and administrative (SG&A) expenses – indirect expenses are those most appropriate to gauging whether or not supply chain operations are run efficiently. All 'hidden' costs pile up under this figure to generate unwelcome surprises in the year-end financial report.

From the balance sheet

- Inventories – a financial item that clearly puts the supply chain under the microscope.

- Accounts receivable (AR) – the amount of money owed from the customers is a clear sign of the ability of the supply chain management team to fulfil demand expectations. This value can be excessive due to poor credit control.

- Accounts payable (AP) – the way the company manages relations with its suppliers and compensates them.

With a healthy list of operational and financial metrics with which to work, the purpose is to build a model that allows you to correlate these metrics so that any activity measured with one set of metrics will immediately have a corresponding effect on the other. The model proposed represents a bridge between financial performance and operational supply chain decisions.

When to use

The 'value tree' model provides an early step in closing the gap between supply chain managers and the finance directors. The existing misalignment between cost reduction, operations excellence and value creation defines what can be called the 'internal' gap, as it is generated within the company's own walls. The internal gap is important when we consider that a company must first enable internal collaboration before exposing itself to partnerships in the open market. Most companies are still operating with silo structures, where product development, procurement, manufacturing, sales and logistics focus solely on their own processes, independent of their colleagues in other departments. To change this, companies can use the model to look at their own processes with a view to optimizing and aligning them more closely with business strategy before implementing applications to support that strategy.

Establishing internal collaboration is important to prepare the way for a stronger and more sustainable rapport with external supply chain constituents. Collaboration is based first of all on trust, which must be shared by both parties. Sharing and agreement suppose that both parties speak the same language to communicate options and decisions. The most important aspect of collaboration is the common language that brings together the intentions and objectives of each counter-party.

Much of the value of the model is in the language it provides to bridge supply chain management and finance, and in its contribution to closing the external gap between company investors, shareholders and the company's board. The role of the supply chain manager can be elevated if he or she can provide evidence as to how the actions performed as part of the supply chain management operations, guided by the correlations illustrated in the model, can positively impact the company's overall profit. The model breaks down the initial indicator (ie economic value added, or EVA[1]) into components and subcomponents, creating a cascade of correlated factors that translate the initial financial measure of corporate value into the 'leaves' of the value tree. The elements of accounts payable, accounts receivable, property and equipment are at the furthest reaches of the tree. These are the metrics that constitute the interfaces that plug supply chain management into finance.

How to use

In measuring corporate performance it is helpful to embrace EVA, which is graphically illustrated by the 'value tree' in Figure 8.2. The term 'value tree' expresses the topology of the model, which graphically represents the parent–child correlations as branches of a tree.

The important factor of the model is that it simultaneously represents elements of both the balance sheet and the income statement. In fact, profit and all its correlated branches on the top side of the value tree are part of

FIGURE 8.2 Value tree model

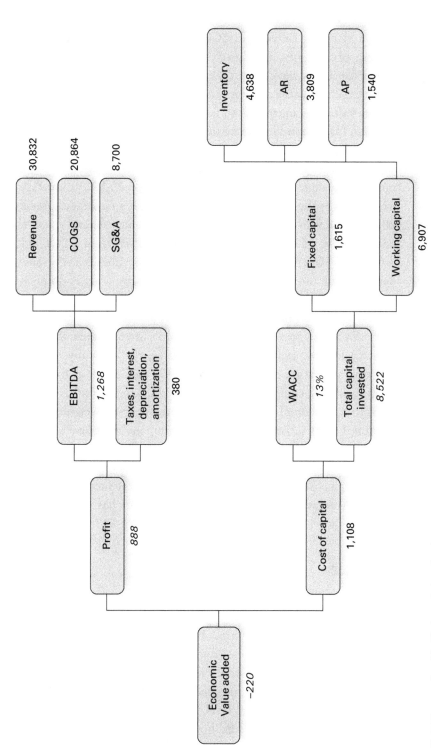

SOURCE: reproduced by kind permission of Enrico Camerinelli

the income statement report. So, too, are revenue and expenses and their related elements COGS and SG&A, expressing the company's ability to achieve profitability. The lower part of the tree represents items whose values can be extracted from the balance sheet, in which working capital and fixed capital are both important elements.

The value tree must be read from right to left. Starting from the middle top, EBITDA (earnings before interest, taxes, depreciation and amortization) is the result of revenue minus expenses, where expenses is the combination of COGS and SG&A costs. The first calculation we see from the numbers is that the company has revenue of 30,832 (monetary unit is irrelevant for the purpose of the example) and an average cost of sales of 20,864. The firm has SG&A costs of 8,700 which remain relatively fixed, and its tax value is 380. These figures yield EBITDA of 1,268 (ie Revenue – COGS – SG&A) and a profit after taxes (ie EBITDA – taxes, interest, depreciation and amortization) of 888. The company is doing well as it produces a positive profit after taxes.

The company's income statement figures, however, do not tell the whole story. We must now refer to the bottom part of Figure 8.2, again from right to left. To generate 30,832 of sales, the company employs 6,907 working capital (ie Inventory + AR - AP) and 1,615 of fixed capital (eg plant, property, equipment). The sum of working capital and fixed capital leads to total capital invested of 8,522. Assuming a weighted average cost of capital (WACC[2]) of 13 per cent, the company must bear a cost of capital of 1,108 to repay shareholders and lenders a fair return. The company's final EVA is -220, meaning that to generate revenues of 888 the company is bearing a cost of 1,108 to pay investors and creditors for the use of their capital. A negative EVA means that the company has destroyed value, as it would be generating a less than adequate return on investment (ROI).

Example

The supply chain manager can use the elements at the borders of the model as interfaces that enable a more detailed breakdown of the metrics into practical, actionable items. Using the information from these interfaces, supply chain managers can organize action items for the resources that fall under their control. An important part of the supply chain manager's role is to act as an intermediary between the higher-level decision makers and the operational level where the company's resources execute the strategies decided by the board. All the data needed for decision making at the higher level are highly aggregated and directly linked with basic raw data that come from operations and specific transactions. These regulate the minute-by-minute decisions that govern activities at the operational level below.

The following example clarifies how to use the model. The CEO's long-term performance strategy is measured in terms of total return to shareholders (ie EVA) – the value generated by the company and the return expected by its shareholders. To support the CEO's decision on what actions to take in order to achieve the expected return, the model breaks down the EVA as the result of profit and cost of capital. The first component quantifies the ability of the company to keep costs under control to generate profitable return. The second component measures how well the company generates cash flow relative to the capital it has invested in its business. When the profit is greater than the cost of capital, the company is creating value. When it is less than the cost of capital, value is destroyed. The model goes beyond this initial correlation of factors to further break down the value items into more manageable components.

It can be seen that there is a wide gap, both in terms of the level of detail and in the ability to link such distant levels of resources that must ultimately work for the same company with the objective of making it more successful and profitable. A 'facilitator' is needed to bridge both sides by translating high-level directives, such as increasing EVA by 5 per cent, into operational indications, such as studying and engineering a leaner changeover time for a specific highly expensive asset in order to reduce non-value-adding activities in favour of more profitable operations. The ability to break down high-level financial indicators and transform them into their constituent cost elements provides invaluable support to operators at the lower level, who establish their decisions according to extremely detailed and specific guidelines and workflows.

The opposite is also true. It is up to the supply chain manager to aggregate and articulate – in a value-based fashion – all the activities that make up the company's daily operations. The ability to capture the essence of the value generated from activities at the shop-floor level, such as reducing throughput time, and translate it into an indicator that is relevant to the finance team, such as a review of prices due to improved delivery performance, is among the skills now required by a supply chain manager.

The model works in both directions. First, moving from left to right, it links expected financial performance results (ie the EVA) to the actionable practices of supply chain management that will most likely lead to an improvement in those results. The user of the model will then be able to assess the current status of the company in terms of financially related results – delving into the language of the executives at decision level – and then convert the improvement actions into operational practices that are more easily executable by the resources at the operation level. Second, it has to support the supply chain manager in translating the language of supply chain management performance into strategic business objectives that belong at the decision level. That is, by moving from right to left, the model enables evaluation of the consequences of decisions taken to tailor the supply chain to the needs of the market, which must be represented in terms of high-level performance metrics (ie EVA).

Further information

Enrico Camerinelli's book, *Measuring the Value of the Supply Chain – Linking Financial Performance and Supply Chain Decisions*, can be found at https://www.routledge.com/Measuring-the-Value-of-the-Supply-Chain-Linking-Financial-Performance/Camerinelli/p/book/9780566087943

Notes

1 A registered trademark of Stern Stewart & Co.

2 WACC represents the weighted average cost of capital in the sense that it averages the two components of cost of capital: capital from debt (loans from banks) and capital from equity.

8.3 Calculating return on investment and payback period

Introduction

Return on investment is a financial measure used widely within companies to decide whether investment in an asset such as technology, machinery or software is going to be cost-effective and how long the payback period is likely to be. The tool can also be used to compare investment in different projects, thus enabling the company to decide on the most efficient and cost-effective investment. The higher the ROI and the shorter the payback period, the more attractive the investment.

When to use

When you are contemplating the introduction of new equipment or technology to improve processes and/or reduce cost.

Seeking improvements in a process can require investment in new equipment, technology or software. As a manager you are likely to need to justify such an investment. You will therefore need to know the cost of the enhancement along with other costs such as training, annual maintenance, loss of performance during implementation, etc, together with the potential savings and, once calculated, the time frame for the return on your investment.

ROI time-frame expectations are reducing and therefore the more accurate the report and the shorter the time frame, the more likely the investment is going to be considered.

How to use

When deciding to introduce a new solution into the business you need to understand the total costs of the project. This not only includes the cost of the hardware and software but also the cost of implementation, staff costs, training and peripherals. You also need to know what your operation is achieving at present (the base case) without the enhancement and what it is likely to achieve once the enhancement has been introduced. Having calculated these figures, you can then work out what your savings are and, as a result, your ROI and the timescale over which the new system will pay for itself.

Example

During a recent voice picking trial a client calculated that its ROI, by replacing barcode scan picking, was approximately 25.4 per cent in the first year, with a payback period of nine and a half months. The method of calculation was as follows:

$$\frac{\left(\text{Gain from investment}\left[\text{or savings made}\right]-\text{cost of investment}\right)}{\text{Cost of investment}}\times100$$

A similar calculation was the payback period. This is calculated by dividing the net investment by the benefit accrued. This basically measures how long an investment takes to pay for itself. It does have drawbacks, however, as it does not properly take into account finance costs and opportunity costs, opportunity cost being what must be given up (the next best alternative) as a result of the decision. The figures were as follows:

Pick productivity savings	£52,800
Increased accuracy savings	£33,600
Total savings (TS)	£86,400
Investment in voice (I)	£68,900

Therefore $(£86,400 - £68,900)/68,900 = 25.4\%$

Payback period $= £68,900/£86,400 \times 12$ months $= 9.6$ months

This isn't a totally accurate picture as no account was taken of the extra training costs and the effect on the business during the early stages of implementation, etc. However, as the voice system is likely to last at least five years, this looks like a good investment.

A risk analysis should also be undertaken to confirm that these potential savings are accurate and can be achieved with the introduction of voice. This gives the company a reasonably accurate picture of the potential ROI achieved through the introduction of voice technology.

One drawback of using payback period as a method of choosing which investment to go for is that it doesn't take into account the cash flow outside the payback period, as is illustrated in Table 8.4. Project A has the shortest payback period; however, projects B and C have the greatest profit/saving.

TABLE 8.4 Payback period comparison

	Project A	Project B	Project C
Initial investment ('000)	240	240	300
Year 1 profit/saving	80	60	60
Year 2 profit /saving	80	60	60
Year 3 profit/saving	80	60	60
Year 4 profit/saving	10	60	60
Year 5 profit/saving	0	60	60
Profit/saving over 5 years	250	300	300

▨ Payback period

Further information

Marsh (2013) provides step-by-step guides and templates for different finance models. An ROI payback calculator for voice picking can be found at http://www.bcpsoftware. com/solutions/voice-technology-solutions/voice-payback-calculator/

References

LXE, Inc (2009) Maximize the power of your workforce: learn how hands free solutions can bring value in a tough economy

Marsh, C (2013) *Business and Financial Models*, Kogan Page, London

8.4 An engineered approach to calculate equipment ROI, by Aaron Lininger

Introduction

Too many companies buy warehouse equipment and technology on a 'best case' scenario. Using an 'engineered' approach to evaluating the ROI provides a more accurate picture of cost and productivity benefits. This is an alternative to the method discussed in tool 8.3.

Many investments fail to deliver promised gains because vendors' initial estimates of cost and productivity benefits are often based on a 'best case' scenario. Those estimates often prove to be inaccurate because each facility has unique physical, process and data constraints, making it difficult to determine what a new technology or piece of equipment can accomplish in a particular environment.

An 'engineered' approach is a more effective method for evaluating potential capital investments. It entails studying the current state of operations at a 'micro' level and pinpointing the specific elements affected by introducing a new technology. The degree to which each element will be affected can be assessed using work-study techniques and/or realistic estimates made by experts. This approach develops a savings estimate reflecting the reality of a particular facility, thereby improving a company's insight into bottom-line impacts of cost-saving initiatives and reducing the potential for costly mistakes.

When to use

When contemplating the purchase of new technology or equipment.

How to use

Step 1

Identify specific aspects of an operation the company is targeting for improvement, and how each will change as a result of introducing new technology or equipment.

Step 2

Consider how this solution will impact other areas of the operation, both upstream and downstream processes, as well as maintenance and support functions – if at all.

Step 3

Consider the impact on a facility's physical layout and traffic patterns. For example:

- Can the equipment be positioned so as not to impede the traffic flow?
- How will the equipment interact with other pieces of equipment in the workspace?
- Will the pre- and post-trip inspections or preventive maintenance programmes need to be modified and/or introduced to ensure the safety of those working with it or in its vicinity?

Step 4

Understand the degree of reliability the new solution must have and the maintenance needed to support the new solution.

Step 5

Gather a baseline value (often measured in time for labour savings) for each step of the task being examined. Each step is broken into smaller steps called elements. Elements unaffected by the new technology can be ignored, allowing the buyer to isolate the true differences between the operation before and after the new solution has been implemented. Methods of collecting the times to carry out each element include stopwatch studies and time-and-motion studies.

Step 6

Project how each element will be affected after implementation. Under ideal circumstances, a potential buyer would introduce the equipment or technology into a facility, train individuals in how to employ it, and then study how it performs and what impact it has in the environment in which it will actually be used. Testing the solution at a facility can reveal unforeseen pitfalls and shortcomings as well as provide fact-based information for subsequent discussions with the vendor. Because many capital investments are large and complex, it may not be possible to test them like this. In such cases, simulation models can be used; however, it is imperative to document all assumptions as they will form the framework for any conclusions drawn from the data.

Step 7

Calculate the differences and apply them to the labour model and affected processes in order to determine the new solution's cost and productivity implications (see Table 8.5).

Example

The management team of Company A's distribution centre (DC) attended a trade show where a vendor was showcasing a new electric pallet jack that automatically advances to its next location without the operator touching the controls. Company A's DC uses pallet jacks during order selection, which is the largest use of labour in the facility. The vendor claims that its automatic pallet jack will improve productivity in order selection by up to 30 per cent by eliminating the steps operators take to return to the equipment controls, allowing them to walk directly to their next location.

When scaled to its facility, the 30 per cent productivity improvement represented huge financial savings for Company A; even achieving one-third of that would be worth serious consideration. Before making a large capital expenditure, the company opted to take an engineered approach to evaluating the technology.

The company already had baseline numbers for the potentially impacted areas:

- the steps to and from the pallet jack to the pick location;
- the steps from the case-placement location back to the equipment controls;
- grasping of the controls;
- the acceleration constant for their fleet of equipment.

The vendor allowed Company A to test one of the automated pallet jacks at its facility to help in the decision-making process and hopefully close the sale. Company A invested several weeks in training an individual so that the pallet jack would be operated as the vendor intended. An engineer then studied the equipment under normal operating conditions, focusing on generating values for the affected elements of the picking process. In studying the new equipment, the engineer discovered an additional factor to consider: a system-response delay before the equipment moves forward. Table 8.5 shows a summary of the values collected.

The element values indicate that potential savings exist but overall savings cannot be determined until the appropriate frequency of occurrence for each element is applied to each value. In the absence of simulation capabilities in a labour management system, the frequencies can be calculated using the following:

- total cases selected;
- total locations visited;
- percentage of cases selected after short travel (from 9 feet to 40 feet between selection bays; manual travel will still be used for longer distances);
- percentage of locations visited after short travel (from 9 feet to 40 feet between selection bays).

Once the company calculated those frequencies and knew the elemental times, it simply had to 'do the maths'; see Table 8.5. Several factors were not considered in this calculation, including maintenance-support hours and the impact on congestion delays. With these factors excluded, the values shown represent a 'best case' scenario. Based on the cost of the additional investment in this technology, the results of the study would need to yield at least a 10 per cent saving to justify serious consideration of such an investment.

After calculating a solid value of the projected labour gains, the management team decided not to purchase the equipment unless the vendor was able to significantly reduce the price or further enhance the equipment to provide additional gains at the same price. The vendor's projected gains of 30 per cent were actually closer to 20 per cent and new pallet jacks would only affect 25 per cent of the total labour component of order picking, thus bringing down the overall savings into the neighbourhood of 5 per cent. Other factors not included in the trial results include improved health and safety of the operators.

This methodology can also be used for increased accuracy in resource planning (see tool 1.8).

(Adapted from 'A better way to calculate equipment ROI' by Aaron Lininger, a manager at West Monroe Partners LLC, which first appeared in the Quarter 2 (2012) edition of CSCMP's *Supply Chain Quarterly*.)

TABLE 8.5 Engineered approach to ROI using time-and-motion studies

Element	Baseline (seconds)	Future state	Difference	Frequency 1	Frequency 1 data	Frequency 2	Frequency 2 data	Labour savings (hours)
Steps to first case	3.0	2.5	−0.50	100,000	Locations	30,000	% locations after short travel	−4.17
Steps with first case	2.9	2.25	−0.65	100,000	Locations	30,000	% locations after short travel	−5.42
Steps to additional case	2.5	2.4	−0.10	125,000	Cases	43,750	% cases after short travel	−1.22
Steps with additional case	2.5	2.4	−0.10	125,000	Cases	43,750	% cases after short travel	−1.22
Return to drive short distance	3.0	0.0	−3.00	100,000	Locations	30,000	% locations after short travel	−25
Grab equipment controls for travel	1.0	0.0	−1.00	100,000	Locations	30,000	% locations after short travel	−8.33
Pallet jack acceleration/ deceleration	5.0	6.0	1.00	100,000	Locations	30,000	% locations after short travel	8.33
System response time	0.00	1.0	1.00	100,000	Locations	30,000	% locations after short travel	8.33

Labour hours reduction	−28.7
Current labour hours	580
New labour hours	551.3
% impact	4.95%

8.5 Supply chain financial ratios and metrics

Introduction

An understanding of finance is essential for the majority of managers in today's business world. Supply chain and logistics is no exception so we have put together a list of financial ratios that can impact supply chain operations.

Financial ratios are used as a tool to analyse the financial situation of your business through its financial statements. The following ratios and metrics are used substantially within the supply chain.

Return on assets (ROA)

This ratio determines how efficiently assets are being used to generate income; it is expressed as a percentage. A high return on assets can suggest a rapid turnover of assets or a high profit margin, or both.

$$\text{ROA} = \frac{\text{Net profit before income tax}}{\text{total assets} \times 100}$$

Return on capital employed (ROCE)

ROCE can be calculated in a number of different ways. Calculations can be made with actual figures or averages. It has the advantage of being simple to use but it doesn't take into account the timing of cash flows. ROCE is calculated as follows:

Average profit before interest and tax (PBIT)/Capital employed × 100

Where PBIT or operating profit is defined as sales minus operating expenses before the payment of interest and taxes

Where Capital employed (CE) is defined as share capital plus reserves plus long-term loans *or* fixed assets plus working capital (net current assets).

For a specific investment of, say, $120,000 and average profit returned over a period of 5 years of $24,000, we get a ROCE figure of 20 per cent.

Discounted cash flow and net present value/internal rate of return

According to Marsh (2013), these are the most widely used methods of investment appraisal as they take into account the timing of cash flows. As money changes value over time, we need a method that takes account of this.

The net present value (NPV) calculation compares the price of the investment to the level of future savings that it will provide. One simple example of an NPV calculation is to consider whether you would rather have $100 today or $120 a year from today. To arrive at an answer in this example, you would have to decide how much interest could be earned in a year on the $100. If you could earn more than 20 per cent you would accept the $100 today, because your earnings after one year would be greater than the $120 you would otherwise receive.

To calculate the NPV on an investment, several pieces of information are needed. First, determine the total cost of the project. Second, calculate the annual savings for at least the first four years after implementation. Finally, determine the rate of return required by the company on capital investments.

Example

Assume you spend $300,000 today for a WMS that will provide estimated savings of $100,000 in the first year and $150,000 in years two to four. Note that the present-day value of these savings is less than $100,000 and $150,000, respectively. Your objective in calculating the NPV is to determine the value of those annual savings today and compare it to present-day cost ($300,000).

Assume that your management requires a return of 15 per cent on all capital investments. At 15 per cent, the first year's savings of $100,000 is worth $86,960 at the present day. Present-day value of $150,000 savings for years two to four is $113,415, $98,625 and $85,770, respectively. Add the total savings in today's dollars and you get $384,770. Because the total saving in today's dollars ($384,770) is greater than the total price of the WMS ($300,000), the investment can be justified.

Operating profit/net profit

$$\frac{\text{PBIT}}{\text{sales}} \times 100$$

Where PBIT = Sales – operating costs. This measures the profit of a company before the payment of interest and taxes.

Days payable outstanding

$$\frac{\text{Accounts payable}}{(\text{Total annual cost of goods sold} / 365)}$$

This measures the average number of days a company takes to pay its suppliers.

Days sales outstanding

$$\frac{\text{Accounts Receivable}}{(\text{Annual Revenue} / 365)}$$

This measures the average number of days it takes a company to collect its money from its customers.

Inventory turnover ratio

$$\frac{\text{Cost of goods sold}}{\text{Average inventory value}}$$

A low number here may indicate that either your stock is slow moving or that there may be problems such as the presence of obsolete stock, low customer demand or order quantities are too high for the demand, resulting in little or no movement. Low numbers are typical in a spare parts operation where stock is held just in case.

Inventory days of supply

$$\frac{\text{Current total inventory value}}{(\text{Total annual cost of goods sold} / 365)}$$

This measures the quantity of inventory on hand in relation to the number of days of usage to be covered.

Distribution cost as a percentage of sales

$$\frac{\text{Total distribution costs}}{\text{Total sales}}$$

$$\frac{\text{Total distribution costs}}{\text{Total cost of goods sold}}$$

Both these metrics can be used to benchmark against other companies. Total distribution costs can include both warehousing and transportation costs. It can also be widened to include inbound costs.

Other financial metrics include:

- Fixed cost versus variable cost split.
- Cost increase versus sales revenue increase.
- Inventory value change versus sales value change.

All of these are compared with previous years' figures.

References

Marsh, C (2013) *Business and Financial Models*, Kogan Page, Philadelphia

SmallBizConnect (nd) [accessed 1 May 2013] Small business toolkit: key
    performance indicators, http://toolkit.smallbiz.nsw.gov.au/
    part/6/30/143?&lang=en_us&output=json

Problem-solving tools

9.1 Brainstorming

Introduction

Brainstorming is an organized problem-solving discussion. It is when a team of people get together to produce ideas for the solution of a problem or for a new service or product. A cross-functional team is seen as ideal, as sometimes people are too close to a problem to come up with workable solutions.

When to use

When solutions for a particular problem are hard to come by and it needs a team of people to come up with some new ideas or solutions.

How to use

Assemble a group of people together in a room to suggest as many ideas as possible in the hope of arriving at a solution to an ongoing problem or for a new strategy or service.

Brainstorming is normally seen as a group activity; however, recent research has suggested that individuals should spend time alone, thinking of potential solutions before coming together with colleagues to discuss their various ideas. This overcomes some of the issues of people being reticent about coming forward with ideas in a group environment.

All participants should write down their ideas on Post-It™ notes and place them on a wall or white board. These can be discussed as they're placed on the wall or discussion can take place later; see Figure 9.1.

FIGURE 9.1 Brainstorming using Post-It® stickers

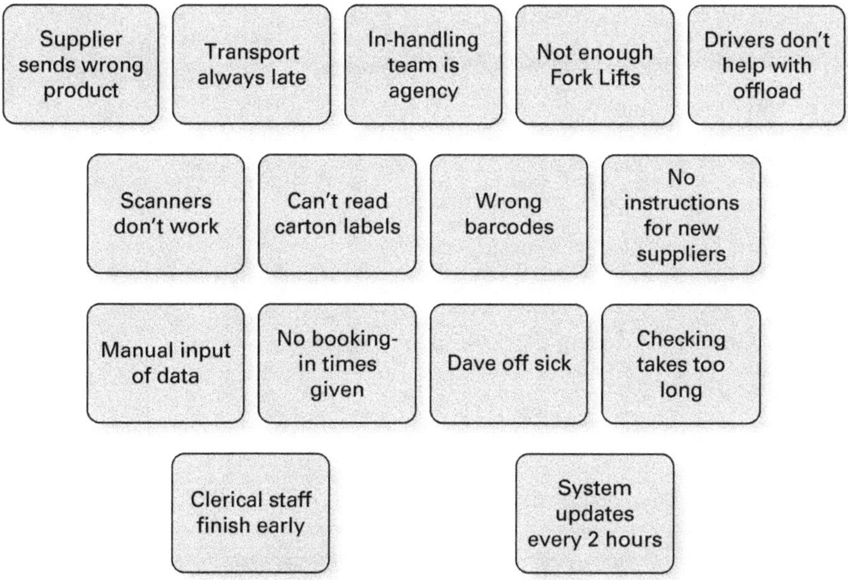

| Supplier sends wrong product | Transport always late | In-handling team is agency | Not enough Fork Lifts | Drivers don't help with offload |

| Scanners don't work | Can't read carton labels | Wrong barcodes | No instructions for new suppliers |

| Manual input of data | No booking-in times given | Dave off sick | Checking takes too long |

| Clerical staff finish early | System updates every 2 hours |

Method

Turner (2003) proposes the following steps:

1 Choose a cross-section of people.

2 Set aside sufficient time with no interruptions.

3 Clearly state the problem or topic and make sure everyone understands.

4 Ask each team member to present his or her ideas, one at a time, in sequence (team members can pass if they don't have anything to add).

5 Record all the ideas exactly as given. No judgements are made until the end of the session.

6 After all the ideas are listed, check for clarification from the team members.

7 When the ideas dry up, it's time to stop.

8 The group then examines each idea in turn, expanding on them, categorizing them and perhaps combining or eliminating some.

9 Put time limits on the discussions.

It may be possible to group the ideas and put them under headings that can then be used as key areas to take forward (see Figure 9.2).

The rules for brainstorming are:

- No criticism of the person, just the idea.
- State ideas quickly.
- Basic ideas initially.
- Don't worry about stating the obvious.
- Don't worry about repeating ideas.
- Link ideas and try to improve on others.
- No questions during the session.
- Quantity is good.

FIGURE 9.2 Affinity diagram

Suppliers	Systems/ process	People	Transport	Equipment
Can't read carton labels	Manual input of data	In-handling team is agency	No booking-in times given	Not enough Fork Lifts
Wrong barcodes	No booking-in times given	Checking takes too long	Transport always late	Scanners don't work
Checking takes too long	No instructions for new suppliers	Dave off sick	Drivers don't help with offload	
Supplier sends wrong product	System updates every 2 hours	Clerical staff finish early		

Once the ideas are exhausted, they are grouped together under specific headings as shown in the affinity diagram example in Figure 9.2. Note that a problem can initially be put under multiple headings. By going through a process of 5 Whys (see tool 9.3) we can determine exactly where the problem lies.

Further information

See Stevens, M (1996) *How to be a Better Problem Solver*, Kogan Page, London.

Reference

Turner, S (2003) *Tools for Success: A manager's guide*, McGraw-Hill, Maidenhead

9.2 Cause and effect analysis, or fishbone or Ishikawa

Introduction

Cause and effect analysis was introduced by Professor Kaoru Ishikawa, a quality management guru, in the 1960s. The technique was then published in his 1990 book, *Introduction to Quality Control*. The diagrams created with cause and effect analysis are known as Ishikawa diagrams or fishbone diagrams (because a completed diagram can look like the skeleton of a fish).

Cause and effect analysis was initially developed for quality control; however, it has now been extended into other areas, including problem solving. For instance, you can use it to:

- understand the specific cause of a problem;
- uncover holdups in your processes;
- discover why and for what reason(s) a specific process isn't working.

When to use

This tool can be used to think through the causes of a problem that is affecting your operation. It helps you look for the root cause as opposed to the symptoms. It is based on producing a diagram that gives a visual representation of the problem. It enables you to consider all the potential factors causing the problem, not just the more obvious ones. By bringing your team together you are able to brainstorm (see tool 9.1) the problem and produce a diagram detailing all the potential factors. I find that being able to visualize a problem is very effective.

How to use

Identify the problem and write it down on the right-hand side of a piece of paper or screen (see Figure 9.3). Then decide on the major factors that may be contributing to the problem; these can include technology, people, equipment, processes, environment, information etc. Draw lines at an angle away from the horizontal line and record the major factors at the end of each line or 'rib'. Collect the causes within each of the major factors that contribute to the effect. Brainstorm by asking each person in the team to provide potential causes and plot them on the 'ribs' within each of the major categories.

Use the 5 Whys tool (9.3) to delve deeper into each of the potential causes. Discuss how these impact the ultimate problem and concentrate on those that have the greatest impact. Once the diagram is completed, each area can be analysed in detail to find the root cause of the problem.

FIGURE 9.3 Fishbone diagram

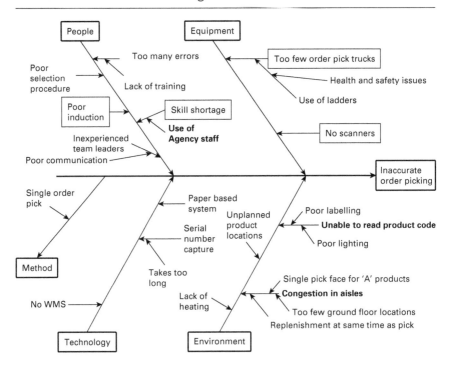

Further information

See http://www.mindtools.com/pages/article/newTMC_03.htm

9.3 The 5 Whys

Introduction

If you are a parent you will have often heard your children ask why things are as they are. They repeat the question until they are satisfied with the answer. It's the same in business. Although called the 5 Whys tool, we need to keep asking 'why' until we get to the root cause of a problem.

This is a simple problem-solving tool that helps users get to the root cause of the problem faster. It can also be used in conjunction with cause and effect analysis (tool 9.2). The tool is based on the philosophy that a problem provides an opportunity to fully understand the causes and thus treat the cause rather than the symptoms.

When to use

The 5 Whys tool attempts to get to the root cause of any particular problem.

How to use

1 Define the problem, eg Customer X is very unhappy.

2 Put together a cross-functional team of people.

3 Ask your team why Customer X is very unhappy and capture the responses, eg we delivered late again.

4 Ensure that all staff are open and honest with their responses.

5 Continue to ask why until no more answers can be given, eg we didn't finish the pick, we were a person short, we didn't plan for this volume, we were given the wrong volume information.

6 Use the answers to identify the problem and the actions that need to be taken, eg the sales team got their forecast wrong and we need to discuss how this can be improved.

The tool enables you to drill down more than you would normally to find the exact cause of the problem. A simple example from Toyota is as follows:

1 Our forklifts keep breaking down – why?

2 Shrink wrap gets caught in the drive motors – why?

3 The warehouse floor gets very messy – why?

4 The team throw shrink wrap on the floor – why?

5 They don't use the bins provided – why?

6 They are in the wrong locations and constantly full.

7 *Answer:* relocate bins and empty more often.

The chart shown in Figure 9.4, adapted from a design by Six Sigma-Material, is a good way of mapping out the problem and the potential causes. If we take

FIGURE 9.4 5 Whys chart

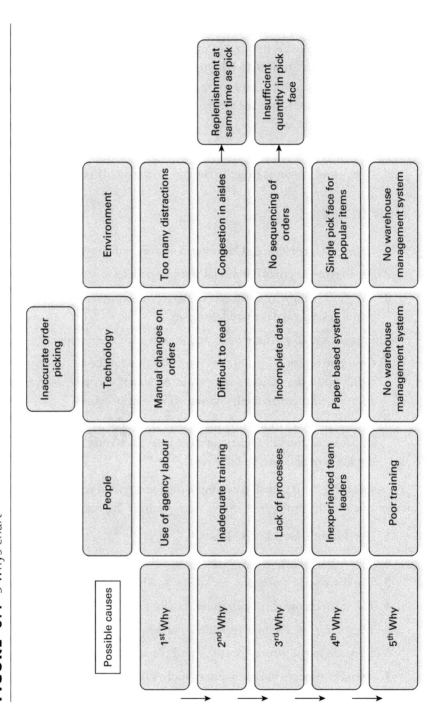

the example of the wrong items being sent to a customer, there are a number of potential causes. In this diagram we have looked at three potential areas: people, technology and the environment (in this case the working area).

Note that we may need to ask more than five questions to get to the root cause of the problem and there could be a number of reasons for the poor accuracy. The point is to take this exercise seriously, ask the difficult questions and get to the bottom of the problem. For example, two of the streams in the figure end with the fact that there is no warehouse management system, and the reason for this could be a lack of budget. Keep drilling down until you can proceed no further. Note that it can also branch off into other directions.

To concentrate resources, the following need to take place:

- Address each major cause in turn.

- Assign *one* person to the corrective actions of each root cause.

- Assign *one* person to the preventive actions of each root cause.

- Agree on a specific completion date for each assignment.

- Record all the names of the people involved in the exercise.

- Record the date the exercise was completed.

References

http://www.six-sigma-material.com/5-WHY.html [accessed 3 March 2013]
Turner, S (2003) *Tools for Success: A manager's guide*, McGraw-Hill, Maidenhead

9.4 The 8-D approach

Introduction

8-D is a quality management tool. An 8-D resolution and corrective action approach concentrates on resolving problems permanently, with the primary objective of preventing any reoccurrence. The premise is to get to the root of the problem as soon as possible rather than use a trial-and-error approach to problem solving. The 8-D approach provides excellent guidelines, allowing us to get to the root of a problem, and provides ways to check that the solution actually works and that the same problem is unlikely to recur.

When to use

When a potential problem has been identified and it requires a team approach.

How to use

The 8-D process follows a structured path with an emphasis on documenting every stage of the process. It also stresses the need to involve people from outside the problem area to get a different perspective.

8-D is especially useful as it results not just in problem solving, through utilizing a tried and tested process, but also produces an ongoing standard and a reporting format that can be utilized in many different circumstances.

It is enhanced as a problem-solving tool by introducing other tools at various stages of the process. For example, the 5 Whys tool (tool 9.3) and root-cause analysis can be used at stage D4 to discover the root cause of the problem. FMEA (failure mode and effects analysis) can be used at stage D5 to check the effectiveness of the solution.

Figure 9.5 provides a step-by-step guide to the 8-D problem-solving process. A worksheet for the 8-D approach can be found at http://thequalityportal.com.

Example

Problem: incorrect delivery to the customer:

D0 – We know we have a problem as the customer has told us so.

D1 – We form a team to investigate the problem:

- the champion: the owner of the problem who ensures sufficient resources and support are provided; in this case the warehouse manager;

- the team leader: gets the job done; in this case the outbound supervisor;

- the writer: ensures the integrity of all the documentation; in this case the general manager's PA;

- the time manager: ensures milestones and tasks are completed on time; in this case the human resources manager;

- the outside expert: possesses vital skills and comes from outside the department; in this case the operations manager.

D2 – Describe the problem. 'We received a number of calls from clients complaining they received the wrong deliveries. This occurred over a period of the last three days. We're not sure where the issue is but it's not stopped, we had another call this morning.'

D3 – Develop an interim containment action. Allocate staff to check every order before it leaves the warehouse and record any incorrect orders and who picked them.

FIGURE 9.5 The 8-D process

D0   The planning stage – do we have a problem?

D1   Establish a team

- The champion – the owner of the problem who ensures that sufficient resources and support are provided
- The team leader – gets the job done
- The writer – ensures the integrity of all the documentation
- The time manager – ensures that milestones and tasks are completed on time
- The outside expert – possesses vital skills and comes from outside the department

D2   Describe the problem

- What's wrong with what?
- When did it happen?
- Where did it happen?
- What is the size and seriousness of the problem?

D3   Develop an interim containment action (ICA)

- Buy time until a permanent corrective action is implemented
- Protect the customer from the effect(s) of the problem
- Contain the problem from a cost, reputation and quality perspective

D4   Define the root cause and identify the escape point

- Verify the root cause – use the 5Whys approach (see tool 9.3)
- Undertake a root cause analysis
- Isolate the point in the process where the problem could have been detected and identified earlier but wasn't

D5   Permanent corrective action (PCA) for root cause and escape point

- Identify the best possible PCA so that it doesn't happen again
- Ensure that it is easier to identify the escape point
- Produce a timeline for completion

D6   Implement the PCA

- Produce a project plan and timetable for implementation
- Implement and validate the PCA
- Remove the ICA if PCA is working
- Monitor the results

D7   Prevent reoccurrence

- Modify the existing systems, policies, practices and processes
- Make further recommendations if required

D8   Recognizing the efforts of the team

- Undertake a before-and-after comparison
- Ensure that the documentation is complete
- Reward the team members appropriately

D4 – Define the root cause and identify the escape point. Use the 5 Whys tool (9.3) to discuss the problem and identify possible causes. Could the problem have been identified earlier?

D5 – Permanent corrective action (PCA). In this example the error was a problem with the use of agency labour and their lack of product knowledge. PCA is an induction for *all* temporary labour, with an emphasis on product knowledge and awareness. Key performance indicators to be extended to all staff. A time frame of six weeks to introduce an abridged version of the company induction programme for temporary labour.

D6 – Implement the PCA. Induction scheme for all new and existing temporary staff. KPIs set up and monitored for existing and temporary staff. Full checks on all orders leaving the warehouse to be removed if accuracy levels have improved.

D7 – Prevent recurrence. Warehouse procedures to include induction for all temporary staff prior to deployment.

D8 – Recognizing the effort of the team. Team dinner organized for members and partners.

Conclusion: by following through this process, not only is the initial problem detected but a temporary fix is put in place immediately while a long-term solution is sought. The final act is to reward all those individuals who were involved, both within the team and in the implementation of the final solution.

References

8-Discipline Problem Solving, Noshir Khory, PhD, Motorola, Automotive and Industrial Electronics Group, 16 October 2000, report supplied by Mark Bergkotte.
(Worksheet provided by The Quality Portal team at http://thequalityportal.com)

APPENDIX 1
Useful websites

With a large amount of business undertaken online and most people utilizing the internet to search for their service providers and for up-to-date information, we have compiled the following list of useful websites. There are many others; however, we hope that this list will help you find what you are looking for in the field of logistics. This list can be downloaded from http://howtologistics.com where it is constantly updated.

Name	Website	Description
AIM Global	www.aimglobal.org	Auto ID information
American Society of Transportation and Logistics	www.astl.org	Professional body
APICS – The Association for Operations Management	www.apics.org	Professional body
Apprise Consulting Ltd	www.appriseconsulting.co.uk	Consultancy
British Association of Removers	www.bar.co.uk	Trade association
British International Freight Association	www.bifa.org	Trade association
British Quality Foundation	www.bqf.org.uk	Professional body
Burman Associates	www.burmanassociates.com	Consultancy
Capterra	www.capterra.com	List of logistics IT companies
Chartered Institute of Logistics and Transport	www.ciltuk.org.uk	Professional body

Name	Website	Description
Chartered Institute of Purchasing and Supply	www.cips.org	Professional body
Constructor Group	www.constructor-group.co.uk	Racking company
Council of Supply Chain Management Professionals	http://cscmp.org/	Professional body
DC Velocity	www.dcvelocity.com/	Magazine/blog
Department for Transport UK	www.dft.gov.uk	Government department
European Foundation for Quality Management	www.efqm.org	Quality organization
Food Storage and Distribution Federation	www.fsdf.org.uk	Trade association
Freight Transport Association	www.fta.co.uk	Trade association
Georgia Institute of Technology	www.scl.gatech.edu	S/C Institute
GS 1	www.gs1.org	Barcode information
Health and Safety Executive UK	www.hse.gov.uk	Health and Safety
How to Logistics	http://howtologistics.com	Online toolbox
IFW	http://www.lloydsloadinglist.com/	Logistics news
Inbound Logistics	www.inboundlogistics.com	Magazine/blog
Institute of Chartered Shipbrokers	http://www.ics.org.uk/	Professional body
Institute of Operations Management	www.iomnet.org.uk/	Professional body
Institute of Supply Chain Management	www.ioscm.com	Professional body
Kogan Page	www.koganpage.com	Publisher

Name	Website	Description
Labyrinth Consulting	www.labyrinthsolutions.co.uk	Consultancy
LinkedIn	www.linkedin.com	Professional network
Lloyds Loading List	www.lloydsloadinglist.com	Freight community news
Logistics About	www.logistics.about.com	Newsletter
Logistics Handling	www.logisticshandling.com	Logistics news and blog
Logistics Management	www.logisticsmgmt.com	Magazine/blog
Logistics Manager	www.logisticsmanager.com	Magazine/blog
Logistics Viewpoints	http://logisticsviewpoints.com/	Logistics news
Logistics World	www.logisticsworld.com	Directory
Manufacturing and Logistics IT	www.logisticsit.com	Magazine/blog
Materials Management and Distribution	www.mmdonline.com	Magazine/blog
Modern Material Handling	www.mmh.com	Magazine/blog
Occupational Safety and Health Administration US Department of Labor	www.osha.gov	Health and safety
Road Haulage Association	https://www.rha.uk.net/	Trade association
Storage Handling and Distribution	www.shdlogistics.com	Magazine/blog
Supply Chain Almanac	supplychainalmanac.com	Magazine/blog
Supply Chain and Logistics Certification Network	www.astl.org	Professional body
Supply Chain Brain	www.supplychainbrain.com	Magazine/blog
Supply Chain Digest	www.scdigest.com	Magazine/blog

Name	Website	Description
Supply Chain Market	www.supplychainmarket.com	Newsletter
Supply Chain Management Review	www.scmr.com	Magazine/blog
Supply Chain Standard	www.supplychainstandard.com	Magazine/blog
The Chartered Institution of Highways & Transportation	www.ciht.org.uk/	Professional body
The Logistics Guild	http://www.thelogisticsguild.com/	Logistics information
The National Industrial Transportation League	www.nitl.org	Professional body
The Warehousing Education and Research Council (WERC)	www.werc.org	Professional body
Toyota	www.toyota-forklifts.co.uk	Truck manufacturers
Transport for London	http://www.tfl.gov.uk/	UK government department
Transport Intelligence	www.transportintelligence.com	Research
Transport Research Foundation	http://www.trl.co.uk/	Logistics research
UK Chamber of Shipping	www.ukchamberofshipping.com	Trade association
United Kingdom Warehousing Association	www.ukwa.org.uk	Trade association
UTAS	http://utas.libguides.com/	Maritime library guide
Warehouse and Logistics News	www.warehousenews.co.uk	Magazine/blog

APPENDIX 2
Imperial/metric conversions

A number of countries continue to use both imperial and metric measures. The following table helps to convert from imperial to metric and vice versa.

Function	Imperial (A)	Metric (B)	Converting A to B multiply by	Converting B to A multiply by
Length	Millimetres (mm)	Inches (in)	0.03937	25.4
	Centimetres (cm)	Inches (in)	0.3937	2.54
	Metres (m)	Feet (ft)	3.2808	0.3048
	Metres (m)	Yards (yd)	1.0936	0.9144
	Kilometres (km)	Miles	0.62137	1.6093
	Kilometres (km)	Nautical Miles	0.53995	1.852
Area	Square centimetres (cm²)	Square inches (in²)	0.155	6.4516
	Square metres (m²)	Square feet (ft²)	10.7639	0.0929
	Square kilometres (km²)	Square miles (mi²)	0.3861	2.59
	Hectare	Acre	2.4711	0.4047
Cube	Cubic centimetres (cm³)	Cubic inches (in³)	0.061	16.387

Function	Imperial (A)	Metric (B)	Converting A to B multiply by	Converting B to A multiply by
	Cubic metres (m³)	Cubic yards (yd³)	1.308	0.7645
	Cubic metres (m³)	Cubic feet (ft³)	35.3147	0.0283
Volume	Litres	UK Pints	1.76	0.5683
	Litres	UK Gallons	0.21997	4.54611
	UK fluid ounce	Millilitres	28.413	0.03519
	US Gallons	Litres	3.78541	0.26417
	UK Gallons	*US Gallons*	1.2009	0.83267
Fuel usage	Miles per UK gallon	Kilometres per litre	0.35400	2.82490
	Miles per UK gallon (mpg)	Litres per 100 km (lpk)	282.48/mpg	282.48/lpk
	Miles per US gallon (mpg)	Litres per 100 km (lpk)	235.22/mpg	235.22/lpk
	Miles per UK gallon	Miles per US gallon	0.8327	1.201
Weight	Tonnes	Long Tons	0.9842	1.016
	Grams	Ounces	0.0353	28.35
	Kilograms	Pounds	2.2046	0.4536
	Kilograms	Hundredweight	0.01968	50.802
Speed (lift)	Metre per second	Feet per second	3.2808	0.3048
Speed travel	Kilometres per hour	Miles per hour	0.62137	1.6093
Temperature	Centigrade (c)	Fahrenheit (f)	$(9/5)*Tc+32$	$(5/9)*(Tf-32)$

In this example T is the temperature, eg if temp is 26° Celsius the formula is $(9/5)*26+32$ = $1.8*58$ = 104.4 °F. If temperature is 97.4° Fahrenheit the formula is $(5/9)*97.4-32$ = $0.555556*65.4$ = 36.33 °C.

APPENDIX 3
Automatic identification (autoID)

Introduction

Automatic identification methods have made a great difference to accurate visibility of inventory in the supply chain. The most common methods in use in supply chains are 1D (one-dimensional) and 2D (two-dimensional) barcodes, and radio frequency identification (RFID).

Clearly it is much quicker to read a barcode or RFID tag than to enter a 10 to 20-digit product identity on a keyboard. However, it is the accuracy of such an operation that makes the big difference. Studies indicate that a trained keyboard operator will make an average of one mistake per 300 key strokes. In contrast, the worst accuracy rate for barcode reading is approximately one error per 300,000 readings, but may be as low as one error per 10 million operations for certain types of barcode.

Since barcode labels are easily affixed or can be directly printed onto virtually any material (mailing tubes, envelopes, boxes, cans, bottles, packages, books and more), they are the most cost-effective and accurate solution for capturing data.

When to use

Barcodes and RFID systems are used to allocate identities to materials and products with a unique identity per SKU. Anybody can implement a barcoding or RFID system in their own operation for items in the warehouse or to track production orders through the factory, for example. Note, however, that if you want these identities to be recognized outside your business, they must be registered with a national body, thus ensuring that the identity is unique in the world.

How to use

The first stage of an autoID project is to be clear about why you want to implement barcodes, and what benefits you are expecting. Different barcoding and RFID systems exist. In this section we will concentrate on 1D and 2D barcodes.

When barcodes are used on a widespread public basis, such as printed on an internationally sold item, it is important to register the symbology to protect the data, especially from product/code copiers. However, if the barcode is for in-house use, it does not need to be registered. Registering a barcode is a simple process that can be performed through third-party online sites or through barcode global organizations such as GS1.

All symbologies have some limitations on the number (size) and type of characters that can be encoded (set). Barcodes can encode numeric only, alphabetical only or alphanumeric character sets. The values of these digits are determined by standards managed by GS1, Global Standards One, formerly known as the Uniform Code Council (UCC) in the United States and EAN International in the rest of the world. GS1 is now the single worldwide origination point for UPC and EAN numbers. Table Appendix 3.1 lists the different types of barcodes and their typical applications:

TABLE APPENDIX 3.1

Barcode	Application
EAN – 13	Character Set: Numeric only; Character Size: 13 fixed-length; Fault Tolerance: High; Application: International retail and grocery standard (Europe)
UPC – A	Character Set: Numeric only; Character Size: 12 fixed-length; Fault Tolerance: High; Application: Retail and grocery standard (United States)
AN – 8	Character Set: Numeric only; Character Size: 8 fixed-length; Fault Tolerance: High; Application: Small packages in retail (Europe)
UPC – E	Character Set: Numeric only; Character Size: 6 fixed-length; Fault Tolerance: High; Application: Small packages in retail (United States)
Code 128	Character Set: Alphanumeric (uppercase/lowercase), punctuation, controls; Character Size: Any; Fault Tolerance: High; Application: Best for full ASCII character set
Code 39	Character Set: Alphanumeric (uppercase only), punctuation; Character Size: Limited by reader; Fault Tolerance: High; Application: Military, government
GS1 DataBar Omnidirectional	Character Set: Numeric only; Character Size: 14 fixed-length; Fault Tolerance: High; Application: GTIN in small format

(Continued)

TABLE APPENDIX 3.1 *(Continued)*

Barcode	Application
GS1 DataBar Expanded	Character Set: Numeric only; Character Size: Variable-length; Fault Tolerance: High; Application: GTIN, applications in ID fields
GS1 – 128	Character Set: Alphanumeric; Character Size: Variable-length; Fault Tolerance: High; Application: Many uses in supply chain: lots, containers, batches, retail
MSI/Plessey	Character Set: Numeric only; Character Size: 3 to 16 fixed-length; Fault Tolerance: High; Application: Grocery
Code 32	Character Set: Numeric only; Character Size: 8 digit (plus one check character) fixed-length; Fault Tolerance: High; Application: Pharmaceutical industry (Italy)

Two-dimensional (2D) barcode symbologies contain information in both the X and Y axis of the symbol. In other words, there are different data encoded in the horizontal and vertical dimensions of the code. To properly decode the data, a scanner must read the entire symbol, in both dimensions simultaneously. This can be done by sweeping the scan line (in the case of a laser or linear imaging scanner) over the symbol, or by using a 2D-array-equipped scanner, which acts as a camera. Since the data can be stored in two dimensions, 2D barcode symbologies allow vast amounts of data to be stored.

There are two kinds of 2D barcode symbologies: stacked codes and matrix codes. Stacked codes consist of multiple layers of linear barcodes and matrix codes encode data using cells within a matrix. Examples of stacked codes are shown in Table Appendix 3.2 and of matrix codes in Table Appendix 3.3.

TABLE APPENDIX 3.2

PDF 417	Character Set: Alphanumeric (uppercase/lowercase), punctuation, controls; Character Size: Variable-length; Fault Tolerance: High; Application: Driver licences, transportation, inventory management, government
Codablock F	Character Set: Numeric only; Character Size: Up to 5,450 characters variable-length; Fault Tolerance: High; Application: Healthcare

TABLE APPENDIX 3.3

Data Matrix	Character Set: Alphanumeric, uppercase/lowercase letters, punctuation, controls; Character Size: Up to 2,335 characters fixed-length; Fault Tolerance: High; Application: Marking small items, printed on labels and letters, industrial engineering for marketing components
QR Code	Character Set: Alphanumeric, uppercase/lowercase letters, punctuation, controls, includes Kanji characters; Character Size: Up to 7,000 numeric characters or 4,296 alpha characters variable-length; Fault Tolerance: High; Application: Automobile manufacturing, mobile phone codes

Further information

AIM Global – www.aimglobal.org

GS1 The Global Language of Business – http://www.gs1.org/

Ten Steps to Barcode Implementation – http://www.gs1.org/barcodes/implementation

Global Electronic Party Information Register (GEPIR). GEPIR is a distributed database that contains basic information on over 1,000,000 companies in over 100 countries. You can search by GTIN (includes UPC and EAN –13), SSCC and GLN numbers or by company name in some countries. http://gepir.gs1.org

Datalogic A D C White Papers

The Growing Requirements for 2D Imaging Technology

GS1 DataBar™ 2010 Sunrise – An Explanation from a Retailer's Perspective, http://www.idautomation.com/product-support/barcoding-for-beginners.html#barcode-Accuracy

Information on RFID can be found at http://www.aimglobal.org/?RFID

www.rfidjournal.com/

INDEX

Note: The index is filed in alphabetical, word-by-word order. Within main headings, acronyms are filed as presented and numbers are filed as spelt out in full, with the exception of named codes and ISO standards, which are filed in chronological order. Page locators in *italics* denote information contained within a Figure or Table.

CPSIA information can be obtained
at www.ICGtesting.com
Printed in the USA
LVHW081535280819
629260LV00006B/127/P